Praise for *Build Your Commu*

MW00533621

'Thoughtful, strategic and tactical, Millington's book will help you see that the real work lies in leading a community that cares.'

Seth Godin, author of *This is Marketing*

'Building a successful, thriving community is one of the keys to success for modern brands. However, very few people understand how to start and nurture a community. Luckily, Richard Millington shares his insights from years of experience and provides a chapter by chapter guide of proven steps that will help anyone successfully launch their own vibrant community. This is the playbook to community success!'

Sarah Leary, Co-Founder, Nextdoor, Inc.

'Richard's book will help any community leader – aspiring or current; in or outside an organisation – gain the tools to not only build their community but also ensure it is valued. Too often, community leaders are stretched too thin and unable to do their work sustainably – Richard breaks down the art and science sustainable community building with a roadmap that provides practical tools and advice.'

Deepti Doshi, Head of Strategic Initiatives, New Product Experimentation, Facebook

Build Your Community

Pearson

At Pearson, we have a simple mission: to help people make more of their lives through learning.

We combine innovative learning technology with trusted content and educational expertise to provide engaging and effective learning experiences that serve people wherever and whenever they are learning.

From classroom to boardroom, our curriculum materials, digital learning tools and testing programmes help to educate millions of people worldwide – more than any other private enterprise.

Every day our work helps learning flourish, and wherever learning flourishes, so do people.

To learn more, please visit us at **www.pearson.com/uk**

Build Your Community

Turn your connections into a powerful online community

Richard Millington

Pearson

Harlow, England • London • New York • Boston • San Francisco • Toronto • Sydney
Dubai • Singapore • Hong Kong • Tokyo • Seoul • Taipei • New Delhi
Cape Town • São Paulo • Mexico City • Madrid • Amsterdam • Munich • Paris • Milan

PEARSON EDUCATION LIMITED
KAO Two
KAO Park
Harlow CM17 9NA
United Kingdom
Tel: +44 (0)1279 623623
Web: www.pearson.com/uk

First edition published 2021 (print and electronic)

© Pearson Education Limited 2021 (print and electronic)

The right of Richard Millington to be identified as author of this work has been asserted by him in accordance with the Copyright, Designs and Patents Act 1988.

The print publication is protected by copyright. Prior to any prohibited reproduction, storage in a retrieval system, distribution or transmission in any form or by any means, electronic, mechanical, recording or otherwise, permission should be obtained from the publisher or, where applicable, a licence permitting restricted copying in the United Kingdom should be obtained from the Copyright Licensing Agency Ltd, Barnard's Inn, 86 Fetter Lane, London EC4A 1EN.

The ePublication is protected by copyright and must not be copied, reproduced, transferred, distributed, leased, licensed or publicly performed or used in any way except as specifically permitted in writing by the publishers, as allowed under the terms and conditions under which it was purchased, or as strictly permitted by applicable copyright law. Any unauthorised distribution or use of this text may be a direct infringement of the author's and the publisher's rights and those responsible may be liable in law accordingly.

All trademarks used herein are the property of their respective owners. The use of any trademark in this text does not vest in the author or publisher any trademark ownership rights in such trademarks, nor does the use of such trademarks imply any affiliation with or endorsement of this book by such owners.

Pearson Education is not responsible for the content of third-party internet sites.

ISBN: 978-1-292-32999-4 (print)
     978-1-292-33000-6 (PDF)
     978-1-292-33001-3 (ePub)

British Library Cataloguing-in-Publication Data
A catalogue record for the print edition is available from the British Library

Library of Congress Cataloging-in-Publication Data
A catalog record for the print edition is available from the Library of Congress

10 9 8 7 6 5 4 3 2 1
25 24 23 22 21

Cover design by Madras

Print edition typeset in Charter ITC Pro 10/14 by SPi Global
Printed by Ashford Colour Press Ltd, Gosport

NOTE THAT ANY PAGE CROSS REFERENCES REFER TO THE PRINT EDITION

Contents

Contents

About the author

Richard Millington is the founder of FeverBee, a community consultancy whose clients have included Apple, Facebook, Google, SAP, Audi and hundreds of famous brands from around the world. Over the past 15 years, Richard has helped almost 300 organisations develop thriving communities for their customers, employees, fans and acquaintances.

Richard has also trained 1100+ community professionals to use principles of psychology, user experience, and a deeper understanding of business goals to grow and improve their communities. Richard has spoken at hundreds of events in dozens of countries around the world and his work has been featured in *The Guardian*, *The Economist*, and a plethora of other media platforms.

Photo by dg-corporate.co.uk

Richard's last two books, *Buzzing Communities* and *The Indispensable Community*, are widely cited for bringing best practices into the field of leading successful online communities.

You can find out more by following @RichMillington and visiting www.feverbee.com.

Acknowledgements

———

Books may have a single scribe but they're nearly always a product of their community.

This book is no exception. In fact, I consider it the product of two communities.

The first community are the people who helped me bring this book to life from scratch.

A thank you to my friend and fellow author Nathalie Nahai for pushing me to dream bigger for this book. A huge thank you to Eloise Cook at Pearson for believing in this project and serving as my editor throughout a year of writing and rewriting. Her thoughts, feedback and encouragement helped me battle the curse of knowledge and make this an infinitely better book.

A special thanks to Bridget Menyeh for pulling together and summarising much of the research that was used in this book. Very few people can take complex and often ambiguous questions and summarise the results of dozens, even hundreds, of academic articles on the topic.

Another thank you to Rick Landers for his help with design and some of the graphics used in this book. I also want to thank my colleague, Clare Layton, who has been my reliable assistant for five years and my accountant, Marit Olson, who has been my accountant for ten years.

Acknowledgements

The amazing community of community leaders

The second community is the thousands of community leaders around the world giving their all to create the best possible experiences for members. The lessons they've learned and shared throughout the years are infused throughout this book.

The list here is too many to thank personally, but special notice to David Spinks for bringing so many of us together via CMX, Rachel Happe and Jim Storer for their analytical insights and research at the Community Roundtable, Carrie Melissa Jones for challenging all of us to be true, authentic communities. Also thanks to Patrick O'Keefe for reminding us to respect our past and Bill Johnston for peering into our future. A special credit to Jono Bacon, Anika Gupta and Priya Parker for their impressive books.

A huge debt of gratitude also to Erica Kuhl, Colleen Young, Evan Hamilton, Monique Van den Berg, Alexa Aliota, Carol Rooney, Liz Crampton, Allison Leahy, Gali-Kling Schneider, Marjorie Anderson, Sarah Hawk, Holly Firestone, Roy Munin, and many more for building and managing some of the best communities in the world today.

A special thanks to Brian Oblinger for helping review and critique the platform chapter of this book (and for doing some of the most impressive community work I've ever seen at Alteryx and now for his own clients).

Everyone needs peers to vent with and bounce ideas off and learn from. A special thanks here to Phoebe Venkat, Kirsten Wagenaar, Wendy Schippers, Alison Michalk, Venessa Paech, Adrian Speyer, Krista Hauser, Dani Weinstein, and others for giving frank and honest feedback on the community sector.

Finally, a special thank you to all of the hundreds of clients and thousands of course participants I've been fortunate enough to work with over the years. I truly feel I've learned more from you than you from me. Thank you.

Publisher's acknowledgements

Image credits:

7 DG Corporate: www.dg-corporate.co.uk; **147 Coleen Young:** Screenshot from Mayo Clinic. Used by permission.

Text credits:

6 Elsevier: Kopelman, S (2009). "The effect of culture and power on cooperation in commons dilemmas: Implications for global resource management". Organizational Behavior and Human Decision Processes. 108: 153–163; **71 MIT Press:** P. Ludlow (1996), High Noon on the Electronic Frontier: Conceptual Issues in Cyberspace, MIT Press. Retrieved from https://mitpress.mit.edu/books/high-noon-electronic-frontier/; **82 Elsevier:** Erin E. Buckels, Paul D. Trapnell, Delroy L. Paulhus, Trolls just want to have fun, Personality and Individual Differences, Volume 67, 2014, Pages 97–102, ISSN 0191-8869, https://doi.org/10.1016/j.paid.2014.01.016/; **112 Oxford University Press:** Adapted from Ridings, C. M., & Gefen, D. (2004). Virtual community attraction: Why people hang out online. Journal of Computer-mediated communication, 10(1), JCMC10110; **169 Elsevier:** Adapted from Kuo, M. S., & Chuang, T. Y. (2016). How gamification motivates visits and engagement for online academic dissemination–An empirical study. Computers in Human

Behavior, 55, 16–27; **179–180 Salesforce:** Adapted from Salesforce. Retrieved from https://help.salesforce.com/articleView?id=networks_reputation_points_setup.htm&type=5/; **200 Mike Tyson:** Quoted by Mike Tyson; **216–217 Tim Ferriss:** Quoted by Tim Ferriss; **107–108 Rick Landers:** Used by permission from Rick Landers.

Introduction

I've got some great news: you're probably a community builder!

If you've ever connected a group of friends, created a space for work colleagues to interact, or connected fans, customers and supporters to help one another, you're a community builder.

Now, your job title might not say 'community builder' and you might be using technologies that look far removed from what a community should feel like but, if any part of your daily life involves connecting people together, you're a community builder.

Welcome to the club!

Community building

It's important to give this work a name.

Far too many of us are doing this kind of work every day without knowing what it's called; it's just been something we do.

You might be the only person in your organisation (or amongst your friends) doing this kind of work. Believe me, that can feel darn lonely. Worse yet, if you're doing it alone you're not learning from the amazing experiences of millions of other community builders out there. It's ironic that community builders often report feeling lonely and isolated.

I know the feeling. For a long time, I too was connecting people online without ever knowing what it was called or that other people like me existed. It was simply something I was roped into doing.

My introduction to communities came through playing video games online. I got a high-speed internet connection at the impressionable age of 14 and it changed my world. I quickly discovered:

1 I could use this lightning fast internet connection to play games against other people online.

2 My main purpose in these games was apparently to serve as cannon fodder for better players to rack up high scores.

3 I loved participating in the community around these games more than playing them. I loved the unique culture, the language and the amazing sense of connection I felt with my fellow gamers. This was my tribe. These were people like me.

I loved one community so much that I began volunteering to write and help manage it. I even began organising and hosting competitive events in the community's name throughout the UK. Within a few years, these volunteering roles had led to my first real paid job managing a gaming community.

As interest in competitive gaming increased exponentially, I found myself in the most fortunate position imaginable. My employers began sending me to events around the world to report back to community members. I spent the latter part of my teenage years in places like South Korea, Singapore, USA, France, Sweden, and many more.

While friends were cold-calling local companies for summer internships, I was on a first-name basis with CEOs of major gaming and tech companies around the world. Building a community had unlocked doors I could never have imagined – and they haven't closed since.

But during all this time, I considered myself a 'gamer', never a community builder. This meant I was restricted to taking advice and wisdom from peers in the gaming industry, when I should've been proactively seeking out and learning from the top community builders. I didn't realise that the experiences and skills forged in the hot furnace of gaming communities (trust me, it's not easy) could be used for a purpose far beyond gaming.

A few years later, I was blessed to do an internship with renowned marketing author Seth Godin in New York. This is when I realised the skills I had been using for years to build communities in the gaming space could be applicable to countless other types of communities.

Over the past decade, I've used and refined these skills to help hundreds of organisations big and small develop their communities. These include big brands like Apple, Facebook, and Google down to small non-profits and individuals just trying to find a better way to stay connected to their friends and families.

I've also hosted workshops and training courses for participants from around the world. I've often witnessed participants have 'lightbulb moments' in these workshops when they realise the work they're doing isn't 'marketing', 'customer support' or just 'following a passion', it's community building. This realisation changes their entire approach. They find a shared vocabulary and a connection with others just like them. Most importantly, they start to get a thirst to become really good at it.

The world needs skilled community builders today

The world needs people like you who can connect, unite and lead us away from loneliness and towards a shared sense of purpose and mission. We need people like you who can help organisations harness the incredible power of getting staff and customers helping and supporting one another. We need someone who can take groups of people and, like electrons in a magnet, get us all aligned so we can achieve something greater together.

Every time you create a connection between two or more people, you're igniting a powerful spark. Sure, some might fizzle out quickly, but others start a fire that continues to burn for years, even decades. Members might exchange advice, work together on a common goal, or may even build a long-term friendship. And when this takes place in a group, you unleash more energy than you can imagine. When our proverbial electrons are aligned in a community, they naturally pull in newcomers and create a shared effort to achieve something far beyond what any single person can achieve alone.

There has never been a more important time to do this – both personally and professionally.

As I write these words, the COVID-19 pandemic has forced a quarter of the world's population into lockdown. Stuck, isolated and alone, we turned to online communities. In just a matter of months, we've seen an explosion of new communities in every conceivable realm. Online Zumba and fitness classes are taking place on Zoom – often supported by a WhatsApp group to chat outside of sessions. Groups of friends are hosting happy hours one or two nights a week. Teachers have taken many of their classes entirely online. We're seeing a surge in the creativity and possibility of community like we haven't seen in generations.

By the time you read these words, the pandemic may have passed but these connections are here to stay. We're seeing the dawn of a new era unfolding before our eyes – and we need people like you to drive us forward.

Building a community unlocks personal and professional benefits that are difficult to conceive when you begin.

For me, it unlocked amazing opportunities, incredible friendships which continue until this day, and a career that I've loved for over a decade. For others, building a community became the ultimate stepping stone to an amazing job, speaking opportunities, and tackling previously impossible goals.

But perhaps the biggest benefit is the feeling of making a difference. When you see how your members are benefiting from a community, you know you matter.

Community building for organisations

Many of you reading this book right now are doing this professionally – perhaps for a business, non-profit, or other type of organisation. You're not alone. Every single day a growing number of organisations are turning their employees, customers and members into an online community. The results of these efforts are incredible.

For example, in countless business communities, customers are volunteering their time to help each other solve problems. Think for a second about how strange that is. They're essentially doing customer support for free.

Would you ever volunteer to provide free customer support for any of the products around you today? Your refrigerator manufacturer? Cosmetic brand? Or insurance provider? Would you ever get home from a busy day at work, hook yourself up to your insurance provider's support system, and begin answering your fellow customers' problems?

But a community provides the motivation that makes that happen. These members aren't doing free customer support – they're helping their community. They're supporting people just like themselves.

And this isn't just happening in the whacky cult brands we've all heard about, it's happening in brands ranging from beloved Sephora to Best Buy. Even the hated telecom companies have (amazingly) found people willing to volunteer their spare time to answer customer questions, write product documentation, and share their top tips on using products. Community is increasingly taking over functions previously handled by paid employees – and achieving better results. When a customer support rep replies with the right answer, only the recipient will see it. When a member shares it in the community, thousands might see it. This often unburdens customer support staff from answering the same repetitive questions every single day and lets them focus on the tougher challenges or top customers.

Even this is only a fraction of the value a community offers organisations. These communities also help customers learn more about your products, services or mission and have a better experience when using them. A community enables customers to tell an organisation exactly what they need. Better yet, members can vote on each other's ideas and the best naturally rising to the top.

And we're still not close to exhausting the benefits of a community. Communities also drive advocacy, help organisations identify future employees, can stop a potential PR disaster dead in its tracks, and plenty, plenty more.

Build your community

Build Your Community is the playbook to achieving these goals.

It's the book I wish I had when I began this work 20 years ago.

While the technology will change every day, *Build Your Community* explains the evergreen principles of building communities that have been present in almost every community project I've ever worked on. If you can learn and master these principles, you have a blueprint you can use to build any number of communities you like.

This book is going to take you step by step through the process to launch and manage a community for almost any kind of group you can imagine. Sure, we'll spend some time covering the technology, but we're going to go far deeper into understanding what makes a community tick and how to attract and keep your audience highly engaged. Whether you're building a community for your business or for your passion, this book is going to help you forge your community from your connections.

I hope you find this book as valuable as I found the experiences I went through to write it.

chapter 1

Why create a community?

There are plenty of great reasons why you (or your organisation) might create a community.

You might create a community simply because you enjoy connecting friends and acquaintances together. You might love seeing people have a good time with one another and knowing you've had a role in new relationships which have formed. It feels fantastic to watch people becoming friends through a community you've created.

You might do it for a hobby. Creating a community around an activity usually makes it more enjoyable to participate in the activity. Participants can share advice, support one another, and coordinate doing it together. Almost every hobby is better enjoyed with others.

You might do it to create a movement or tackle a problem. By connecting people together you can collaborate to solve a challenge you might face. This problem might range from something as big as preventing climate change to helping each person through their own personal struggles.

You might do it to achieve some personal goals. A friend of mine hosts a regular, exclusive gathering of top people in his industry. The attendees get to feel special when they make the list and they have a private place to have intimate discussions with one another. My friend gets invaluable connections to the top people in his industry. Creating a community can turn you into a connector and place you in a position of power. It can help you build a reputation and can lead to new career opportunities, speaking opportunities, or *ahem* book publishing contracts.

You might be building a community on behalf of a business or organisation which needs to connect employees, members, customers and fans together. You might want to improve how employees collaborate, increase customer loyalty, or learn what your audience wants so you can serve them better.

You might build a community to earn money for yourself. There are over a thousand forum creators today earning several hundreds of thousands of dollars a year through a combination of sponsorships, advertising, and offering unique products and services for their audiences (most of the major social media platforms are an extreme aberration of this category). Once you have a large audience flocking to your community, there are a myriad of ways to earn a living from it.

No reason is more valid than any other, but you should be very clear about your goals before you begin. Knowing why you're building a community doesn't just help you align your entire approach to ensure you achieve your goals; it helps you motivate yourself to get through the difficult times along the way.

In this chapter, I'm going to explain how a community can help you and your organisation. Whether you're building a community for a local club or a multinational conglomerate, a community can help you achieve your goals faster, cheaper and better than any other approach. I'm also going to highlight what's required, how long it will take to achieve your goals, and the right language to use to persuade others of the importance of your community.

What makes a community approach completely unique?

What's unique and special about a community instead of any other approach?

It would be a lot easier to create a simple website about a hobby or host an event for a topic you're interested in. If you're a business, many benefits of a community might seem similar to things you're already doing. Your customer support team is already answering customer questions, and your customer success team is training and guiding them through the product. You're probably already gathering research to learn what your customers want.

What makes a community approach completely unique?

Two things. First, in a community you don't have to do everything yourself. You don't have to answer all the questions, create all the content, or run all the activities yourself. Members step forward to do these things. This makes a community the single best approach to grow and scale your efforts to support, educate and engage your audience.

Second, a community creates a deeper relationship between members. A community forges relationships that help members feel a sense of belonging and togetherness. It turns new customers into lifelong buyers and disparate friends into a close-knit community eager to help and support one another. No other channel can do that.

By turning your audience into a community, you're creating an environment that motivates members to do things they would never usually do – things that are incredibly valuable for you and to each other.

As mentioned in the introduction, few of us get home from work and volunteer to do customer support or start documentation on how to use our printer. Why would we? The effort is too high and the rewards are non-existent. But an online community flips the scales in your favour by creating powerful rewards to do these kinds of things.

By creating a community, you're creating opportunities for members to feel useful, important and liked by other members. You're giving members the opportunity to become leaders in their field and feel like they're helping hundreds, even thousands, of people every single day. This is only possible within the social dynamic a community creates.

In a community every single person who has solved a problem can help the next person with that problem. Every person who spots a gap in your documentation and can fix it. Anyone with ideas for your organisation can share them and see if others agree. They can vote and collaborate on implementing them together too – and they do this to feel part of a team. The best communities even have members advocating for them, tackling every possible customer problem, and collaborating on future products they want to see.

Only a community can create the social dynamic for this to happen. No one in a community is working for free, they're working for things which they value even more than anything you could pay them. They're working to better themselves and feel better about themselves by helping others.

This doesn't mean communities are without their flaws and problems. As we will learn in this book, communities are less like a solar panel harnessing natural energy and more like a nuclear reactor. They take time to set up and get going. They need careful maintenance to prevent a blow-up. But once they get going, they create a chain of self-sustaining interactions which can supercharge everything you do.

What are the different types of communities?

You probably participate in a lot of different types of communities today – and the type of interaction is different in each group. In a WhatsApp group with your friends and buddies, I'm betting you typically have long rambling conversations about anything and everything.

In a Slack community with your work colleagues, I'm betting you're primarily coordinating and sharing updates on upcoming work projects (with a few cat memes thrown in to lighten the mood).

On forums for topics you're interested in, you might just browse the latest questions and answers – maybe contributing when you can.

There are many many ways of classifying communities. You can classify communities by the audience you're targeting (developers, advocates, customers, employees, fans, members). You can also classify communities by the type of interest that brings them together (communities of place, practice, identity, circumstance, action). You can even classify communities by the platform they use (forums, chatrooms, social media) or interactions which take place (ideation, learning, success etc.).[1]

I prefer a simpler approach which categorises communities into four broad areas by the benefits they offer members: mutual support, exploration, influence, and belonging.[2] This helps us create a taxonomy which can represent any other type of community.

1 Mutual support

Many of the major communities today are support communities. They are places members can ask and answer each other's questions. You can find examples of these communities in almost every topic imaginable. You probably belong to a group or two which revolves around members asking and answering questions.

This type of community has several advantages. They are relatively easy to get started, very useful to members, and can help you support thousands, even millions, of people without a paid support team. They are the greatest tool for scaling customer support channels available. They are also fairly easy to measure compared with other types of communities.

However, support communities suffer from unparalleled participation inequality. Typically, a small group of superusers (more on them later) answer the majority of questions. These superusers need to be carefully motivated and looked after if the community is going to succeed.

Another downside of support communities is members only tend to visit when they have a question and leave when they get an answer. It's fiendishly hard to get people to stick around once they have got an answer to their question. The churn rate can be high and it also can be tricky to keep information relevant and up to date over the years.

2 Exploration

Exploration is a broad category that covers many sub-groups of community. The most common are communities of practice, customer success, ideation, and some hobbyist groups. In an exploration community, members proactively share what they're doing, get feedback from others, and try to improve.

The key difference between this and a support community is its proactivity. In a support community members are reactive. They wait for questions before sharing knowledge. In an exploration community members proactively share information. For example, in a support community you might ask how to fix your iPhone. In a success community you might post about some productivity apps you've discovered for your iPhone.

Outside of overly complex nomenclature, a community of practice is a form of exploration community. Members are proactively sharing information, documenting resources, and trying to get better within a chosen topic. Most internal communities for employees are essentially communities of practice for members to improve and build upon what they're doing.

Exploration communities are more likely to feature different types of media (blogs, videos, audio, photos) and often can create documentation or resources for other members. These communities are great for increasing loyalty, satisfaction, and save you time when members create articles and documentation to use your products better. Another major benefit of these communities is they give members a reason to visit every day to see what's new. Members don't wait for a problem to decide to visit.

The downside is they are harder to get going (why would a member want to start sharing what they're learning and doing?) and if you're not careful they can become filled with self-promotional spam (see LinkedIn).

It's worth noting that many communities initially begin with customer support before becoming a support/exploration hybrid with features like ideation, blogs, and other technologies for members to proactively share and learn from one another.

3 Influence

Influence-based communities are those where members collaborate together to improve something they would be unable to improve alone. The most common type of these are collective 'movements'. These are common in cause-related sectors, political campaigns, and any field where people are looking to collaborate together to make a change.

The traditional field of community organising sits squarely in this category – but so do many communities of cult brands like Supreme or Harley-Davidson where there is no single community manager, but hundreds of different blogs, groups, and websites each contributing in their own way.

The defining characteristic of these communities is they often lack a single person who coordinates all the activity. Instead they have numerous groups each working distinctly to achieve common goals. The community of people behind Wikipedia and most developer communities are good examples.

It's common in many software products (and obviously in open source technologies) for members to each contribute in their own form – often by submitting code or reviewing the contributions and submissions of others.

The upside of these communities is when members support something; *they really support something.* They often go to extreme lengths and invest an incredible amount of energy to make it succeed. They can be self-sustaining, inclusive, and self-perpetuating.

The downside is you need to overcome the collection action problem to get a movement started and you may yourself have responsibility without control. It can be very hard to maintain and manage contributors when there are thousands, perhaps even millions, of people each contributing separately to your cause. Most movements have had at least one, and often several, major blow-ups where members behaved in a way which damaged the brand and reflected badly upon all members.

Collective action problem

Collective action problems were best defined by American political scientist Geoffrey Mancur Olson Jr. His 1965 book, *The Logic of Collective Action,* argued that when the effort within a group to create a public good is concentrated amongst the few and the rewards are diffused across the many, individuals are motivated to 'free ride' on the contributions of others.[3] This is seen in the high lurker (learner) rate in the majority of online communities.

There are ways to overcome this. You might only enable active participants to enjoy the benefits of 'public goods' created by the community, might create an identity and social norm in which members are expected to contribute (or feel ashamed if they don't), or try to forge an identity in which members feel 'people like me contribute'.[4]

4 Belonging

The final type of community is that with a primary goal to provide members with a sense of belonging. This often isn't stated explicitly. When you spend time with your friends and family at home, bars, or restaurants, there probably isn't a 'come here to get your sense of belonging' notice at the entrance. But that is still the major benefit. In these kinds of groups, often nominally centred around a common interest, you're probably not spending most of your time giving support to one another or exploring a topic, you're simply hanging out and talking about whatever comes up.

These communities often don't have a clear purpose other than to pursue a common interest with like-minded others and experience a sense of belonging. These are communities where people can feel they truly belong, they get to know one another, and care for one another. I spent countless hours talking to fellow gamers in my earliest communities about topics other than gaming.

The purpose of these communities is to build and sustain a powerful sense of community amongst members and enable each member to be who they are. The advantage of these types of community is they provide amazing value to members. It can truly give your audience a place where they feel they belong. The downside is it's hard to sustain this community as it grows (and they can be especially prone to fights and conflicts).

If you're building a community for an organisation, you might also find that communities designed solely to create a strong sense of belonging are harder to connect to a clearly measurable corporate goal.

You can see a summary of each type of community below along with its common terminology and pros and cons.

Community type	Pros	Cons
Support (customer support, member support, health, circumstance etc.)	Easy to measure. Offers direct value. Relatively easy to get started. Scales support to more people at no cost.	Hard to keep members engaged. Small number of members answer a majority of questions. Tricky to keep information updated.
Exploration (customer success, ideation, communities of practice, employee)	Easier to keep members engaged. Create valuable resources. Improves expertise of entire group.	Harder to get started. Difficult to sustain high quality (can become self-promotional).

▶

Community type	Pros	Cons
Influence (movements, developer, cult brands, advocacy, collaboration)	Community largely self-organises. Sustains incredible contributions on the web.	Lack of control – can bring harm upon a brand name. Hard to overcome collective-action problem.
Belonging (interest, groups of friends)	Builds a 'true' sense of community spirit. Provides indispensable benefits to members.	Hard to sustain as the community grows. Prone to flights and conflicts.

You need to be deliberate about the *type* of community you create. Each type of community will result in different kinds of interactions taking place. Think of your community a little like a factory. How you calibrate the machines changes the output. You need to calibrate the interactions in your community for the experience you want members to have and the results you want.

The missing category

Do you notice what topic is missing above? Communities for members to talk about you and how wonderful you are. That's not because these kinds of cult communities don't exist, it's because they're almost impossible for organisations to deliberately create. They lack a clear purpose. By far, the biggest reason behind a community's failure is trying to get members to do something they have no interest in doing. Just because your customers loyally buy from you or you have an audience who read your site often, doesn't mean they want to spend their spare time talking about you and how great you are.

If you don't believe me, ask yourself a simple question: *how much of your spare time do you spend participating in communities of other brands – even brands you really love?* I'm guessing the answer is zero (or close to it). Now ask a few friends the same question. The result will be the same.

Examples of successful communities

If you need a little inspiration, here is a fairly random selection of examples (both brands and non-brands) of different types of communities. Remember, many of the best examples are on platforms not open to the public.

They might be in your private WhatsApp or Facebook groups, maybe with some colleagues on Slack or on a rare subreddit.

Type	Community
Support (customer support, member support, health, circumstance etc.)	Apple (discussions.apple.com) Fitbit (community.fitbit.com) Spotify (community.spotify.com) Sonos (en.community.sonos.com)
Exploration (customer success, ideation, communities of practice)	Launch Forth (launchforth.io/) Lego Ideas (ideas.lego.com) BackYard Chickens (https://www.backyardchickens.com/) Microsoft Teams (microsoftteams.uservoice.com) Salesforce (success.salesforce.com) SAP (community.sap.com) Sephora (community.sephora.com)
Influence (movements, developer, cult brands, advocacy)	Supreme Community (https://www.supremecommunity.com/) Kaggle (Kaggle.com) Github (github.com) Autodesk Advocates (https://autodeskadvocates.influitive.com/) Cision City (https://citizens.cisioncity.com) Cvent (https://cvent.influitive.com/)
Belonging (interest, groups of friends)	CoinTalk (https://www.cointalk.com/forums/) Airline Pilots Central (https://www.airlinepilotforums.com/)

Don't be afraid to evolve your community over time. Your community might begin with one benefit and later expand to include others. Likewise, don't be afraid to offer multiple benefits at once. The only thing that really matters is you're crystal clear about the type of community you intend to create, the trade-offs this involves, and the value you're offering members.

Once you've decided this, you can start clarifying the goals of your community.

What should the goals of your community be?

If you're building a community for a business, you might've nodded along so far while thinking: *'This all sounds great so far Rich, but my boss doesn't want vague niceties, she wants specifics. How will the community specifically help my business?'*

Or, if you're really unlucky, she might ask the dreaded question: *'What's the ROI of the community?'*[5]

What is return on investment?

Return on investment, in its strictest definition, is simply the ratio of what you earned against the investment you made. If you invest a dollar and get two dollars back, you have a 100% ROI.

An ROI ratio is essentially a crude tool organisations can use to compare different activities against one another and allocate their money to achieve the biggest possible results. If your advertising campaign achieved a 20% ROI and the community achieved a 40% ROI, an organisation should theoretically invest less in advertising and more in community.

In practice, it's far more complicated. Many activities, for example, have a law of diminishing returns past a peak level. And very few organisations are measuring the true ROI of the community. Typically they want to know the value of a community and how it can be measured.

The goals (or ROI) of a community created for personal motivations and those created on behalf of a business are very different. If you're creating a community for your own passions (or perhaps on behalf a non-profit), then the benefits of a community we've covered above (support, exploration, influence, and belonging) are often enough. You're creating a community to provide tremendous value to members. You might use more complex language to describe the goals, but this alone might be enough.

However, if you're building a community on behalf of an organisation you need to dig a little deeper into what a community can (and can't) offer. You also need to know *how* a community provides those benefits.

Step 1: Identify possible goals for the community

How do communities benefit organisations?

There are plenty of reasons why a business might create a community. I've listed the most common in the table below.

Value	How is this value achieved?
Reducing customer support costs (scaled support)	Customer support staff don't need to answer questions if other customers are doing it for free. Every answer can also be found via search. A single good response might be seen by thousands of people. Every person who finds a solution in the community doesn't need to call customer support.
Learning what customers want/need	A community keeps you close to the pulse of what members want and need. Not only can members suggest ideas, you can also track data to see which topics are most popular, and what members are struggling with. This saves a lot of time compared with running a focus group. A community is also a great place to test your products and marketing campaigns before launching them to the public.
Increasing customer loyalty and satisfaction (satisfaction, NPS, retention)	As members learn more about the products and get to know their fellow customers, they're less likely to move to a competitor and more likely to keep buying from you. They're also likely to become more satisfied with their purchase. A community can significantly increase net promoter score, customer satisfaction, and the lifetime value of a customer.
Attracting new customers	Community members might advocate for your brand, share your content, publish reviews and provide case studies. You might also identify members as sales leads through behaviours in the community. Community content can also be integrated into the sales path, which increases conversions. You might also benefit from visitors who found you via search engines signing up to be a member.

▶

Value	How is this value achieved?
Membership fees and advertising	Some organisations charge a membership fee to be a member. Others sell advertising. A handful let third parties run campaigns or host focus groups to gather research. All of these directly generate revenue.
Reduced recruitment costs	You can post adverts and recruit members from the community instead of traditional channels. This is less common than other benefits, but still happens.
Saving staff time and improving results	An internal community can help staff both share and properly document content. This stops them duplicating work and lets them build and improve upon the knowledge within the organisation. It also helps members collaborate with one another and saves a lot of time.

You might have noticed the problem with the table above. It seems to overlook many, if not most, of the amazing benefits of a community.

What if members are sharing incredible product insights which let you quickly fix bugs before they upset thousands of customers? What if they warn you about a potential PR disaster? What if they provide you with amazing case studies and material for your sales team? What if they help you develop a best-selling product?

This is why pure ROI metrics are about as well suited for communities as they are for PR campaigns or your company's commitment to having environmentally friendly packaging. You're probably not calculating the return on investment of any of these – at least to a dollar value.

Is it important your community delivers a great return on investment? Absolutely.

Is it the best way of measuring the value of a community? Absolutely not.

Strict measures of ROI capture only a fraction of the value your community will create. So, while you need to be clear about how a community helps the organisation, the real benefits of the community show up just below the level of profitability. They are the antecedents of profitability. We need to give these things a different name. I call them the *visible impact* of a community.

The visible impact of your community

Last year, I was sitting in a stakeholder engagement meeting with a client's head of sales.

These stakeholder engagement meetings typically have two major goals. The first is to make sure the community isn't treading on any toes. If we're planning to launch a community, we don't want to inadvertently upset someone who could potentially scupper the project. The second is to see how the community can support their work. A community can support almost every area of the business and I was curious to see how the community could support his goals.

During the meeting, he took me through the slide deck he used for prospects. I noticed the slide deck included only two case studies. Both of these case studies were more than three years old. When I asked why he didn't have more case studies, he sighed. The problem, he explained, was it took forever to create good case studies and it was a nightmare getting approval to use them. He told me his sales team was too busy chasing down leads to create case studies.

I sensed an opportunity and asked him a simple question.

'How would you like a lot more of these – created by members of the community?'

He seemed sceptical, but was open to it.

A few months after we launched the community, we set up a template for case studies and offered members a one-off chance to earn 10x the number of points (more on these later) they typically would earn in a month if they wrote a case study and *gave us permission to use it in marketing material*. We also promised to promote the best case studies to other members. In that one month alone we received 11 new case studies each with images and permission to use them. When we ran the challenge 8 months later, we received a further 37.

Today, his sales slide deck is *packed* with a diverse set of case studies covering almost every sector my client works in. The head of sales has specifically mentioned that prospects seem amazed by their quantity and quality of case studies and he believes it's been a major factor in converting more prospects into customers.

I can't tell you what the dollar returns of these case studies are, but it's pretty clear it's having a big impact. This kind of impact can and does happen all the time. You just need to know how to create and capture it. Most organisations are harnessing only a small fraction of their community's potential value. They're letting the rest rot away because they don't have a system for capturing and utilising these sorts of impacts.

Every day, your community is telling you precisely what they want and need. They're telling you what bugs to fix, how they feel about different elements of your product, and plenty more. They're creating stories you can use for your press releases, testimonials, for new customers, and helping one another use the product even better.

The first step to harnessing this impact is to set it as a goal for the community. Once it's a stated goal you can put together a system to capture it. You might not

13

be able to measure the number of dollars earned for each spent, but the visible impact will be clear to all.

Not sure what the impact of your community could be?

If you're not sure how a community can help your organisation, you can do what I do in FeverBee's consultancy projects and start building a list of problems you and your organisation face.

You can put these together yourself or, even better, bring your colleagues and key stakeholders into the fold and learn as much as possible about their challenges. This is more important than you might imagine. When researching my last book, I discovered a near direct correlation between the amount of time someone spent engaging and learning about their colleagues and the level of support they subsequently feel they have gained.[6]

Two things happen when you engage with colleagues. First, your colleagues feel listened to and consulted about the community. This means they're more likely to support it. Second, you get to prod and probe not just into the broad idea of what they need but the very specifics of when and how they need it.

For example, one acquaintance had a community that was generating really useful insights and feedback for his company's products. But this feedback was never being used by the engineering team. So he began attending the meetings of the engineering team to figure out why. He discovered that the community feedback was great, but he was sending it at the wrong time. The engineering team needed the feedback before each engineering sprint (a period of rapid work) where they set their priorities. Once the feedback came at the time when it could be used the community became indispensable to them.

You might also find you need far fewer members than you anticipated to deliver a huge impact. Quick Base for example, persuaded a handful of community members to leave reviews of their product on the biggest comparison site in their sector. Within weeks, they were the number one ranked product in their category. This generated millions of dollars in revenue.

In 2018, I worked with a client to set up mentoring groups for new customers. Veterans of the software would join and mentor small cohorts of newcomers each month. This directly increased the conversion rate of customers using the free version of my client's software into the paid version.

Once you have a list of challenges your colleagues face you will soon spot possible community solutions. I've created a list of the most common types of impact on the following page. It's not comprehensive, but it might help as a useful starting point.

Stakeholder	Goals, challenges, and possible impacts
Executives/CEO	• Ensuring the company looks innovative and customer-centric by being close to the pulse of the community. • Helping transform the business into a customer-centric organisation. • Identifying long-term trends. • Retaining best staff members.
Engineering	• Getting great feedback to fix product problems. • Identifying and fixing problems/bugs. • Getting the best insights about (or from) customers. • Prioritising what needs to be fixed and in which order. • Identifying trends by location and other data.
Sales	• Identifying new sales leads. • Increasing search traffic. • Turning members into advocates. • Integrating the community into the sales funnel. • Collecting great case studies for our sales/marketing teams. • Getting top members to publish reviews on major comparison sites.
Marketing	• Testing and improving marketing campaigns. • Sourcing great content ideas. • Increasing awareness of new products. • Gathering testimonials and use cases. • Testing marketing copy in the community.
Success/loyalty	• Building a repository of all our best official and unofficial product information. • Increasing the number of customers who develop their first apps/make their first use of a product. • Helping newcomers create their first success in using your products and keeping them around is an impact. • Improving customer satisfaction / NPS score. • Building a powerful sense of community amongst our customers.
PR	• Early warning system of potential PR disasters. • Developing use cases and interesting stories for journalists. • Capturing a desirable demographic of participants.

By the time you've completed this process, you should be able to list at least half a dozen possible goals of the community. The next step is to prioritise them.

Step 2: Prioritise your goals

It's important when you launch a new community not to try and tackle too many goals at once. I'd usually recommend beginning with just one clear goal and then expanding over time. But this means you need to decide the order you might tackle each goal.

If you're working alone or for a non-profit, your goal is likely to be the thing that delivers the most benefits to members. If you're working for an organisation, you need to also align your goals to the needs of the organisation.

There are three ways to establish priorities.

1 **What does your boss want?** The easiest way of prioritising your goals is simply asking your boss what she wants. Sometimes you might just be given a clear goal to aim for. This doesn't mean you can't have more goals later, but it does mean you have a clear goal to begin with.[7] If you are given a goal, make sure it's not something vague like 'increase engagement'. Try to make it specific like 'generate 30 reviews and make us the leader in our category' or 'answer 20% of customer calls via the community'. You don't want any ambiguity here about whether you achieve your goals or not.

2 **What is the biggest problem to solve?** The second approach is simply to begin with the biggest problem to solve or whichever goal would yield the most valuable results to the organisation. Often people have conflicting ideas about which problems to solve – so go with the problems of your colleagues who have the most influence and interest in the community first and work your way down.

3 **What is the easiest problem to solve?** The third option is to try and bank a quick win to build momentum. If your organisation isn't broadly supportive of your community or you're a little unsure of going it alone, start with the quickest possible win. This is often behaviour a few members can do (i.e. creating reviews, testimonials, or ideas) that shows an immediate impact. Once you gain support, you can tackle more goals with more resources.

Each approach has pros and cons. Getting a goal from your boss is easy, but I've often found that senior executives don't understand communities well enough to set goals and end up setting goals that are vague or aren't a good fit for a community.

If you get a good, clear goal then go with this. If you don't, then (if there is a good level of support for the community) go with the goals of the individual(s) with the most interest and influence over the community. If, however, the level of support for the community is minimal, go with the easiest goal to prove some success.

What if stakeholders don't agree?

I've often found myself in the difficult position in a consultancy project where stakeholders don't agree what the goal of the community should be.

When this happens I invite stakeholders to a workshop where we go through a series of activities where everyone can highlight their challenges, voice their concerns, and collaborate together to prioritise their goals.

You might still have to make a judgement call and not every stakeholder might agree, but at least everyone had a chance to be heard and give their opinion – as well as learning the opinions of others.

Step 3: Build your community roadmap

Once you have goals listed by priority, you can start building your community roadmap.

Your roadmap is a simple snapshot plan of your community which highlights what your community plans to achieve and by when. My roadmaps are divided into three stages: short, medium, and long term.

A community roadmap for personal communities and non-profits

A personal or non-profit roadmap might look like the table on the following page. Notice the gradual expansion from creating a sense of belonging, to exploration, to support. You don't have to go in this direction, but it helps to know your focus initially and how you will expand beyond that focus to provide the most value to members and the organisation over the long term.

Short term (0–1 year)	Medium term (1–2 years)	Long term (2–5 years)
Reach a critical mass of activity with 50+ posts per day.	Sustain a critical mass of activity with 75+ posts per day.	Reach maturity with 150+ posts per day.
Create a powerful sense of exclusivity and belonging amongst the first 300 members (survey measured).	Sustain a powerful sense of belonging as the community grows. Give members control over how the community is run.	Maintain a powerful sense of belonging. Hand over a majority of the running of the community to its members.
Collaborate to create the definitive guide to getting started in [topic].	Create one community-created guide every two months tackling the most popular topics.	Create one community-created guide every two months tackling the most popular topics.
	Create an area for members to file a 'field report' on what worked and didn't work for them.	Sustain and feature the top 20 'field reports' to other members each month.

As the community grows, so do the benefits it offers members. Remember, we're not tackling the strategies or tactics yet, we're simply determining the goals of the community.

A community roadmap for a business

A community roadmap for a business or large organisation is different. It focuses on the benefits of the community to the organisation. You can find an example below:

Short term (0–1 year)	Medium term (1–2 years)	Long term (2–5 years)
Resolve 25% of customer support questions via the community.	Resolve 50% of customer support questions.	Resolve 75% of customer support questions.
Generate 30 great testimonials.	Generate 50 great testimonials.	Generate 75 great testimonials.
Post 10 approved case studies.	Post 30 approved case studies.	Post 60 approved case studies.

Short term (0–1 year)	Medium term (1–2 years)	Long term (2–5 years)
	Build a knowledge base of customers' best advice.	Build a knowledge base of customers' best advice.
	Validate our engineering priorities using community data and ideas.	Validate our engineering priorities using community data and ideas.
		Test marketing and PR copy in the community before launch.
		Embed community participation into the employee training process.
		Generate reviews on key community comparison sites.

You should generally assume that as the community grows and delivers better results, the community will receive additional investments which will enable us to tackle more goals.

As you can see in the example above, you begin by setting achievable goals in your first year and steadily expand as you demonstrate results. Notice how achievable these results seem. Keep the goals as simple as possible when you get started to avoid setting unrealistic expectations. You can always raise the bar later, but it's harder to lower it.

To create a roadmap you can use our template available from: www.feverbee.com/buildyourcommunity.

Step 4: Turn your goals into behaviours

The next step is to determine the behaviours members need to perform to achieve these goals. For each of your goals above, you need to list *precisely* what you need your members to do. This is how you set your objectives for the community. If you're working for a business, you're most likely to be measured by these objectives, so be careful in deciding them.

Sometimes this process is easy. If you want to help the sales team gather great testimonials, you need members to create testimonials. If you want to gather product feedback, you need members to send emails or create posts giving feedback.

Sometimes this is more difficult. If you want to increase satisfaction or retention, what kind of behaviours lead to that? It might be solving problems, learning to use your products, having a great community experience, or one of a dozen other activities. This in turn might mean you want community members to complete newcomer programmes, training courses, read top articles etc.

To help you think about the potential behaviours you might want members to perform in the community, I've added many of the most common ones below.

Goal	Behaviour to achieve the goal
Increase customer satisfaction (loyalty)	• Asking product questions and getting quick feedback • Reading information about the product's superiority • Reading advice on getting more from the product • Using the product/service with friends • Earning points or status that make switching difficult
Generate and identify leads	• Creating content that attracts high search traffic • Sharing problems that self-identify the member as a good lead • Downloading product information that self-identifies the member as a useful lead • Asking pre-purchase related questions • Searching for product information
Advocacy/ spreading word of mouth	• Sharing community content with friends • Writing reviews and testimonials
Reducing customer support costs	• Asking product questions in the community • Answering product questions in the community • Searching for the answer in the community • Tagging, updating, and documenting product questions
Generating product ideas	• Suggesting new ideas • Posting product feedback • Voting on ideas • Participating in focus groups • Responding to surveys

Goal	Behaviour to achieve the goal
Increasing reach/reducing advertising costs	• Subscribing to the mailing list • Opening emails from the brand • Clicking on links in the email
Recruitment	• Answering questions that demonstrate expertise • Viewing job advertisements posted in the community • Sharing job advertisements posted in the community
Improving productivity/ reducing duplication of costs	• Asking for help in the community instead of via email • Answering questions in the community • Tagging and sharing documents • Tagging people with skills and expertise • Updating documents • Inviting people to share their expertise
Donations/ fundraising/ collective actions	• Starting a petition • Signing a petition • Sending a donation • Raising money from friends
Better informed members (non-profit)	• Asking questions in the community about personal challenges • Posting personal experiences • Reading the experiences of others

This is far from a comprehensive list, so feel free to add your own. Remember a community creates dynamics for amazing contributions to happen – but you can't anticipate it will magically happen. Far too many community efforts try to generate as much engagement as possible without being precise in what kind of engagement they need. If you aren't clear about what you want members to do, the odds on them doing it are extremely low.

What verb is it? (Be specific)

You shouldn't use vague verbs in your objectives. For example; 'sharing best practices' is vague. Does that mean replying to discussions, posting content, creating videos or something else?

▶

You, your colleagues, and your audience might have completely different interpretations of what that means. A far better objective is getting members to 'create long-form blog posts tackling major challenges our members face'.

Try to replace verbs like 'sharing', 'collaborating', and 'supporting' with more specific verbs and phrases like 'creating blog posts', 'replying to questions', and 'joining groups' so everyone understands what you're trying to achieve.

Once you have decided what members need to do to achieve these goals, add them to the template below each phase.

Short term (0–1 year)	Medium term (1–2 years)	Long term (2–5 years)
Resolve 25% of customer support questions via the community.	Resolve 50% of customer support questions.	Resolve 75% of customer support questions.
Generate 30 great testimonials.	Generate 50 great testimonials.	Generate 75 great testimonials.
Post 10 approved case studies.	Post 30 approved case studies.	Post 60 approved case studies.
	Build a knowledge base of customers' best advice.	Build a knowledge base of customers' best advice.
	Validate our engineering priorities using community data and ideas.	Validate our engineering priorities using community data and ideas.
		Test marketing and PR copy in the community before launch.
		Generate reviews on key community comparison sites.

Short term (0–1 year)	Medium term (1–2 years)	Long term (2–5 years)
Key member behaviours at each stage		
Asking questions in the community instead of filing a ticket or calling customer support. Answering questions in the community.	Asking questions in the community instead of filing a ticket or calling customer support. Answering questions in the community.	Asking questions in the community instead of filing a ticket or calling customer support. Answering questions in the community.
Creating video testimonials.	Creating video testimonials. Requesting video testimonials from other members.	Creating video testimonials. Requesting video testimonials from other members.
Posting case studies in the community. Reading and learning from the case studies of others.	Posting case studies in the community. Reading and learning from the case studies of others.	Posting case studies in the community. Reading and learning from the case studies of others.
	Writing long-form advice articles on key topics in the community.	Writing long-form advice articles on key topics in the community.
	Voting on the current engineering roadmap.	Voting on the current engineering roadmap.
		Giving feedback on marketing copy.
		Posting reviews on comparison sites.

Every behaviour should be clear and precise. Using the above example, we now know when we launch this community we need members to ask questions in the community, answer questions in the community, create video testimonials, publish their case studies, and read the case studies of others. Our entire approach will be designed to get members to do that – this is especially important when we try to decide what technology to use.

WARNING – Don't get sucked into the engagement trap!

Far too many community programmes try to generate as much engagement as possible. This is like firing a scattergun and hoping you hit something. More engagement can help, but it can also hurt as well.

Bigger communities have more problems you need to deal with. They attract more trolls, they are harder to manage, and tend to become less intimate for the kind of members you want to attract. It doesn't matter how much engagement you have if members aren't doing what you need them to do.

Never let yourself be measured solely by the level of engagement you create. It's unsustainable and doesn't help you achieve your goals.

By this point you should be able to speak confidently about the goals of your community, the behaviours you need members to perform, and the type of community you're trying to build. In the next chapter you will learn what motivates members to participate in communities and the strategies you might deploy to persuade members to perform the behaviours you've listed here.

Summary

An online community transforms the passion, expertise, and resources of your audience into indispensable assets for you, your members, and your business. A great community produces a great ROI, but it's hard to measure and show that. The real value of the community appears just below the surface of profitability. We call these the 'visible impacts' of the community and they can support many areas of an organisation and help you achieve your personal goals.

If you want your community to have a great impact, you need to design it with the right impact in mind. First, determine what type of community you're building. Each type has its pros and cons. The strategies and technology you use will be heavily influenced by the type of community you're building.

Next, speak to your colleagues and find out what they need and list out the potential problems your community can solve. Prioritise these and put them into a short-, medium-, and long-term roadmap.

Finally, determine which behaviours you need to achieve which goals. You can list these by year too. These are your objectives. Once you have clear goals and objectives, both for today and tomorrow, you will find everything else becomes much easier.

Checklist

---

1 Speak to colleagues to develop a list of problems your community can solve.

2 Prioritise these problems by the severity of the issue, the ease of solving it, or by the influencer of the interested stakeholder.

3 Create a roadmap with short-, medium-, and long-term goals for the community.

4 Turn these goals into objectives (behaviours that members need to perform to achieve these goals).

5 Determine the metrics of success for your community.

6 Get your entire plan approved by stakeholders.

Tools of the trade
(available at www.feverbee.com/ buildyourcommunity)

- FeverBee's Template Roadmap
- Questions To Ask Stakeholders
- FeverBee's Strategy Template
- The Community Guide to Measuring Return on Investment
- Templates for Hosting a Community Workshop

chapter 2

Who is your community for?

The secret to a thriving community is *relevance*.

Think about how many people are fighting for your attention right now. Instead of participating in your community, your members could be enjoying clips of the *Daily Show* on YouTube, catching up with friends on WhatsApp, or binge-watching a new series on Netflix. The war for attention is ferocious.

Even if your audience feels a compelling need to ask questions, learn from others, or share their expertise, there's no guarantee they will do it in your community. They can also do this on social media, in other communities, or by talking to their friends and colleagues.

So, why would they decide to visit and participate in your community?

If you can't answer this question, your community is doomed.

Your audience will only visit and participate in your community if it is the most relevant method for them to satisfy their needs and desires at a given moment. These needs and desires will vary throughout the day. When you're waiting for a bus, you might simply want to kill time and visiting Facebook might be the most relevant way to do that. When you're at work, you might need an answer to a software question and the software company's community might be the most relevant way to do that. Yet while these needs and desires vary by the hour, day, and month, the principle remains the same. Your community needs to be the most relevant method for your members to satisfy their needs and desires at some point in their lives.

Relevance is the magnet which draws your members in and keeps them coming back.

Relevance shapes what features you add and remove on the community platform. It determines what activities and discussions you initiate. And, most importantly, it guides who you invite to join your community. Every decision you make about your community should be designed to make it the single most relevant place for your audience to satisfy their needs and desires.

Relevance often falls into one of two categories. A community is either relevant to a large number of people for a short amount of their time (i.e. support communities) or is relevant to a small number of people for a large amount of time (interest and belonging-related communities).

Facebook thrives because you get to express yourself and keep in touch with what friends are doing better than anywhere else. The Apple community thrives because it's the best place to get help for people who don't want to call customer support when their iPhone tracker breaks. The Fenty Beauty community thrives because it's the very best place to show off your look and get featured on the homepage of a top brand.[1]

Who is your community relevant to?

If you're trying to be relevant to everybody, you'll end up being relevant to nobody.

Your audience is simply too diverse. Your audience isn't a homogenous mass of people with identical needs and aspirations. They have different backgrounds, different experiences, and might even work in completely different fields. Some might be enthusiastic newcomers to the topic and others might be grizzled veterans. What is relevant to one group may be completely different for another.

For example, newcomers may want advice on how to get started in the topic, recommendations on what products and services to buy, and tips to avoid making common mistakes. Veterans might want exclusive news and insights, advanced tips, and to feel recognised for their experiences.

Deciding who the community is for (especially at the beginning) is the critical decision you will make about your community.

This isn't an easy option. You might have dozens of options. Imagine you're building a community for product managers. You can build a community for product managers by their level of experience (newcomer, veteran etc.), by their location (product managers in New York, London, New Delhi etc.), by their sector (technology, retail, sports etc.), or even by the type of company they work for (small, medium, large enterprise etc.).

These decisions will determine how relevant the community is to your audience. If you're a product manager working at a Fortune 500 company, you will probably find a community *exclusively* for product managers at Fortune 500 companies far more relevant than a community for any product manager from any field. This can be the difference between one in ten discussions being relevant to you and nine in ten discussions being relevant to you. In turn, that's the difference between a community you visit every day and one you might remember every few months.

The secret is to narrow your target audience to get started. For example, if you're building a community about a passion, say baking bread, the kinds of discussions and information which will be relevant to professional bakers is very different from weekend amateurs. While the professionals may want to discuss the pricing and comparative abilities of commercial ovens, amateurs may just want to know which yeast to use or how to stop baking lopsided loaves.

It becomes a lot easier to attract people in the beginning when you've zeroed in precisely on who you're targeting and what you want.

Exclusivity is a powerful tool

In 2012, a provider of healthcare services reached out to me with a very familiar problem: *their members weren't participating.*

They wanted to create a community which would attract influencers and buyers of healthcare services to participate in their ecosystem. They had hired a well-known design firm to put together the communication plan, a small community team to try and drive a high level of engagement, and spent a huge sum of money on a fancy technology platform.

The platform had everything you could possibly want. It had areas for discussions, private groups, blogging, gamification, social media integration, and more. It was packed full of features very few people were using.

Every few months they would try a new campaign, competition, or promotional blitz to attract people to the community. Each effort would drive a spike in activity. But these newcomers vanished almost as quickly as they

▶

had arrived. The community was an expensive ghost town. By the time the company reached out to me, they were coming to the conclusion they needed to change to a new community platform.

I felt this would be a mistake. The problem wasn't the platform they were using, but the audience they were targeting. Moving a ghost town to another platform doesn't magically populate it with people. The community simply wasn't a place where their audience wanted to spend their time. The problem was they were trying to appeal to too many people at once. It wasn't relevant enough to any of the audiences they were targeting.

We tried a different approach. Instead of trying to create a community for everyone and hope influencers and senior purchasing managers in the healthcare sector drifted in, we created a community solely for the top people. We created a list of the top 217 people in the sector and launched an exclusive group just for them.

Each person on the list received a personal invite to the private group from the CEO explaining why they (specifically) were being invited, what the group was for, and who they would get to connect with.

Once they were in the group, we initiated and solicited discussions on topical issues (which we uncovered in our audience research), hosted private online webinars and offline events, and helped introduce people to each other. Most importantly, we invested hours each month reaching out to each participant to find out exactly what they needed – then we followed up to ensure they were getting this a few weeks later.

It would've been impossible to do this kind of work in a community with thousands of members. But because we had narrowed the audience, we only needed to reach out to five to ten people per day to contact everyone each month.

The results were immediate. The majority of the group made at least one contribution each month and discussions have been active ever since. Members of the group have constantly told us how this tiny community is in their work and how they feel they've finally found their peers. This community has become a private place for top figures in the industry to openly share and help one another.

Most importantly, my client directly tracked $4.3m in increased purchases directly as a result of relationships and conversations which began in our new community. The group might be small compared with the mega-communities, but it connected my client to all the key players in the industry. Better yet, they realised this group didn't need a fancy, expensive platform. They simply needed exclusivity and the VIP treatment.

If you want your community to be a priority it has to have unparalleled relevance to the lives of your members. This is what ensures your audience visits your community out of habit at the start of their day instead of hoping they get around to it at the end of the day. If you can't make your community relevant, your audience will never make it a priority.

Daily relevance vs long-term relevance

We can split relevance into two categories: things that are relevant to you today and things that are relevant to your long-term goals.

In the long term, you probably want to be happy, healthy, and wealthy with good relationships with your spouse, family, friends, and peers. But today you might be looking for tips to increase engagement in your community, trying to find a good restaurant to meet your buddies tonight, or looking for the right time to ask for a pay rise.

Understanding the difference between what's relevant in the short term and long term can be critical to making your community succeed. It's always tempting to build a community around big, noble, long-term goals. But, in my experience, it's far better to position the community to serve these immediate, daily needs.

A few years ago, I was hired to save a dying community of teachers. The community had been running for almost five years, but activity had been declining for the past two. I was the third consultant brought into the project. The previous two had undertaken research, discovered that teachers were too busy, and recommended the community should require less time to use. None of these recommendations had worked.

They had listened to what teachers were saying but hadn't properly understood what they needed. Making the community easier to use didn't make the community more relevant to teachers right now. People make time for things which are important enough anyhow. The problem was the community wasn't relevant to their daily needs.

If this community of teachers are saying they're too overwhelmed with work and don't have any time, the solution is so obvious it's easy to miss it. I helped my client reinvent the very nature of the community. Lack of time was the most pressing problem for teachers so we reinvented the community to solve that very problem. We turned the entire community into a place for teachers to swap their time-saving tips.

We brought in productivity experts, let teachers track how much time they had saved with each idea, and we highlighted our time-saving ideas of the week.

We created a 'quick time-saving tips' area as well as photos and videos showing some of the tips they had used.

Activity in the teachers' community rose slowly in the first month after our changes and then rapidly over the coming few months. Within six months, the community had surpassed its peak activity. The key was identifying what was relevant to our members today. Once we had nailed that concept, it became easier to build our engagement plan.

The word 'today' is critical here. Sure, teachers still cared about the long-term future of the profession, discussing salary issues, and deeply wanted to help their students. But *today* they were simply too busy to ever make it a priority. Once the community was about their biggest challenge *right now*, it became a priority.

Another great example comes from a struggling community for sales and revenue professionals I worked with in 2018. The community had been created with the broad goal of helping members share advice and expertise. However, our research showed sales professionals most needed case study templates, proposal templates, and the right language to use in their sales calls.

Instead of continuing to drive people to participate in discussions, we sourced 150 templates from a tiny group of members (and linked to others across the web) to get started. Then we told members if they wanted access to this treasure trove, they needed to share their own templates and resources (notice how we're solving the collective action problem here). Each new template was added to the pot which in turn attracted more people to share their own. This virtuous cycle also drove discussions around the best types of templates to use for each situation and steadily increased participation in the community.

If you want your community to thrive, don't be vague about the benefits or broad in its purpose, but ensure the community is aligned to the needs of your members right now. No one needs to join 'just another community'; they want to join a community which serves their daily needs.

This is critical in every type of community. Even if you're running a small WhatsApp group with close friends, you still want to solve the immediate needs of your members. That might be having fun, feeling like they belong, or planning an upcoming trip.

When you're trying to get a community off the ground, it's usually best to find the smallest possible segment you can delight by solving their daily needs.

This raises the obvious question however, *how do you find out what the daily needs of your audience are?*

Step 1: Set up and run a survey

The most obvious way to find out what your audience wants is to ask them.

If you're building a community as a hobby for a small group (fewer than 100 people), you can reach out to the vast majority of them over a few weeks and ask them. The answers will be invaluable.

If you're working on behalf of an organisation, however, you have two common approaches. The first is easy – select one of the personas or archetypes your organisation has already created. Many, if not most, organisations already have segments or customer personas you can use. Check with your marketing or sales team. If you're lucky, they might even have divided their customer base into separate email groups based upon these segments. This will save you plenty of time.

If your organisation doesn't have this (or you're not able to use them), you need to do the research yourself. The easiest way to identify your segments is to use a survey. There are plenty of useful tools available. The cheapest and easiest to use include SurveyMonkey, Google Forms, and Typeform. You can also use more advanced tools like Qualtrics and SurveyGizmo. For simplicity, I tend to prefer SurveyMonkey.

Your survey should try to probe into the demographics, behaviours, and psychographics of your audience (you can find our template surveys for both existing and new communities at www.feverbee.com/buildyourcommunity).

I've included a breakdown of each of these below:

Question type	Why is it useful?
Demographics	Demographics questions often provide the easiest way to map out and develop audience segments. You might ask questions relating to the member's type (customer, staff, reseller, partner, developer), sector (telecoms, non-profit, retail etc.), age, sex, and location.
Behavioural	Behavioural questions are questions about what your members have done (and do). The most common are questions related to years of experience as a customer, community member, or working in that sector/interested in that topic. This is important because the needs of newcomers to your field are often very different from the needs of experts and this provides an easy means of segmenting members. It's also useful here to ask questions about what brings them to an existing community or where else they get useful information.

▶

Question type	Why is it useful?
Psychographics	Psychographic questions are where you start digging deeper into your audience's character traits, needs, and desires. It's good to ask them what areas of the community they find most useful, their primary interest in the topic, and to identify potentially useful pain points. We typically use rating and ranking features for these kinds of questions.

Not every question is relevant for every community. Feel free to adapt the survey to suit your situation. Ideally you should be aiming to ask no more than seven questions. The fewer questions you have, the more people will complete the survey. Push back against colleagues who try to add more questions to a survey. If you don't know precisely what you will do with the answers, don't ask the question.

Try to avoid offering incentives for completing the survey. The number of people who take the time to complete a survey is a good indicator of the number of people likely to join the community when you get started. This will be useful information if you need to make membership projections later.

How to find people to survey

You can usually find survey recipients from your existing customer list, your mailing list, newsletter list, or (if you have no audience to begin with) through social ads and promotions through other channels.

If you're reaching out to an audience who doesn't know you at all, you might be forced to offer a small incentive to get people to respond. Typically a chance to win a small prize might be good enough – but only do this if you have to.

To have a high level of validity, aim to get at least 285 responses.[2] Collect a lot more if you can, but 285 is usually the minimum. This usually means you need to send the survey to around 2500–5000 people. Don't worry too much if you can't do that, but be aware the more responses you gain the more valid the results will be.

Step 2: Identifying your segments

Now comes the finicky part. In the survey, you're looking for clusters of members with distinct shared needs, behaviours, or interests. Go through the questions one by one and compare future responses by answers to each question.

Some tools, such as SurveyMonkey, make this simple by offering a comparison tool which lets you filter and compare answers between clusters of people formed from other questions (i.e. you can compare challenges listed from people who joined the community within the past year against veterans). You might use answers to a sector question (retail, technology, non-profit etc.) as a means of comparing later answers looking for significant differences.

This isn't as scientific as you might hope, but you should be able to find some clusters as you play around with different filters. You will probably have some hunches about what the different clusters might be. So test your hunches. Often it's factors like age, location, or what kind of work they do which help decide the unique segments amongst your audience.

SurveyMonkey even offers a statistical significance option to reveal whether the filter you're using does produce meaningful differences in responses (or whether those differences could be caused by random chance). I've created a video showing how to do this on www.feverbee.com/buildyourcommunity.

List the different segments you find

Each time you find a potentially unique segment, list the segment and outline what makes the segment unique. You're not looking to neatly split every possible member of the community into distinctive groups, you're simply trying to create an outline of possible segments you might target. Ideally, you want to find distinct segments with unique daily needs you can satisfy better than any other channel.

You can turn these into full personas if you like, but simply listing the unique interests of the segment usually suffices. A typical example might include:

Segment	Summary from research
Newcomers (using our products for 0–1 year)	• Drawn to the community by an immediate product problem and wants a response without being attacked for asking a dumb question. • Looking for examples and guides they can follow. • Worried about being overwhelmed with too much information too soon. • Typically ask for help via customer support and via friends they know who use the product (by email).

▶

Segment	Summary from research
Intermediates (using our products for 1–2 years)	• Most interested in Q&A and long-form content if well organised. • Will sometimes browse questions and answer some if they know the answer. • Visit most frequently to get the latest product news and updates.
Veterans (using our products for 2+ years)	• Visit frequently out of habit to see if there is something new they can learn from. • Care greatly about the signal to noise ratio. Too much beginner-level content in the community. • Like to quickly scan the community and will open several tabs at once to respond to relevant questions at the beginning of the day. • Want a more private place to chat with fellow-veteran users and feel a part of the company's mission.

You can also dive deeper into specific segments using two qualifiers (i.e. veterans who live in the USA) or newcomers who use specific products etc. Don't be afraid to look at any number of answers to compare your members and identify the unique needs of each.

Step 3: Selecting your first segment(s)

Now you need to decide which of these segments you will serve to get started.

You can make this decision in one of two ways.

The first is to serve the segment you feel would be most valuable to the organisation. You can list each segment by their value and begin with the one at the top. For example, if you're building a customer support community, you might launch your community helping customers with a single type of problem or focus solely on newcomers and gradually expand. Likewise, you might build a community just for your most loyal customers, most passionate fans, or those with the most experience in the topic.

The second approach is to look for the segment most likely to participate in a community. This is typically the easiest way to get a community going. This is usually either the segment you have the best relationships with already, the segment which has a clear passion for something your community could provide, or the segment with the least competition for their attention (hint: it's generally best to avoid areas of high competition to get started).

How many segments should you target at once?

This should raise a fairly obvious question: 'Can't I target multiple segments at once?'

You certainly can, but you increase the risk of not satisfying any segment's desires well enough. As we'll soon see, serving any single segment is a lot of effort. Trying to serve more is like hosting multiple parties at once. It's usually far better to focus on supporting one single segment and expand from there.

This doesn't mean you need to forbid members of other segments of your audience from joining. It just means you need to be clear who your focus is on to get started.

Step 4: Conduct interviews to identify use cases

Now it's time to go deep in understanding what your audience desires.

It's critical to spend time with your audience at events and in person. I've spent several days sitting with prospective members at their offices or in coffee shops trying to get the full picture of what they need. When this isn't possible, you can try and schedule phone interviews to talk to prospective (or current) members of your community.

I recommend interviewing around three to five members of each segment (ideally in person or on voice chat) to get a deeper sense of who they are and what they need.

For example, the community of sales professionals from earlier were clear that they wanted templates of proposals and case studies, but it was only in the interviews where I could find out precisely what type of templates they needed and in what format (e.g. sales proposals in presentation format). Once I knew that, we could make sure this community was filled with these very templates when we launched.

You can find these interviewees either through your existing mailing list or by inviting people to put themselves forward in an email to your audience. Remember an interview isn't a survey. You might begin with a few broad questions, but you should push deeper to get the precise context and background information. It's one thing for a member to say they like useful information, it's another to describe what precisely they're working on now and the exact materials they need (and in what format). I also like to ask questions about their needs (or challenges), ambitions, and who they consider their peers or feel similar to.

Using your interview data, you should be able to identify precisely what members need. We can then turn these needs into specific 'use cases' for the community. You can see an example below (targeting a newcomer segment).

Member need	Use case
Not be overwhelmed with information.	• Newcomers receive a restricted set of information upon joining the community focused only on the next actions they need to take.
Get guided through the journey of what they should tackle at each stage.	• Newcomers advance through a structured 30-day programme of discussions, mentoring, and in-house expertise.
Feel confident enough to ask a question without being attacked.	• Newcomers are partnered with an experienced mentor with whom they can ask and answer questions. • Newcomers join a private group to ask beginner-level questions and not risk being embarrassed in front of others.
Get advice on their particular situation.	• Members can share screenshots of what they're working on and see the screenshots of others to get instant feedback.
Know if they're doing it right.	• Members share and track their progress against others also going through the same stage of progress.
Easily find relevant information and documentation.	• Members receive pop-ups in the product directing people where they can see questions and answers relating to this phase.
Feel connected to others in their exact situation.	• Members can see the number of days a member has been using the product in their profile information.
Feel a sense of achievement at achieving minor things.	• Newcomers advance through a graduation when members have surpassed 30–60 days (along with a reward /discount/referral code).

What is a use case?

Put simply, a use case simply describes how your community might be used by your target audience. If members say they need information, a use case might be searching for information about a topic within that community, asking a question for that information, or reading information that has been posted by other members.

Use cases turn a list of emotive needs and desires you gather from your members into concrete actions people need to perform within the community. You will use these later to select your technology and design your community.

Hopefully now you can see the contours of your community beginning to take shape. You should now be able to get a clear sense of what your community is going to be about and what will happen within the community. In the next chapter, you will learn how to take these use cases above and begin designing the perfect community experience for your audience.

In later chapters you will also learn how to use this framework to create content and discussions your members will love. Remember the purpose of this process is to help your community explode into life (or reinvigorate an existing community). You do this by making sure it's the most relevant place for your members to satisfy their daily needs.

Summary

The war for your members' attention is ferocious. If you want your community to thrive, you need to satisfy the daily needs of your audience better than any other channel. However, the needs of your audience are too diverse to satisfy them all at once. Instead you need to segment your audience by unique needs and decide which you will target at first. You can run a simple survey to understand these segments and select the best ones for you.

Once you know your chosen segment(s), get to know them intimately. Attend the same events they do, interview three to five members of the audience, and drill as deep down as you can go into understanding what they need. As you get to know them, you should be able to list a number of needs and turn these into use cases for your community.

These needs and use cases will inform every decision we later make in your community. Your unrelenting mission is to make the community the most relevant place possible for your members to solve their daily needs and desires.

Checklist

- -

1 Create a survey for your members.

2 Use filtering to create segments of your audience.

3 List unique segments.

4 Select best segment to launch community.

5 Interview members to identify needs.

6 Develop a list of needs for each segment.

7 Turn these needs into specific use cases.

Tools of the trade
(available from www.feverbee.com/ buildyourcommunity)

- -

For surveys

- SurveyMonkey
- Qualtrics
- Google Forms
- Typeforms
- FeverBee's Survey Templates
- FeverBee's Audience Interview Questions
- FeverBee's Segmentation Templates
- FeverBee's Use Cases Template

For interviews

- Zoom
- Skype (w/SkypeRecorder)

chapter 3

Creating your community experience

If you haven't tried to develop your own community website before, it can feel like walking through a minefield with a blindfold on. There are a whole bunch of things which can blow up (and you don't even know about them yet).

I've seen organisations flush millions of dollars down the drain through terribly designed community websites. Almost nothing causes community leaders more stress than trying to create a new community website from scratch. Like building a home, it often winds up being far more expensive, time-consuming, and difficult than you ever anticipated.

This chapter is going to guide you through the process of building a home for your community. Whether you're creating a community for a few dozen members or coordinating the efforts of millions of customers, your community needs a place where members can engage and interact with each other. While some organisations invest millions of dollars in a community platform, others create something that works really well for their members for less than a few hundred dollars. And if you're going this alone and forgo a few features, you can even develop an effective community platform for free.

In this chapter you're going to learn what community platforms are available, how to select the right community platform for your audience, and how to design your community platform. I'm also going to highlight some of the common mistakes to avoid and how to deal with other issues which may arise.

What's the difference between a community platform and a community website?

Let's begin by distinguishing between two key terms; *community platform* and a *community website*. They're often used interchangeably but they mean very different things.

A *platform* is a set of technologies which you will use to create your website. Facebook, for example, is a platform where you can host groups.

A community *website* is built upon a platform and is the home for your community. It is what your members will see and how they will interact with one another. For example, the Spotify community *website* is built upon the Khoros *platform*. The Khoros platform also hosts the communities for Fitbit, HP, and Sephora websites and many others.

To keep things simple and avoid confusion, I'm going to refer to any interface you create on a platform as a 'community website' (even though this won't be strictly true if you use a tool like WhatsApp or Slack).

It's best to think of this process like finding a house to live in. Some community platforms offer something akin to pre-built homes. You can simply slap your name on the letterbox and move in. Others give you the materials and expect you to assemble it yourself. You can customise it exactly how you want, but it will cost you time and money.

What type of platform should you use?

Before deciding what platform to use, you need to figure out which approach you plan to take. You have five broad options here:

1 Build your own platform

You can simply build your own community platform from scratch. The main benefit of this is you don't need to pay a licence fee (more on that soon) and you can customise it anyway you like. Most of the major sites you can think of like Facebook, LinkedIn, Reddit, and Stack Overflow were also custom-built. Some large brands have recently taken this route too.

However, be warned this is exactly like building your own house from scratch. If you haven't done it before, you're going to find it's more complex than you imagine. Even if you hire experts, you're still going to face challenges you don't expect. Many people who try this approach soon realise it's far more trouble than it's worth. It's hard for any organisation to create a community experience comparable to one provided by one of the major platform providers.

The major community platform providers have more skills, knowledge, and experience in communities than you do. Their entire organisations are designed to do precisely this one thing extremely well. When you purchase a platform, you're not just paying for the technology, you're also saving yourself from making a tonne of costly mistakes. The major benefit of creating your own platform (ensuring it has every possible feature you could want and saving on licence fees) is usually outweighed by the trouble you will face making it work in practice.

The only two groups who should attempt this are the very largest organisations with a tonne of expertise and resources or the start-ups who have nothing to lose and are keen to try something new and risky.

2 White-label platforms

White-label platforms are pre-built community platforms which you can brand as your own. You can best think of these as prefabricated houses. They're fully built for you, you can move in today, and they're cheaper compared to other options.

However, it's cheaper because (like a prefabricated home) every website looks almost identical. These platforms work by offering the same product to everyone instead of customising each website to each community. You can change a few things, but you're largely restricted in what you can do.

The term 'white label' means that it's your name, rather than the name of the platform, that appears on the community. This is what separates these platforms from Facebook groups, LinkedIn groups, Reddit, and other platforms which are free – but carries the platform's branding rather than your own.

So why not just use one of these free platforms instead of a white-label platform? The main reason is not only can you customise white-label platforms more, but being a paying customer means you can expect someone to answer the phone when you call with problems (try getting Facebook on the phone when you're not happy!).

It also means the platform provider won't suddenly delete your group from existence without explanation as happens often on Facebook. Imagine spending years building up a Facebook group and one day finding it has disappeared due to a vague complaint and you have no means of getting it back. You can also expect better communication about what's coming up and give feedback to a real person. You also won't typically have advertising in your community (especially from competitors!). Remember the reason social media tools are free is because you're helping them sell advertising to your members.

There are plenty of small white-label platforms to choose from. Three of the most popular are Mighty Networks, Tribe, and Hivebrite. All three of these platforms allow you to select what features you want (discussions, private groups, online courses, file sharing etc.), customise the design a little, and launch your community in a matter of minutes.

At the time of writing, both Mighty Networks and Tribe are free for the most basic options with costs rising to $57 per month to $87 per month with premium features and support. Hivebrite offers a more advanced range of features with prices beginning at $5k per year. If you have limited budget and technical capacity, these are a great way to get your community started and test different ideas before upgrading later.

The big advantage of using white-label tools is they're typically quicker to launch and a lot less risky than investing a large sum of money on a fancy community website (especially before you've got thousands of members ready to use it). You don't have to pay a lot of money upfront and hope people show up.

The obvious downside is these platforms don't have many of the features of enterprise platforms. It can be tricky to connect these platforms to your existing databases and you can't customise the platform the way you might want. It can also be really hard to leave these platforms when you want to move on.

For example, if you can't move your community's data from one platform to another, you need all your members to recreate their accounts and lose all the previous conversations and expertise they've shared. That can be extremely painful.

3 Open source platforms (and self-hosting)

Let's go back to our house analogy for a second. You don't just need a house, you also need somewhere to put the house. In technology terms, this is called *hosting*. Your website, for example, is hosted on a server somewhere. You pay a fee for the use of that server. Communities are the same. When you pay for a community platform, you're not just paying for the community technology, you're usually also paying them to host the community for you.

This means they act as your landlords. You pay them a licence fee and they keep the software updated, maintain it, and generally fix things when they go wrong (although some might charge extra for this). The upside of this is someone else takes care of the dirty work. The downside is it costs money.

An alternative option between creating your own site and using a white-label platform is to use open source software. This is software provided by an organisation (or community of coders and developers), which you can download for free and customise as much as you like. You also host it yourself (on a web server either you own or, more likely, rent from a third party such as Amazon web services).

The upside of this approach is it's inexpensive, you begin with something that works (i.e. you're not developing something from scratch), and you typically have a community you can call upon for support. The downside is you often still need to spend plenty of time customising it to your whims and you have to take care of all the fiddly bits yourself. These fiddly bits include upgrading the software every time it's updated, ensuring there's no major security risk, and fixing things which break. Unless you have an advanced level of technical expertise (and experience working with open source software), I'd suggest avoiding open source options for now.

4 Enterprise platforms

The luxury homes of the community platform world are fully fledged enterprise community platforms. Most of the largest customer communities today are hosted by around half a dozen enterprise platforms. The reason for this is simple. Big brands have very specific needs and don't want their big new community initiative hosted on a cheap platform with limited features.

Technically, enterprise platforms are also white-label platforms. They give you the software and you can slap your name and logo on it. Most of your members won't even know whose software they're using. The difference is the range and depth of features enterprise platforms offer.

These features typically extend far beyond just question and answer forums. Members can typically share blog posts, publish their own documentation (knowledge base), earn points through their contributions and get a ranking (gamification), livestream themselves, submit and vote on the ideas of others (ideation), create and join groups, and much, much more.

Enterprise platforms also tend to offer more advanced search, onboarding (more on this later) features, and better abilities to integrate with your existing systems. This last feature, integration with your current database, is important. You don't want your customers to have to remember different usernames and passwords. At this level, integration does not only mean the seamless ability to sign on (or stay logged in) when a customer moves from your company website to the community, but also to track community and purchase activity all in one place.

For example, your customer support team would know what questions a customer has asked in the community before and what answers they've viewed. They can use this information to avoid telling customers things they've already tried and guide them to the best solutions. You can also get interesting data about what customers really want based upon their participation in the community.

Enterprise platforms also typically offer more customisation, advanced privacy and security options, and additional services to help you run and grow your community. At large companies, it will be impossible to gain approval for any software that doesn't match the company's security requirements – this often means you're forced to use enterprise platforms by default.

At the time of writing, the top enterprise platforms are Salesforce (Community Cloud), Khoros (formerly Lithium), Telligent (Verint), inSided, Higher Logic, Vanilla, and Discourse. While there are certainly a plethora of other contenders, it's often best to stick with a known name. The reason for this is simple. If you've spent a tonne of time and money setting up your community on a platform, you don't want to find out your platform vendor is struggling financially and may either shut down the business or not be able to compete with better platforms.

What are you buying?

It's important you know what you're buying with an enterprise platform. As we've mentioned before, you're not buying the software, you're licensing the right to use it for a specific period of time (typically around three years).

The licensing fees for these platforms reflect their breadth of features. They tend to range from tens of thousands to a few million dollars per year. In our experience, most organisations can expect a cost ranging from $80k to $400k per year. You might also purchase premium support packages to get immediate help if things go wrong.

There are two major downsides to using an enterprise platform. The most obvious is cost. The cost to set up a platform includes not only the licence to use it, but also the implementation fees. This is the cost of designing and configuring your community to function and look the way you want.

Another downside is time. After you've gone through a lengthy procurement process you still need to set up the platform, integrate it with existing systems etc. This frequently takes three to six months from the date you sign the contract to going live with the community.

Both of these are driving another major downside; *risk*. The greater the cost and the longer it takes to set up, the greater the pressure for the community to prove itself and become an instant success. If this doesn't happen, your colleagues might quickly begin to question the value of your community. If the community doesn't catch on, you could still be paying hundreds of thousands of dollars a year for the rest of the contract.

5 Use free tools

You might be thinking that setting up a fancy enterprise platform sounds like an almighty amount of trouble. Does your community really need a fancy platform to host activity? What if you don't have a few thousand dollars a year to spend on your community platform? Why not just use the same social media tools you and your audience are using every day?

Your audience already spends hours every day on social media, the platforms are free to use and in many cases have the most advanced features available. You can get started right now and let these platforms take care of all the fiddly stuff.

You can create a pretty decent community experience using tools that are available right now. You can use Twitter, Slack, WhatsApp, or Facebook Groups as a place for members to talk to one another. You can create and share blog posts on Medium, host webinars on Zoom and GoToWebinar, send emails out on Mailchimp, Aweber, Constant Contact, and maybe use event software like Bevy, Meetup, and Eventbrite to help coordinate the efforts of thousands, even millions, of people without directly controlling them.

Using tools like Zapier you can also integrate other great software like Tettra (for members to share resources with one another) and Donut (to build bonds between members). You might even end up creating a better community experience than you would've done with a more expensive platform.

The major benefit of this is it's cheap and you're often getting a best in class experience in many key features. It's also relatively quick to get started, you have a lot more flexibility and someone else takes care of all the hard work. Often you're using the tools members are already using so you don't need to keep persuading them to visit a new place.

Another major benefit is it can be empowering for members. You can go where they are, benefit from siphoning from existing audiences (Reddit, Stack Exchange etc.), and support members who are deciding to create a new group, blog, or contribute in their own way.

However, this approach also has major downsides. You have *no control* over many of these platforms, and the reach (the number of people who will see your messages) on platforms like Facebook can be as low as 0.1%. This means just 1 in 1000 of the people who like or follow your accounts will see any update you post.

The lack of control can also be a problem when things go wrong. If your members start abusing one another and sharing false information your brand suffers even though there's nothing you can do to stop it. There's nothing to stop competitors slipping in and wreaking havoc either.

You also don't get any useful data. Want to know how many people are viewing and participating? Tough luck. Want to know if your efforts are having a big impact? You're going to struggle to find out. You will have no idea how many of your customers are engaging in the community.

Finally it can also be a discombobulating community experience if your members have to jump from one tool to the next without any central website driving and coordinating all activities. There's no 'town centre' experience that sits as the beating heart of your community. You can create a single page connecting all these things – but it's unlikely most of your members will see it.

While this might not be a great approach for top brands, it can be the perfect approach if you're developing a community for a topic you're passionate about, and for a smaller group or local club, this can be a great option. A growing number of DIYers are creating their communities precisely in this way.

Comparing different approaches

You can use the comparison table of the different approaches below to help guide the best approach for you.

	Licence cost	Hosting cost	Implemen-tation fees	Expertise required	Customi-sation	Features
Custom built	None	$,$$$	$$,$$$ – $$$,$$$	Extreme	High	Variable
White label	$$$		$$$	Low	Low	Low
Open source	None	$,$$$	$$,$$$	High	High	Medium
Enterprise platforms	$$$,$$$		$$,$$$	Medium	Medium	High
Social media	None	None	None	None	Low	Low

If you're working at a large organisation, you don't want to launch something which doesn't function perfectly, has a gaping security flaw, or just doesn't look good. This will probably drive you to one of the largest enterprise platforms.

If you're working in a small to medium-sized organisation, you should either use a white-label platform or create your community experience using inexpensive social media tools. If you have some unique needs or have advanced technical skills, you might try an open source approach (but be sure you know what you're doing).

Note that these are approximate rules of thumb rather than rigid rules. And before making a decision about which approach to take you should first make a membership projection. This is especially important if you're expecting more than a few hundred people participating.

You can always pay more, but never pay less

It makes sense that a community platform vendor will charge you by the number of members who use your community. An organisation with a million members should be paying more than one with a thousand members. However, it's slightly more complicated than that. Platform vendors aren't running a meter where they look precisely at how many people used your community last month and then send you the bill. Instead many predict how many members you're likely to have and place you on a pricing tier.

For example, a typical enterprise community might charge the following:

Tier	Pricing
Up to 500k visitors	$90k per year
500k to 3m visitors	$210k per year
3m to 6m visitors	$330k per year

While this makes things simple, it comes with a sneaky catch.

If you attract more members than predicted, you will have to pay for the next tier (or incur additional charges). However if you attract fewer members than predicted, you still have to pay for the predicted number of members. This means (using our table above) if you sign a contract on a 500k to 3m tier and you only attract a few hundred visitors, you're still paying $210k per year. But if you attract more than 3m, you get moved up. It's a bit of a racket. All vendors will happily let you upgrade your account if you get more people than expected, but very few will let you downgrade your account if your estimates (or their estimates) were too high.

▶

This is important for one simple reason; it's in the best interests of a community platform provider to make you believe you will have as many members as possible. Asking a community platform provider how many visitors you can expect is like asking a shop owner how many items you should buy. You will probably end up buying far more than you need. It's therefore best to be conservative in your predictions.

I know communities that launched, failed to gain traction, and then still had to spend the next few years painfully paying for millions of visitors who never arrived. To avoid this you need to make a good estimate about the number of visitors you're likely to attract. If you have an existing community, you have some data to work with. If you don't, you need to make a projection.

How to make an accurate membership projection

To make an accurate membership projection, you're going to need access to three types of data.

1 **Web traffic.** You want to know how many people are visiting your organisation's homepage today. We will use this to make estimations for how many will visit the community later.

2 **Click-through data.** This shows how many people click on the various tabs and menu options from your homepage and elsewhere in the community. This shows what percentage of visitors might visit a community.

3 **Audience data.** You want to know how many people you could potentially promote the community to when you launch it.

You can see the types of data and where it might help below:

Type of data	Software	Specifics
Website traffic statistics	Google Analytics, Adobe Analytics, Mixpanel, Matomo	Find out how many people visit your organisation's website each month.
Click-through data	Google Analytics, Crazy Egg, Adobe Analytics, Mouseflow	Find out how many people click through from your homepage to navigation tabs / subpages.
Potential sources of members	Mailing lists, loyalty schemes, promotional opportunities	Find out how many people you can reach with a message when you launch.

Don't worry if you can't get access to this kind of data, we will come to a solution for that soon.

Now you have three methods to make an accurate membership projection. These are:

1 **Estimate by web traffic.** This is the most common option. You look at the number of current visitors you get to your website and estimate how many of them might then visit the community. For example, if you have one million monthly visitors to your main website and you know a typical navigation tab is clicked by 10% of them, it's reasonable to assume your community will attract 100,000 visitors each month (assuming the community is also on a navigation tab).

   The problem with this method is it ignores search traffic. For most public communities, the majority of people will visit via search engines as opposed to navigating through your organisation's website. As a rough rule of thumb, you can look at how many people arrive at your organisation's website by search and estimate around 20% to 30% of them will instead land upon a community page within two to three years.

2 **Estimate number of active users.** Sometimes you want to know how many active users (people logged in) your community will have. This is important if you're using a platform like Salesforce or Slack which charges by the number of active users instead of the number of visitors.

   This has the potential to be a lot cheaper or more expensive than other platforms depending upon how many people are likely to log in to your community as opposed to reading the content for free. It's also important if you're planning to build a community which isn't open to the public.

   A simple way to estimate this is to look at how many visitors log in to your main organisation website today. For example, if you know you have 5000 people asking and looking up answers to questions on your website today, you might estimate a percentage (say 10%–20%) of these will instead ask questions in your community.

   Another way is to assume 1%–10% of your current mailing list might regularly log in to your community if it isn't open to the public.

3 **Estimate by similarly sized organisations.** If you don't have access to the data above, you can look at organisations of a similar size and make an estimate based upon that. If a similarly sized competitor attracted 20k members in the first few years, you can use that as an approximate estimate.

   Be careful though. It will take your community years to reach the same size and level of participation as an existing community. Also some organisations have a frustrating tendency to inflate their metrics in public statements to look good.

You might notice that the estimates we're using here of how many people who currently visit your homepage might visit or log in to the community are far too broad to make a specific projection.

This is because it varies significantly by community and by the topic. The goal isn't to be 100% accurate but instead be accurate enough to make an informed decision about what pricing tier you should be on. You should be able to at least know if you should be on the 0 to 500k tier, the 500k to 3m tier, or the 3m to 6m tier. If it's close between two pricing tiers, pick the lowest one.

To help you make a more specific projection, you can use our handy member projection tool available at: www.feverbee.com/buildyourcommunity. You drop in your own metrics and come up with our best estimate of how many members you're likely to have engaged and are visiting your community.

Now you know how many people you're likely to attract, you can start thinking about what you need these people to do in your community and begin shortlisting possible community platforms.

WARNING – Not everyone will visit or participate!

Be careful! Just because you have a 10,000 strong audience doesn't mean you will have 10,000 community members. Debenhams, a fashion and beauty retailer in the UK, has 1.3m members in its Beauty Club loyalty scheme, but since its launch in 2017 the community attracted only 75,000 community members. Only a few thousand of which were ever active. The community was shuttered in July 2020.

Turn use cases into technology requirements

In the last chapter, we turned our member needs into use cases. These are the specific things members want to *use* the community for. Before we can shortlist our platforms, we need to turn these use cases into more specific technical requirements.

If you're going to use a white-label platform or social media tools, you can probably just list out the broad use cases and then start looking for platforms to match. If you're going to use an enterprise or open source platform (or build your own), you need to be very specific in how your community needs to work.

Programming a dumb robot

If this is your first time doing this, it can be a little confounding.

You might want to get help from someone with experience in turning use cases into technology requirements. It's best to imagine yourself programming a dumb robot. You have to be very precise.

For example, if you want newcomers to have their own personal journey in your community where they receive different emails from veterans you need to think about how that might work. You might need a community platform that can segment members by date joined and assign them to different email lists automatically. You need to be able to create a series of editable emails that are sent on a specific, editable schedule to each group.

In a community, for example, you can't say you need newcomers to receive different emails than veteran members. Instead you need a platform with an email tool capable of assigning members to different groups automatically and then you need a series of emails you can edit and schedule for each group. You have to be as clear as possible about how this might work on the technology side.

I recommend listing both the use case and the technology requirement here. Often you might find platform vendors or developers who will see this later and who might have a better way to achieve the same use case. But for now list the primary use cases of your community and try to list the specific technology requirements. Here is an example:

Use case	Technology requirement
Limit information to just the core basics to get started.	• Admins can hide and restrict content that newcomers share within the community for a specified period of time.
Prevent the newcomer from receiving any email not aligned to their immediate journey.	• Admins can automatically assign newcomers to a broader email list after a specific period of time.
Structure the community as a 30-day programme of discussions, mentoring, and in-house expertise.	• Admins can create a separate series of emails just for newcomers.

▶

Use case	Technology requirement
Buddy each newcomer with an experienced mentor to proactively reach out and guide members through.	• Veterans (members of a specified rank) see newcomers who have recently joined. • Veterans can send direct messages to newcomers.
Create a private group to ask beginner-level questions and not risk being embarrassed in front of others.	• Admins can create private groups that only newcomers can join.
Have a place where members can share screenshots of what they're working on and see the screenshots of others.	• Members can drag and drop images to the community from their desktop. • Members can easily upload images from their phone. • Members can remove screenshots from the community. • Admins can pre-moderate images in the community.
Let members share and track their progress against others also going through the same area.	• Admins can set onsite notifications members receive to update their profiles. • Members can update their profiles with the latest metrics and apps they're working on. • Members can see their progress against the progress of others in their cohort on their profiles.
Have pop-ups in the product directing people where they can see questions and answers relating to this phase.	• Admins can set pop-ups which can appear for a fixed amount of time and for specific target audiences. • Admins can customise pop-ups with text, images, and video. • Admins can create a guided series of pop-ups which show members what they need to do based upon a member's previous activity.
Include the number of days a member has been using the product in their profile information.	• Admins can customise member profile field options with the ability for members to set when they became a customer.
Have a graduation when members have surpassed 30–60 days (along with a reward/discount/referral code).	• Admins can set onsite reminders and emails based upon how long a member has been a member of the community. These can include hyperlinks, images, video, and text.

You don't need to list every single thing your platform needs to do. Most platforms have a default set of features which will come as a standard. Things like being able to register an account, browse discussions etc. are pretty much a given. You do need to ensure, however, that your primary use cases are being supported by the platform beyond the features that are present in every platform.

Shortlist community platforms

Once you know what features you need, the approach you will take, and how many members you can expect, you can start shortlisting possible community platforms. You can use our community platform comparison tool here (www. feverbee.com/communityplatforms). This tool will let you calculate the number of members you anticipate, set a budget, and showcase a list of relevant features offered by each platform. You can also see examples of communities on each platform.

You can also find a breakdown of some of the most popular platforms in the table below. Be warned this isn't a comprehensive list and technology changes fast. By the time you read these words the landscape may have changed significantly – so do your own research!

Social media and other inexpensive tools	White-label platforms	Open source platforms	Enterprise platforms
Facebook groups	Ning	Drupal	Khoros
LinkedIn groups	Mighty Networks	Discourse[1]	Salesforce
WhatsApp	Tribe	Vanilla	InSided
Telegram	Hivebrite	Joomla	Telligent
Mailchimp	YourMembership	ELGG	Vanilla
Zoom	Meetup		Discourse
Citrix	Circle		Higher Logic
GoToWebinar			Yammer
Slack			Microsoft Teams
Bevy			Sharepoint
Eventbrite			
Reddit			
Twitch			
Stack Exchange			

From this tool and your research, you should be able to narrow down your options to a handful (usually two to three) of platforms and select the best one for you.

Developing the RFP

If your budget is limited (i.e. less than $50k) you can usually look at the examples and test each platform before making a decision. If you're looking for a platform at the enterprise level, you probably need to create a request for proposal (RFP) from platform vendors to gather specific information and requirements.

The purpose of the RFP is to be able to compare community platforms in the fields that matter most to you. This means you begin by prioritising your needs. This is typically a combination of your use cases detailed above and any specific technical requirements you have.

It's critically important in the RFP stage to gather feedback from relevant stakeholders about what needs to be in it. You might be surprised to learn that legal, PR, marketing, technical, and procurement teams might all have different requirements about branding, privacy, security, and service support. The RFP should never be sent to a vendor before it has been approved by key stakeholders internally.

To develop the RFP, you need to list the priority of each feature you need. Not every platform is going to let you do everything you want. It's common to rank the priority of each feature on a 1 to 3 (or 1 to 5) scale when evaluating possible options. This priority lets you weigh each platform and make the best decision for you. Typically:

1 = Nice to have, but not essential.

2 = Very important, but can survive without.

3 = Essential, a showstopper if not present.

For example, members being able to change usernames might be a fairly low priority 1 feature – good to have, but hardly critical. Whereas members being able to authenticate themselves using their existing current system login information might be a priority 3 feature (essentially a showstopper if it doesn't work).

If you need some help, you can find our RFP template here: www.fever-bee.com/buildyourcommunity

It's also important in the RFP stage to distinguish between features which come 'out of the box' and that require custom development. For example, a platform vendor might say their community platform can enable members to suggest and vote on each other's ideas. They might not mention that this requires a $20k investment and three months of development to make it work. Many of the problems which occur in the community development process come from the confusion between what a community platform is able to do when you get access to it and what requires a significant amount of time and resources to make it work.

The RFP process should take approximately two weeks. While this process should be free from intuition and personal judgement, in our experience you can often learn a lot about the working relationship and level of support you can expect from a vendor by how they engage with you during this process.

Negotiating and signing the contract

If you're using a white-label platform, you can usually purchase the platform with a few clicks of a button. If you're using an open source platform, you simply download the software and get started. However, if you're using an enterprise platform you will likely go through a process of negotiating and signing the contract. Even if this entire process is handled by a procurement team you should be aware of what you're paying for.

A few things are important here:

1 **Most contracts are for three years.** A typical community contract at an enterprise platform will last for three years. Many platform vendors apply significant discounts to encourage the client to sign a three-year contract. This isn't simply about greed, it often takes that much time to get a community up and running. You might spend three to six months on the development of the community alone and a further few years growing the level of activity.

2 **Know exactly what's in the contract.** A typical community contract at an enterprise platform will specify some combination of the following:

- **A licence for a specific number of annual visits (often <500k, <3m, <6m).** Make sure this matches your membership projection. As we've discussed, some platforms (i.e. Salesforce) charge primarily by the number of active users of the community. At the time of writing this is $2 per unique logged in member and $5 for each member who contributes 2+ times per month. If your community is primarily customer support, this might be significantly cheaper given that the majority of people view answers without having to log in or register. If it's for people to discuss a topic in general (i.e. Sephora's Beauty Community), this might become a lot more expensive.

- **A licence for a number of applications calls.** If you're integrating the community with additional features that might request information from the community vendor, there may be additional costs here to consider.

- **Cost for additional features (gamification, knowledge, ideas etc.).** It's common for additional features to be bundled together at different pricing tiers. Be sure that you're getting the features you expect. It's not uncommon for features like gamification or a knowledge base to be charged at $10k to $20k per year extra in addition to your licence fee.

- **Support services (customer support, speed of response agreement).** You might be getting premium support services, which will explain how quickly you can expect a response and through what medium. Be warned that if the level of service you can expert isn't specified in the agreement, you might find yourself not getting the level of support you need to develop your community.

- **Training costs.** This includes both training to use the platform, ongoing 'tune up' workshops, and strategic advice in managing the community. You might be able to negotiate a deal to have these included for free. As a general rule, anything which doesn't cost the platform vendor significant effort to offer can usually be included for free.

- **Implementation and development costs.** If the vendor is also developing and designing the platform, there will also be a considerable implementation fee here. We will cover implementation in more depth later.

Make sure you're making full use of the support services you're paying for. You need to know exactly which activities are within your realm of responsibility and which are not. Be aware that even minor help requests or questions to your vendor can be considered *billable* time that you pay for.

3 **Have everything prepared.** The moment the contract begins (and you gain access to the platform), you are paying for the community. Even if you haven't launched the community to the public yet, you are still paying for it. This means you need to make sure you have developers, designers, and an implementation partner ready to go from day one. One former client gained access to their platform and then learned they wouldn't have access to the company's developer team for five months. They spent almost $80k in fees during this time for a platform they couldn't do anything with yet.

Before you sign a contract, you should have your ducks aligned. This includes:

- an implementation partner or developers lined up and ready to go
- internal technical staff ready to support the development (i.e. helping with integration and single sign on)
- a relatively clear idea for the design of your community.

Signing the contract is like launching the starting gun for your community. You want to be ready to spring to action.

Finding implementation partners

Some organisations are surprised that after paying for an expensive platform, they often get something which doesn't look great. This is like buying an expensive home and finding it empty when you arrive. It has huge potential, but you need to do plenty of work to get it up and running. Even if you're using an inexpensive white-label platform, you're still going to need to spend some time to set up and design the site.

Many community platforms will offer to design and develop the platform for you at an additional cost. Others will refer you to recommended 'implementation partners' who do this work for you. Implementation partners are essentially the plumbers, electricians, and decorators of your community. They are third-party firms who specialise in your vendor's software. They are often certified by the vendor and may even be paying the vendor to receive referrals as part of a 'partner programme'.

The benefit of working with an implementation partner is typically speed and experience. They can move fast, have experience working with lots of different organisations, and can create a very customised experience. The downside is cost. They don't come cheap. If you have developers on your team you can take this on yourself. However, be warned that if you don't have experience, this is just like doing plumbing yourself. You might save money now but end up spending a lot more further down the line.

Two roles of implementation partners

Implementation partners should do two specific things:

1 **They should integrate with your current systems.** If you're moving from one community to the next, they will also take care of the migration.

This essentially means exporting data in a readable format from one platform and then uploading it in another. This sounds simple enough, but can be devilishly tricky in practice. Many fields in vendor databases don't match each other so you need to transform the data to make it work. For example, sometimes one database doesn't allow specific characters to be used and can force members to change their names or profiles – which wreak havoc and upset members.

2 **They should make the community look really, really good.** You don't want the first impression of your community to be a negative one. It doesn't have to be Facebook, but if you're making a big investment, it shouldn't just be a bland forum either.

The cost of an implementation partner depends entirely upon the full scope of work. For most community projects we've been involved with, the fee has ranged from $50k to $500k. A mid-range of around $80k to $250k is usually about right for an enterprise community platform without too much complexity. You might be able to find some solo developers or smaller agencies for far less; just be careful to ensure they have the credentials to do the job.

Each platform will recommend different vendors. You can find our list of recommendations here: www.feverbee.com/implementationpartners

---

Guiding principles for great community experiences

Whether you hire an implementation partner or not, you should have some strong guiding principles to work with. These help inarguable rules that help create a great community experience for your members. These include:

1 **Minimise time and effort to get rewards.** Community members, similar to visitors to any other website, have a limited amount of time and effort they will invest in your community. The more time it takes for members to find what they need, the less likely they will participate. This is important in every design decision you make. You want to minimise the effort and maximise reward. For example, you're going to miss out on a lot of activity if members need to scroll down and make several clicks to find what they want.

2 **Clearly show what's new and what works.** For the best part, members want to know what's new in the community today and what actually

works. This means you need to prioritise the latest activity, most popular activity, and areas where members can easily get answers to their most pressing questions.

3 **Keep social density high (but not too high).** Social density is the level of activity that takes place within any given area of the community. The social density has to be enough to sustain a critical mass of activity (i.e. people need to see the questions from each other to answer them), but not so high for it to be overwhelming. You should limit the number of features and areas where members can participate to ensure their attention is focused on the areas that matter.

   As your community matures, you may continue to add and remove features to balance this social density. In mature communities you should spend as much time removing old content and pruning discussions as creating new material. It's easy to believe you serve your community best by providing as many features and as much content as possible, but creating a better experience is often about what you remove.

Designing the community experience

Now we can begin thinking about what the full community experience will look like for community members. The community experience can be divided into three areas:

1 **Structure.** This defines which features are positioned where and how the navigation will work.

2 **Design.** This defines how the community should look and feel.

3 **Functions.** This defines how the community features will work.

While your developers and implementation partners can give you direction, you need to be holding the reins and overseeing the decisions made in each of these categories. Getting any of these areas wrong can undermine your community effort. We can't go through every single aspect of each in this book, but we can cover the major principles to ensure you can develop a quality community experience.

Developing the right community structure

The community structure covers the taxonomy, navigation, themes, and home-page layout.

Taxonomy is a technical term, which essentially means how you are going to classify all the information in your community. This sounds really boring, but it's critically important. Your members are going to create a lot of content and discussions. If there isn't a good system for categorising this content no one else will ever find it.

Sometimes you can borrow from an existing structure you have on your website, in your knowledge base (or documentation), or adapt one provided by your colleagues. At other times you will need to create your own taxonomy for the community (i.e. what will be featured in your navigation bar? Which areas will exist as sub-menus?).

You need to make one critical decision early on. Is all the information in your community (discussions, content and events etc.) structured around your products, interests, or what members are trying to achieve?

For example, imagine you're managing the community at Fitbit. Would you structure the community by each variation of your fitness tracker (Ionic, Versa, Charge etc.)? By the type of exercise members want to do (jogging, swimming etc.)? Or by their goals (losing weight, running further, building muscle, sleep better etc.)?[2] Each option offers a different community experience.

The larger your audience, the more difficult (and important) these decisions become. If you work for a company which has dozens of products, you will probably have to combine some products into a single category to sustain a good level of participation in each area. If any of these become too popular, you might need a separate sub-category just for a niche area within that topic.

As a rule of thumb, try to begin with as few features and categories as possible. It's a lot easier to add features than remove them.

Creating a taxonomy

You should create your taxonomy based around the use cases that draw people to the community and their unique needs within that use case. For example, if you know the prime use cases are to get product help, learn more, share advice, and get started with the products, you might create a taxonomy like that we see over the page:

Home	Search	Get help	Explore (browse)	Share advice	Get started	Member profile/register
		Product category 1	Community blog/ newsletter	Create blog posts	Join a mentoring group	Login/register
		Product category 2	Community library/wiki	Answer questions	Rules and guidelines	Forgotten password
		Product category 3 etc.	Popular discussions	Unanswered questions	Common problems	How to use the community
			Popular content	Current member rankings	Help for first timers	Security, privacy, and legal matters
			Popular members	How gamification works	Insider jokes	
			Known issues		Acronyms and phrases	
			Meet the staff			
			The community story so far …			

If your use cases are different, this will also be different. You can find some common examples at www.feverbee.com/buildyourcommunity

Designing your community

If you're developing a community for your own goals, you have a lot of freedom in how you design your community. You also, however, have to make a lot more decisions.

If you're working for an organisation, your community website should closely resemble your company website. This helps create a coherent experience for members as they move between your company website and your community. This also means many of the decisions you otherwise need to make (how large should buttons be, what colours should we use, what backgrounds make sense?) have already been made for you.

Before you begin designing the site, make sure you have a copy of your company's brand guidelines (if they exist). Use these to design a consistent community experience. However, even with a handy copy of these guidelines, you still have a number of critical decisions about what appears on your community. Decisions that seem relatively arbitrary (should you display the latest or most popular activity first?) have a big impact upon whether and how members will participate.

These include the homepage, banners, and page and newsletter templates.

The homepage

Let's begin with the homepage. This is the page every newcomer and regular member will see when they visit the community. If your community doesn't feel like a thriving hub of exciting activity, members will be far less likely to start and reply to discussions. You have plenty of decisions to make here.

Here are the biggest:

- **Should you show the latest, most popular, or most relevant activity?** A simple rule of thumb, if you're just getting started, you probably want to show the latest activity first. This helps the community seem engaging and active. As your community grows, you want to show the most popular activity. This lets people sort through the content to find the best stuff. If your community reaches 'mega community' status you probably need to personalise the experience to show the most relevant activity to each member.

- **What platform features do you show?** You have plenty of options for which features appear on the homepage. You can show discussions, search, groups, blogs documentation, leaderboards and more.

- **Calls to action.** What are the key calls to action? The most common are inviting members to search for information, register, start discussion, log in, vote, and share content. The more calls to action you have the less likely members will pay attention to any of them. As a general rule, try to limit the homepage to just two to three calls to action. For most communities (search for information, register/login, and start discussion) this should suffice. But let your use cases guide you. Whatever is the biggest priority for your members should be shown on the homepage.

Even the simplest looking community homepages are the outcome of a dozen or more tricky decisions. In fact, the reason why some websites look so simple to use is precisely because they made a lot of difficult decisions during this phase. The more cluttered the homepage looks, the less able the designer was to make the key decisions to ensure members had a great community experience.

Banners

Banners are amongst the most underrated tool in community design today. A good banner can massively increase the number of people who join and participate in a community. We've tweaked banners in the past to increase the registration ratio by 400%+![3]

A banner is essentially a graphic (or interactive graphic) which sits at the top of your community page. The purpose isn't just to look good, but to advertise to your members what the community is about or what they should do next.

Most banners are poorly used. Which is a shame given they are taking up the prime real estate of your community homepage. Far too many communities have banners which are either too big or fail to guide members to the next action. For example, many communities have banners which take up 70% of their homepage. While this might work for your main company homepage, it is a disaster for a community. It pushes community activity *below the fold* (the point at which members have to scroll down for more information). In turn, this forces members to scroll down the page on every visit to see what's new in the community.

This is a clear violation of principle two – it increases effort without delivering an additional reward. On a mobile phone, this problem is exacerbated as members must scroll with their thumbs to find the content they want. No one is going to visit your community several times a day if they have to constantly break their thumb to find the content on each visit. On mobile, which can account for anything from 20% to 90% of your traffic, the banner should be removed or minimised.

To make the banner work for you, there are a few things to get right.

1 **Keep the banner to 1/4 of the height of the display area.** At the very least, you should still be able to see the latest activity *above the fold* in the community.

2 **Keep the search box within the banner.** In most communities, this is what most people want to use. Make sure people can easily see the search box to find the information they want.

3 **Ensure any text supports the unique value of the community.** No one needs a welcome message here. This is like a brand advertising in Times Square welcoming people to Times Square. It's a waste of an incredible opportunity. Instead explain the community's powerful unique use case and what makes it amazing.

4 **Have a clear call to action.** The most common calls to action invite members to register and start a discussion. But don't feel limited to that if you need your members to do something else.

5 **Use conditional logic to serve different banners to different members.** Newcomers may need calls to action to register and get started. Veterans probably want to easily reply to discussions and build their reputation. You can use conditional logic to serve a unique banner to members based upon previous activity. And you can change banners up frequently. If you have an exciting upcoming event or activity, change up the banner to promote it.

A good example of a homepage is the Temenos Kony Community.[4]

It has clear calls to action, a simple navigation structure, and small boxes for major features. Better yet, the latest activity appears above the fold and top members can see where they rank.

Page and newsletter templates

In addition to the homepage and banner, you may also need to create (or adapt) a few standard page templates. Page templates are essentially standard formats for how other types of content (discussions, categories, groups, knowledge articles, and blogs etc.) are displayed.

On a white-label platform, this will be done for you. On an enterprise platform, you will usually have a few templates you can adapt and work from. Make sure they're suited to the needs of your audience.

You want to ensure a consistent experience. You don't want the navigation buttons or design to change as members move between different areas of your community. For example, if you want a sidebar with a call to action to match one of your use cases, this should be within a template. Also be aware that if you're looking for any unique customisations on these, this can take a lot more time than you expect.

When you set up these templates, follow the same principles as before. Ensure the key activity is placed above the fold, restrict the page elements to the core few, and follow the same branding as the rest of the site.

Functions and features of your community

Now we've covered the structure and design of a community, it's time to talk briefly about the features within the community. Many of these we will cover in more depth later in this book.

Almost every feature a community offers also comes with a dozen or more different settings you can tinker with to create a different community experience.

From my experience, it's common to see the sheer number of options available and imagine yourself sitting in the cockpit of an aeroplane. You don't want to mess with any of the settings in case anything goes wrong. As a result you might stick to the default settings. This is a mistake.

The reality is you're setting up a community not flying a plane. You need to explore what each of the settings does and make clear decisions about what you need to change to best support your members.

I'm not going to be able to go through each setting as they vary too much between platforms. However, it is a good idea to go through each setting in turn and see how it impacts the community experience and check that this matches the needs and use cases of your members. Much of the art in developing a great community experience lies in the configuration of the community settings to suit your members' unique needs.

Summary

- -

Developing a community website is hard. Before you begin, you should be clear about your use cases for the community (note, some people call these stories). Once you have your use cases, determine how many members you're likely to attract. This should help you determine which category of technology to use and your likely costs.

If you're projecting fewer than a few hundred members and you have a limited budget, you should take advantage of the free tools which already exist and consider upgrading to something more as you grow and have more resources.

If you're projecting more than a few hundred members, but have a small budget, use a white-label platform which enables members to interact with each other. This gives you a platform to build from but is limited in features and the extent to which you can customise it.

If, however, you're expecting a large number of members (more than a few' thousand), you need an enterprise platform. This gives you access to a full range of features and customisations.

Once you've decided on your approach, shortlist the options and compare them by the weighted use cases to find the best platform for you. Try to find as many examples as possible. For an enterprise platform, you should complete an RFP first and ensure all stakeholders are actively engaged in the process. Remember, if you're using an enterprise platform you will need very talented in-house developers or an implementation partner to develop the site to match your needs.

In the design phase, follow three core principles. First, minimise the time and effort to get rewards from the community. Second, display what's new and what's popular in the community. Third, keep social density high (but not too high). This should guide many of the decisions you make concerning which features to use, where to position activity, and how you design the banner which appears on the community homepage.

Later in this book we will explore the functionality of a community website in more depth. Each feature presents many options in how it works and what members will see. You will learn how to use many of the features which come with community platforms. This includes how to drive more participation with gamification, keep people engaged in smaller sub-groups, and design the perfect welcoming journey to keep community members hooked and coming back to visit your community every day.

Ultimately, the success of developing a community website hangs upon having clear use cases, the right platform, a great implementation partner, and carefully considered instructions for each. If you can pull these things together, you will be well on your way to delivering a world-class community experience.

Examples

- Kony (https://basecamp.kony.com/s/)
- Workshop (https://www.workshop.com.au/)
- HP (https://h30434.www3.hp.com/)
- Apple (https://discussions.apple.com/welcome)
- Fitbit (https://community.fitbit.com/)

Checklist

1 Decide which community approach you need.
2 Make your membership projection.
3 Shortlist and compare possible platforms.
4 If needed, create the RFP.
5 If needed, select an implementation partner.
6 Use your use cases to decide the taxonomy of your community.
7 Design the homepage and page templates.

Tools of the trade
(available from: www.feverbee.com/ buildyourcommunity)

- FeverBee Membership Projection Worksheet
- FeverBee Community Platform Comparison Tool (www.feverbee.com/ communityplatforms)

- FeverBee RFP Template
- FeverBee Community Examples list (www.feverbee.com/communities)
- **Social media**: Bevy, Meetup, Mailchimp, GoToWebinar, Zoom, Twitch, Telegram, WhatsApp, Facebook groups
- **White label**: Mighty Networks, Vanilla, Discourse, Tribe, Hivebrite
- **Enterprise**: Salesforce, Khoros, InSided, Telligent, Higher Logic, Vanilla, Discourse

chapter 4

Setting the rules

Rules have a bad reputation in the online community world. They can seem patronising and authoritarian. Members of many communities are notoriously resistant to rules. Similar to 'Godwin's Law' ('*As an online discussion grows longer, the probability of a comparison involving Nazis or Hitler approaches 1'.*)[1], the more you try to enforce standards of behaviour in the community the greater your chances of being compared to a dictator.

This is a shame because the purpose of rules isn't just to restrict what members can and can't say. The real purpose of rules is to establish and nurture social norms which create a powerful community experience for members.

In her must-read book, *The Art of Gathering*, author Priya Parker shares examples of remarkable rules she has used to transform mundane gatherings into transformative experiences.[2]

At one typical gathering hosted by Priya, attendees were told they can't share what they do for a living. At another, they weren't allowed to talk about their kids. Priya has even hosted events where the first person to check their phone has to pay the bill. Can you imagine attending a gathering where you couldn't talk about your work, your family, or check your phone?

These rules seem extreme, even fascist perhaps. Yet, as Priya explains, remarkable rules knock members out of their typical behavioural routines. This creates the space for remarkable, even transformative, community experiences.

This is true online as well as offline. The most successful communities today aren't those with the best technology, but those with the best culture – a culture shaped and formed through unique rules and social norms.

Stack Overflow, for example, is a community for programmers. The community is notoriously stringent in the kind of questions and responses it wants. If you don't structure your question properly, provide enough context, or don't check if the question has been asked before, it will probably be removed by a tyrannical moderator. If you do it twice, *you* might be removed along with your post.

Likewise, if you provide an answer that doesn't provide enough information or feels more like an opinion, your answer might be deleted. Stack Overflow doesn't want your opinions, it wants high-quality facts.

These rules make Stack Overflow an entirely unique community. Whereas most people managing communities want as many responses to a question as possible, Stack Overflow wants just one ... the right one. The right one is the post which best solves the problem.

If you're looking for an answer to a problem, this is terrific. You don't have to scroll through and test a dozen or more possible solutions to find the right one. But it comes at a cost. It makes the community more exclusive. Stack Overflow isn't for everyone. If you want to shoot the breeze about all things programming you'll find yourself kindly invited to shoot the breeze somewhere other than Stack Overflow. It's also harder for newcomers to feel accepted (and the community frequently reeks of elitism). Yet this criticism is mitigated by one simple fact – Stack Overflow is indisputably the most valuable community for programmers in the world.

The success of Stack Overflow stems from setting and enforcing rules which create a very specific culture, a culture which prizes quality over quantity of participation. The founders knew the type of community programmers needed and established rules with that in mind.

At the other end of the spectrum lies Sephora's Beauty Community (a FeverBee client). Whereas Stack Overflow invites you to ask a carefully framed question, Sephora invites you to start a conversation. At the time of writing, the most popular discussion in the Sephora community is perhaps the very least likely to ever appear in Stack Overflow: 'What are you wearing today?'.

The Sephora community thrives on opinions. That's because unlike programming, answers are less binary. It's hard to argue which shade of lipstick is best. But everyone has a favourite. Over time, an aggregate of opinions might form a consensus. Thus the more opinions the community solicits, the better the community can form a consensus (and the more valuable it becomes to members).

Members are encouraged to talk about what's on their mind and share their likes and dislikes each week. It might not look like it, but the culture of the Sephora community is as carefully cultivated as the culture of Stack Overflow. Members get a place to feel like they belong, to be inspired, and understand what people like themselves do.

This process of setting and enforcing rules to create a unique culture has a name we're far more familiar with, *moderation*.

Moderation

We often think of moderation as just removing the bad stuff. And, sure, removing the bad content is important. It's hard to create any sort of meaningful culture in a community filled with spam, fights, and personal insults. But moderation isn't *just* a battle to keep the hounds of hell at bay. It's also the work that shapes the culture you want for your members.

There are two elements to moderation: (1) establishing rules and (2) enforcing rules.

Establishing rules

Let's tackle establishing rules first. This is where your corporate communication policies, ethical concerns, philosophy towards free speech, your duty of care towards members, and your urge to create something special are going to collide.

A quick warning before we begin, in some areas we're going to tiptoe into legal matters. Always get a lawyer to review your moderation policies and processes to ensure you're abiding by all necessary laws.

Enforcing rules

At first glance, setting rules might seem to be a relatively simple case of telling people what they can and can't do in the community. If they break the rules, you remove them. That sounds simple enough.

Alas moderation is far less black and white than you might imagine. Instead it's deciding which shade of grey you want for your community and trying to keep it that shade as your community grows and matures.

We can break categories of rules into three specific areas we see below. There are rules you create which nurture unique social norms, those which are universal amongst all communities, and those which fall into the category of 'tricky judgement calls'.

Types of rules	Explanation
Unique social norms	Rules that help you create and shape a unique community experience. These are primarily formed and created by you and the community team (i.e. no opinions allowed!).
Universal rules	Rules that provide a safe experience for community members. These are informed by ethical guidelines and the law (i.e. no racism!).
Judgement calls	These are 'grey area' issues which reflect both of the above. These are informed by your brand, communication policies, and your available resources to enforce them (i.e. should swearing be allowed?).

Step 1: Create unique social norms

The first thing you should do is decide what remarkable rules (or social norms) might define your community. Consider Priya's example above. She knew mums spent a huge amount of time at social gatherings talking about their kids. If she forbade that as a topic, it forces the conversation to evolve beyond their comfort zone. What kind of rules might shake your members out of their typical mode of communication and help force the kind of community and culture you want?

Think back to your personas from Chapter 2 here. What kind of personalities are you dealing with? What kind of information do they need? Are they likely to want to participate in a community at the more serious end of the continuum or at the most fun end of the continuum? Do they want to talk about themselves or just about the topic? Creating a unique social norm can completely change the type of interactions you have.

Change My View, for example, is a subreddit[3] encouraging people to post a belief and then call for the opposing view. At the time of writing it has nearly 1m members. It's a completely different type of community experience and the opposite of the flame wars which take place on Twitter every day.

Another great example is ProjectManagement.com – a community filled with project managers sharing templates with one another. Each template has to be original and of high quality to be accepted within the community. Today the community is filled with thousands of templates for project managers to use. That's an indispensable asset to community members.

Almost every kind of online and offline group has unique social norms. Academia has strict norms about accepting and publishing peer-reviewed submissions. 4chan has unique social norms enabling members to post almost anything and everything they want (for better or for worse). Sometimes you want a social norm to compliment an existing audience's personality, other times you might want to become a breath of fresh air by violating typical expectations.

These unique rules might be the single biggest decision you make about your community. For example, if members need ideas and inspiration, then you might ban opinions and instead force members to share their personal stories with one another. Likewise, if members need facts, then you might only allow members to share data, solutions, or facts verified independently.

Decide which social norms might really matter to you. You probably want to set at least one (and no more than three) remarkable rule for your community.

Most decisions here exist in some sort of continuum. It's best to push towards one side or another of a continuum. I've included some examples below:

Social norms for your community

Mundane or noisy?

The advantage of moving towards the serious end of the scale is it delivers high-value information to members. The downside is it can be a mundane experience. High signal communities usually become a place that members visit only when they need information. Worse yet, you start competing with search engines for that information.

The advantage of a fun community is it's a more enjoyable place to visit. Members can feel a strong sense of community with each other and talk about what's on their mind. The downside is it can be noisy and difficult for people to find what they want. It can feel like wading through a lot of low-quality posts to get to useful information.

Don't be afraid to be different from any other community out there, it's usually the best strategy to get a community started from scratch.

When you start considering 'crazy' options like banning opinions in favour of facts, banning questions in favour of stories, or banning solutions which don't include evidence etc. you might create the framework for a truly powerful community experience. And we have barely scratched the surface of the unique rules or processes you can set up to create a truly unique and different community culture.

Aim to come up with between one and three unique rules which set the tone for your community. You might even want to run these by some prospective community members to get their take on what they want to see.

Step 2: Establish your universal rules

Once you've established your unique rules, you can now set clear standards you expect members to abide by. These are the typical rules which prevent your community becoming filled with irreverent internet memes, flame wars between members, and constant trolling. Not only would it undermine the entire value of the community, it would also be an obvious target for detractors looking to cause problems (and it just looks bad).

WARNING – The danger of fighting for free speech!

A quick aside for those free speech advocates out there.

Sure, you might want your community to be the final bastion of free speech on the web. That's a noble goal that many communities have pursued in the past. But be aware that being the final bastion of free speech on the web means you're likely to attract the speech of people who have been booted from every other site.

This is a PR disaster waiting to happen. Anyone with any sort of audience can highlight the kind of speech you're allowing and claim your organisation's failure to remove it is an endorsement of it (which is true). This can easily tarnish both your reputation and your organisation's mission.

It also opens the door for mischief. One client had competitors posting offensive comments in the community and slipping tips to trade journalists that the company tolerated this kind of abuse. These proved devastating in the trade press and led to the community's swift demise.

There are several rules which we consider universal and they should be enforced in every kind of community. These include:

1 **No hate speech.** Any post which is intentionally racist, sexist, homophobic, transphobic, or discriminatory should be removed and the user suspended (if not outright banned). As we'll soon see, while the enforcement of this rule can be open to interpretation, it should still be an indisputable rule.

2 **No illegal activity (or sharing of illegal activity).** Posts which discuss illegal activities, link to illegal activities, share the fruits of illegal activities, or use copyright content should be removed. You should also not allow links to illegal streams or let members share methods to circumvent laws etc. It's just not worth the bother and attracts the people looking to undertake illegal activity.

3 **No self-promotion.** Members should not be allowed to explicitly self-promote their own work except by special permission. As any visitor to LinkedIn can tell you, self-promotion is one of the easiest ways to kill a community. This is usually the most common violation and also covers almost every type of spam.

4 **No personal attacks.** Members should be encouraged to debate issues as much as they like, but personal attacks against the person are forbidden. This keeps discussions on the right side of the line. You're allowed to say *'you're wrong!'* (with an explanation) but not *'you're stupid!'*. Once a member attacks the individual instead of the individual's argument, the argument is over.

5 **No ongoing conflicts.** Online debates often continue forever as two sides become increasingly entrenched in their own views. After members have made a few posts on the same topic (e.g. up to five), it's time to call it quits and lock the discussion.

Below your social norms, list these rules. These rules ensure members can participate without fear of being personally attacked. These are very much black and white decisions.

Now we start to wade into the 'shades of grey' area, your tricky judgement calls.

Step 3: Make your judgement calls

You're going to need to make some tricky judgement calls in some areas of your community. Sometimes your platform vendor will do some of these for you. Other times, your company and communication policies can help.

Some of the most common judgement calls include:

1 **Should members be allowed to swear in the community?** If your answer is yes, consider if you want to be removing posts of members saying *'That's a fucking amazing idea, thank you so much!'*.

2 **Do members have to use real names or can they use a pseudonym?** If pseudonyms are allowed, are there any restrictions on what characters they can use or potentially inappropriate terms? That is, would you be happy with a community with a member called Jackhammer69 or TrumpMEGAFan2024? If not, what usernames are forbidden? Also consider what characters you allow. Remember some languages have characters which don't exist in the English language. You can inadvertently cause offence by banning characters which don't appear in the standard English alphabet.

3 **What profile photos are ok?** This is the same challenge as above. Can members use almost anything as a profile photo or should it be of themselves?

What if members don't want to publicly show a photo of themselves? What if members used a Confederate flag or photos of a controversial political figure as their photo? What about a picture of something that's clearly a sexual innuendo? What if the profile photo reads 'Make America Great Again', 'Black Lives Matter' or 'All Lives Matter'?

4 **Lying and fake news.** Are members allowed to share information which isn't true? This is especially problematic as members often don't believe the information they're sharing is false. Do you want to be responsible for judging what is and isn't true?

5 **Can members have off-topic discussions?** Are members allowed to initiate and participate in discussions about politics, their personal lives, or whatever is on their mind at any particular time? Do you want to stop members talking about something they're excited about at the weekend?

6 **Can members talk in their preferred languages?** Are members allowed to ask questions in their native language? Or do they have to speak in English? (This can be an especially sensitive topic internally.) If you do restrict questions to just English, you must be prepared for some badly worded questions from non-native English speakers trying their best to participate in the community.

7 **How long should responses be?** Are members allowed to respond to discussions with simple comments like 'great', 'nice idea!' or 'sounds good' or are you going to force them to post longer discussions and responses? If so, how long is an acceptable length for a response?

Now you can add your judgement calls and complete your rules. You can use our template here: www.feverbee.com/buildyourcommunity.

WARNING – Will you have the resources to enforce your rules?!

Remember that you need the resources to enforce every rule above.

There is no point setting strict rules for community members if you can't enforce them. Every single rule takes time to enforce. And every second you spend arguing whether a member's photo is a veiled political statement is time you can't spend doing any of the other critical tasks in this book. Be careful not to set stricter rules than you can enforce.

Enforcing the rules

In April 2017, I was invited onto the TV network Al Jazeera for my first (and hopefully last) television news appearance. The topic was community moderation policies. *The Guardian* newspaper had leaked Facebook's internal moderation policies the day before and I was interviewed as a community specialist to talk about them.

Just as I was warming up to my future life in showbusiness, the interviewer hit me with his first question.

'Why is Facebook so secretive about the rules for using the platform?'

My answer (to his apparent disappointment) was they're not. The rules for using Facebook have been available on the site almost since its inception. Facebook isn't secretive about the rules, it's secretive about how it enforces its rules.

This difference is important. Facebook might ban abuse but it doesn't clearly state what constitutes abuse. And the reason for this is simple; if the bad guys know precisely what words, phrases, and images to avoid using, they can slip all sorts of bad content through the net.

The interviewer didn't seem happy and fired back with his next question:

'But then why [repetitive] does Facebook allow beheading videos?'

I began to sense this appearance might've been a mistake. I tried to reply:

'Facebook doesn't allow beheading videos ...'

The interviewer interjected:

'But you can find these videos right now on the website!'

The problem (as I again tried to explain) wasn't with the rules but with enforcement of the rules. Almost all the controversy surrounding the topic of moderation doesn't concern the rules themselves but how they are enforced (or, frequently, seem arbitrarily enforced). For example, a typical moderation system uses machine learning algorithms to flag suspicious content into a moderation queue (other members might flag content too). Then lowly paid moderators in places like Bangladesh and the Philippines process this queue deciding what content should be rejected and what should be approved.

The problem is that every human system has an error rate. Moderators might review thousands of items of content in a day and make the right call 99.9999% of the time. However, if you're getting almost a billion items of content every week this still adds up to hundreds of thousands of mistakes every week.

These mistakes fall into three areas. The first are genuine errors. A moderator might've simply pushed the wrong key or flagged the content badly. The second is because perpetrators of bad content have done something especially sneaky (i.e. editing something illicit into a boring presentation video). The third is simply because the policies themselves are open to subjective interpretation.

This demonstrates just how hard it is to police a community. The more rules you have, the more resources you need to enforce them. Also, the more rules you have, the more things are going to slip through cracks. I'll try and tackle the most common issues you're likely to deal with below.

Preventing bad actors

No, we're sadly not just talking about Nicolas Cage.

If we were, we could simply establish a rule preventing anyone named 'Nicolas Cage' from participating in any of our communities (or, ideally, any future movies).

But what if Nicolas Cage used a pseudonym? Say, Egac Salocin? How would we stop him? What about his dozen or so namesakes? Should they all suffer for Nicolas Cage's dismal acting abilities?

What if *the* Nicolas Cage repented for ruining so many promising movies and promised to do better in the future? Should we let him back in? What if Nicolas Cage claimed someone had been impersonating him? Should he be readmitted into our communities? What is a reasonable length of suspension someone should receive for starring in a movie like *Ghost Rider*?

Bad jokes aside, bad actors (a person engaging in negative activity) are a problem for communities big and small. And these are precisely the kinds of questions you're likely to face when dealing with them. Even the smallest communities can be devastated by a handful of bad actors committed to causing havoc.

What motivates bad actors?

Let's begin with what motivates people to dare come to your community and wreak havoc upon its innocent population.

The literature on bad actors is almost as voluminous as the number of bad actors themselves. We can split bad actors into three types. The type that do it for personal external gain (i.e. spammers, self-promoters etc.), those who do it for personal reasons (i.e. trolling, hurtful messages etc.), and the new crop of 'state-sanctioned' bad actors (i.e. Russian trolls).

The motivations of the first group are fairly obvious. Spammers and self-promoters are typically seeking to make a profit.[4] They have identified your community as a means through which they can peddle their money-making schemes. The majority won't even be real people but instead spam bots – typically single nodes on a large 'bot net' which probes thousands, perhaps millions, of similar communities looking for opportunities to gain free advertising.[5]

Spam accounts which belong to real people tend to either subtly mention their company or products in posts, slip links into posts and signatures, or privately message members who they feel have '*shown an interest*' in the company.[6] If you've visited LinkedIn recently, you get the idea.

The motivations of the second group are more complex and harder to discern. There tend to be three broad causes of their behaviour: the personality and attributes of the perpetrator, the mood of the perpetrator, and the topic being discussed. Each of these presents a different method for dealing with the problems they cause.

Three ways of tackling bad actors

Your approach to tackling bad actors should usually depend upon what caused them to act bad in the first place. We can go through each of these reasons to identify solutions.

1 **Personality problems.** The personality of the perpetrator is the easiest to understand. As one of the largest studies on trolling ever undertaken concluded: 'trolling appears to be an Internet manifestation of everyday sadism'.[7] In short, trolls troll because they have a personality type which leads them to enjoy the act of disrupting conversations.

   While the methodology of diagnosing sadistic behaviour traits has shifted significantly over the years, a 2001 study found 0.2% of the general population met the definition of a sadistic personality disorder.[8] This is a crude measure but reveals something worth considering. Once your community goes beyond a relatively small size (probably around 500 members), you're statistically likely to have at least one person who will gain enjoyment from trolling.

   This person who will enjoy being negative about everything might attack others, and might say things they don't believe simply to get a reaction. Trolls like these can be the most frustrating to deal with because they're often not breaking any explicit rules. They're just being annoying. Members of this group should be warned and then removed if they keep behaving to the detriment of other members.

2 **Mood-related problems.** The second group are those who cause harm when they're in a bad mood.

   This group includes pretty much all of us at some point in time. Right now a tiny percentage of your audience, even some of your favourite people, are having a bad day. This makes them more prone to lashing out at someone else.

Fortunately, a simple reminder can turn things around. This group is often best dealt with a nudge/warning (after they've had time to calm down) or a short suspension from the community. If someone with a good track record is doing something bad, it's best to drop them a quick note rather than whipping out the *banhammer*.

3 **Situation-related problems.** The third group are those provoked by a particular topic. For example, any discussions between climate change believers and sceptics, Obama fans and Trump fans, or vaxxers and anti-vaxxers will almost always descend into furious name-calling and abuse. Yet, even relatively minor issues can spiral out of control in a tit for tat debate. In 2013, Wikipedia editors, a typically serious (and, frankly, tedious) bunch, engaged in a 40,000 word war about whether to capitalise the 'I' on the Star Trek: Into Darkness page.[9]

This group considers accepting anyone else's argument a threat to their own expertise and thus rejects the ideas of others by default.

Situation-related problems are trickier to deal with. Some people have taken to banning difficult topics entirely or severely restricting discussions about them. Often these debates simply need a moderator to step in and close the discussion before it spirals out of control. If members are simply restating or repeating opinions, it's time to close the discussion.

WARNING – Every rule has exceptions!

The big challenge with enforcing rules is there are exceptions to every rule.

You probably can't predict them until you come across them. For example, you will certainly want to ban pornography from your community, but where will you draw the line between art and photography? Would you ban images of Michelangelo's *David* in Florence, *Fountain of Neptune* in Bologna, or a statue of a topless woman in a public park in Kansas? Facebook's overzealous moderators have been criticised for all three in the past.

What if the images are related to sex education? A mother sharing photos of her breast-feeding her children? Would you ban those too?

Even the vilest of content has exceptions. Every moderator worth their salt would remove nude images of underage children. But what if the image in question is an infamous and historically important image of a child victim of a napalm strike during the Vietnam War? Or a mother sharing photos of her kids in the paddling pool on a hot summer's day? If moderators are following rigid rules without exercising their own judgement, you're going to get outcomes in these situations that will provoke a backlash.

You might also be drawn into situations you would really rather avoid. You might ban illegal activity, but legality varies by country. It's illegal in some countries for women to be seen in public without a hijab. Is that really a standard you want to enforce in your community too? Or do you really want to enforce the laws of your country upon other members from throughout the world?

Teach moderators well and let them lead the way

The obvious solution is to let moderators use their own judgement.

A friend of mine who used to work for the *Huffington Post* proudly claimed he hired smart moderators and let them make the judgement calls rather than trying to come up with strict rules for every possibility.

This tackles many of the challenges above, but introduces a new problem: *inconsistency*. Judgement calls are inherently subjective and each moderator's bias and personal views come into play. It wouldn't take you long to find groups on both the left and right of the political spectrum highlighting an egregious difference between how two similar posts were treated. This, they claim, is proof of bias perpetuated against them by moderators employed by the social media company responsible.

Subjectivity comes at a cost to consistency. In the early stages of community, you will probably do most of the moderation yourself and make plenty of judgement calls. However, as you expand, your approach to moderation must also shift to something that works at a far better scale.

Be quick, clear, and decisive

Whatever kind of community you're managing, there are a few best practices to abide by. Aim to resolve problems quickly and efficiently. For example, you don't want to engage in an endless back and forth with a member about whether or not they have broken the rules. You make a decision and the decision is final.

Be clear about what the member did wrong and what the outcome will be. As a rule of thumb, you should spend less time dealing with the offence than the time it took to cause the offence.

For example, it takes a few seconds to ban a member, but it takes a member several minutes to register a new account if he wishes to cause trouble again. If you ban the member's IP address, it takes him even longer. You should never be spending more time with your worst members than your best.

Also remember your community isn't a court of law, it's a community. Treat bad actors as you would a bad guest at your home. You can ask members to leave (or remove members) simply because they're not a good fit. They might have a bad attitude, be constantly toxic, or just be rude to other members. They might not have broken a specific rule, but they're just bad for the community.

Your first job isn't to respect their freedom of speech or some version of their rights; it is to be the protector and facilitator of a growing community. You wouldn't try to collect definitive proof of a bad house guest's behaviour before asking them to leave, you would simply ask them to go.

This doesn't mean removing a member should be the first course of action. While you want to enforce your guidelines, you also don't want members to live in fear of saying the wrong thing.

The scale of escalation

Some community leaders use a simplified scale of escalation for dealing with most bad actors. You can find a typical example below:

Action	Description
1 Reason (minor offence)	Drop member a friendly note to explain the problem with their post and the impact it has upon other members.
	This works best for minor problems, negativity, or when members have caused problems without any clear excessive intended malice for other members.
2 Warn and remove the post (repeated offence, breach of judgement calls)	Deliver a warning. This should mention the behaviour, the damage caused by the behaviour, and what will happen if it occurs again. Be aware that many members will automatically assume a defensive response to any warning. Don't engage, just repeat the warning and end the communication. At this stage you should also remove the offending post(s) from the community.

▶

Action	Description
3 Suspend (repeat breach of judgement calls, breach of universal rules)	If the behaviour continues, the next step is a short-term suspension. This is also a default response to more serious breaches of the community rules. A suspension is typically a term of 1–30 days. Any longer is close to a lifetime ban. Be clear what rule was broken and how long the suspension is for.
4 Ban (repeated breaches of judgement calls, breach of universal rules, constant toxicity)	If a member has consistently caused problems or engaged in serious breach of the universal rules, they should be removed from the community.
5 IP ban (serious breach of judgement calls, rejoining community following a ban)	Banning a member's IP address is the same as banning a member but with one critical difference, it makes it (slightly) harder for a member to rejoin the community under a different name. They would need to use their mobile phone, a VPN, or access the community from a different location. It also bans anyone else who might be using the IP address (i.e. the entire organisation they work for).
6 Shadow ban (constantly rejoining of community following ban)	Some platforms enable you to 'shadow ban' a member. This in essence allows members to keep posting their content but no one will be able to see it. This essentially bans a member without letting the member know they have been banned. This is somewhat cruel and should only be used for members who have shown a repeated desire to cause problems even after being banned.

Each approach serves a different purpose. The key thing is to have clear and consistent policies which are flexible enough at this stage to recognise that not every problem can have a ready-made prescription, yet clear enough that you and your team know what to do in each situation.

Every solution has a cost

You are equipped with an arsenal of tools to fight off the horde of trolls and spammers hammering at your door. You can ban and suspend members. You can pre-approve posts or even members. You can set up spam filters to catch pesky automated spam and recruit an army of volunteers to be on the lookout for sneaky self-promotion hidden in otherwise innocuous links and email signatures.

But in the yin and yang of managing a community, every solution also comes at a cost. Pre-approving members slows participation to a crawl. Someone who has a problem wants to be able to ask their question right now. If they have to wait hours to even ask the question they will give up and go elsewhere.

Likewise, pre-approving posts requires an increasingly expensive moderation team to keep activity flowing. Banning members can also turn disgruntled members into lifetime enemies hell-bent on sabotaging everything you do. You need to find the right approach with the resources you have.

What does moderation cost?

You might be reading this and thinking 'Heck Rich, there's no way I need a team of moderators, my community simply isn't that big!'

Don't sweat, you're probably right. If you're only getting a few dozen posts a day, you (and maybe a few volunteers), can probably handle things just fine. However, you should be prepared for what happens as your community grows. Unless you have the right moderation system in place you're likely to fall victim to an array of problems.

For example, you might rightfully enjoy taking your weekends off. When your community is fine it's not a huge deal if the community goes unsupervised for a day or two at weekends. However, as your community grows, mercurial bad actors quickly realise the best time to publish spam or abuse in the community is on a Friday night knowing it won't be seen until Monday morning.

A post in the Google community once complained of racism in search results for black women compared with white women. By the time the post was seen and responded to by Google it had gone viral and reached mainstream media causing wide-ranging negative publicity.

People can post abuse and highlight issues in small communities too, but the stakes are typically lower. Fewer people are likely to see it and it's far less likely to get traction. As you grow you need to be prepared to proactively change your approach to moderation.

We can divide this approach into three phases.

Phase 1: Small communities (up to 100 posts per day)

In the early stages of a community, when you're receiving up to 100 posts per day, you can moderate the community yourself. You might get a little spam, a few offensive posts, and the occasional issue which needs to be escalated internally. But it doesn't take long to skim through 100 posts and remove the bad apples – especially if fellow members are helping flag them. You can exercise your own subjective judgement in a fairly consistent way to enforce the rules.

Phase 2: Mid-sized community (100–1000 posts per day)

At this point, you're going to need some help. This isn't just because it's time-consuming, but also because of the need for speed. If someone posts an abusive comment when you're small, it's problematic but not a disaster. Once you're getting more than 100 posts a day it becomes a serious problem.

Typically, you hire more community staff who perform moderation as part of a bigger role. However, over time you might want dedicated moderators committed to your community. Many mid-sized customer communities hire moderators from western firms to not only remove posts, but also to appropriately engage, respond, and escalate criticism. This tends to cost $1 to $2 per comment for this service.

One great advantage of moderation companies is not only can they scale up quickly, but they can also help tackle multiple languages without having to open up new offices or go searching for people around the world.

At this stage, you need to set some fairly clear rules and train people to implement them. There will still be plenty of subjectivity, but within fairly clear policies.

Phase 3: Mega-communities (1000+ posts per day)

In the largest communities, moderation is a numbers game. You know how many posts you need to review per day and you recruit the appropriate level of resources to perform that role.

The largest social networking platforms tend to hire moderation firms in developing countries with rigid rules and pay a few cents per post. At its peak, the *Huffington Post* was moderating 500,000 comments per day with a team of just 28 moderators. The average cost per moderated post was just $0.05.[10]

At this level, you need not only rules but extremely clear instructions on how those rules are enforced. This will also include a growing number of exceptions and how best to handle these exceptions.

As your community grows your enforcement of the rules moves from subjective interpretation based upon your opinion to strict rules followed by a paid moderation team. Not many communities exceed 1000 posts per day, but if you do you're likely to need clearer rules that moderators can follow.

The table below shows the types of moderation you should use based upon your community's level of activity and the degree of subjectivity inherent in the approach.

Level of activity	Types of moderation	Subjective or objective?
0–100 posts per day	Community manager personally checks new contributions and removes those which they feel aren't within the rules.	Highly subjective
100–1000 posts per day	Community team of two to three people remove the bad content. A few more precise rules are developed for common problems.	Largely subjective
1000–10k post per day	Community team, volunteers, and paid moderation staff check new contributions. More precise enforcement rules are required to guide moderators and volunteers.	Partially subjective and objective
10k–100k posts per day	Moderation is handled primarily by a third-party moderation team who follow clear rules to determine what content should and shouldn't be allowed.	Largely objective
100k+ posts per day	Moderation is handled by a third-party moderation team who follow codified rules with training and testing to ensure they are adhered to. Rules are increasingly precise to handle situations.	Highly objective

Proactive enforcement and shaping behaviour

Everything we've covered so far is reactive. Someone does something bad and you see the bad signal and spring into action. The problem is you're always playing catch-up. You're never looking to reduce the incidents of bad behaviour in the first place. You're probably missing out on a lot of relatively simple changes you can make to improve how members behave in the community and give yourself less moderation work to do.

For example, in 2019 a field experiment was conducted on a community of 13m subscribers to the Reddit Science community.[11] The experiment was simple. Moderators added a 'sticky comment' that displayed the community rules at the top of a discussion. This comment included information about the norms of the community, welcomed newcomers, named unacceptable behaviour, and described enforcement consequences. Essentially it said 'Comments will be removed if they are jokes, memes, abusive, off-topic, or medical advice. Our 1200 moderators encourage respectful discussion' (notice the social norm at work).

The experimenters then displayed this announcement randomly on some discussions but not others.

A month later, they looked at the results and discovered when the rules were announced to members, rule compliance increased by 8% and newcomer participation increased by 70%. This test hadn't just reacted to bad behaviour, it had proactively reduced the quantity of it – and increased the participation of more newcomers at the same time!

These kinds of proactive interventions can have a huge impact. Another example comes from the video gaming sector. Neuroscientist Jeffrey Lin was hired to reduce the incidents of toxic behaviour in the League of Legends community. Jeffrey quickly discovered only 5% of abuse was coming from dedicated trolls looking to cause problems.[12] The majority of abuse simply came from gamers having a bad day. To tackle this problem, Jeffrey began by sending out warnings to members about their behaviour with colour-printed messages. A typical warning might read:

'Teammates perform worse if you harass them.'

These colour-coded tips alone reduced verbal abuse by 6.2% and offensive language by 11%.

But this was just the beginning. Jeffrey wanted to have an overall improvement in the community and its negative culture. So Riot Games introduced a new idea – *The Tribunal*. Often members weren't aware what they had done wrong. As a result, once their bans were lifted, they simply repeated the behaviour which led to them being banned in the first place. The Tribunal would serve as a jury to their peers. The role of the Tribunal is to review chat logs of gamers reported for bad behaviour and decide whether a gamer deserves punishment or not.

The first incarnation saw gamers receive a report explaining what they had done wrong. This increased the reform rate (the percentage of members who don't reoffend within a time period) to 50% in three months. Next Jeffrey introduced 'reform cards'. These included the Tribunal's judgement and the chat logs explaining precisely what they had done wrong. This increased the reform rate to 70%.

This was impressive, but Jeffrey still had one final trick up his sleeve. Jeffrey and his team used machine learning tools to provide instantaneous feedback. Members now received abuse reports within 5–10 minutes of an offence. The reform rate then rose to 92%.

You probably can't hire a neuroscientist for your community team, but you should consider not just how to remove a bad item of content but how to reduce future bad items of content. As we've seen in the examples above, sometimes very small interventions – like clearly displaying the rules at the top of discussions or quickly explaining what members have done wrong – are enough to significantly reduce bad behaviour.

Summary

Moderation is not a game of 'whack-a-mole'. Well, it's not *just* a game of 'whack-a-mole'. It's primarily about creating the right kind of community culture. This means encouraging the good and removing the bad. You should establish social norms early on and enforce them ruthlessly. These social norms might be the defining characteristic of your community.

However, social norms are hard to enforce if your community is overwhelmed by spam and fights. It's important to develop the right systems to prevent this. You need to make some tricky judgement calls and develop the right approach for your type of community. Remember that the more rules you set, the more time and resources it will take to enforce them.

It's one thing to set the rules, it's another matter entirely to enforce them. There's no point creating a rule you're unable to enforce. As your community grows, you need to move beyond informal policies and subjective decisions to more formal policies with a growing moderation team.

Remember too that enforcement isn't just a reactive game, it's also a proactive one. You have plenty of immediate tools to remove or suspend bad actors from the community. But the biggest wins might be in rethinking your systems and using nudges in the right places to reduce incidents of rule breaking in the first place.

Checklist

- -

1 Clearly list the universal rules for your community to prevent harm and abuse of members.

2 Decide the tone and personality of your community – then make decisions about 'grey area' rules.

3 Determine the perfect experience of members and then set one to three 'remarkable' rules to perfectly position the community.

4 Use our activity chart to plan your enforcement approach.

5 Look at common causes of bad behaviour and consider interventions to reduce them.

Tools of the trade
(available from www.feverbee.com/ buildyourcommunity)

- -

- FeverBee's Community Guideline Templates
- Facebook's Community Standards (https://www.facebook.com/communitystandards/)
- Flickr's Community Guidelines (https://www.flickr.com/help/guidelines/)
- TripAdvisor's Community Guidelines (https://www.tripadvisorsupport.com/hc/en-us/articles/200613647)
- Ubuntu's Community Guidelines (https://ubuntu.com/community/code-of-conduct)
- The Verge Community Guidelines (https://www.theverge.com/pages/community-guidelines)
- Priya Parker – *The Art of Gathering: How We Meet and Why It Matters*
- Timothy Garton Ash – *Free Speech: Ten Principles for a Connected World*

chapter 5

Attracting your first members

Imagine turning up for a party and being the only person there. How long would you wait for others to show up? Probably not too long.

No one wants to be the only person at a party. This is true on the web too.

The first few people to a community are like the first few people to a house party. The promise of a great party might keep them there for a while, but if things don't pick up quickly they will soon be gone. This creates a problem. If each new person leaves before the next arrives, it's impossible to build a crowd that sticks around and keeps newcomers engaged.

It's a classic 'chicken and egg' dilemma. No one wants to join a community which isn't active, but how do you create an active community if no one wants to join an empty community?

This is the core challenge of launching a community from scratch. It's a lot easier to get newcomers to stick around once you have some momentum and a decent number of people actively engaged. But until you have reached that tipping point (where more discussions beget more discussions and your members attract more members), you're in a fragile state.

This tipping point is called *critical mass*.

Critical mass is a term borrowed from nuclear physics. It describes the minimum amount of fissile material needed for a sustained chain reaction. In community parlance, we use it to mean the minimum number of active members to ensure steadily growing levels of activity.

When you launch a community (the moment the website goes live to your audience) you have a relatively short window to reach a critical mass of activity. If you don't reach a critical mass of activity quickly, the community momentum quickly peters out.

In this chapter, I'm going to share a practical method for quickly getting to a critical mass of activity and avoid becoming a costly ghost town.

How many members do you need to reach critical mass?

In 2018, I decided to investigate how many members a community needs to reach critical mass. Using data from almost 200 communities, I looked for differences between communities which did or didn't sustain an upward trajectory of activity. The data varied considerably, but I was able to establish some general rules of thumb.

The communities which succeeded generally achieved three key data points within three months. These were:

1 One hundred contributing members per month (i.e. members starting or replying to a discussion).

2 Three hundred monthly posts (or about ten posts per day).

3 Ten new registrations per day.

Even for smaller groups, like those on WhatsApp or Slack, getting at least 10 posts per day seems key. If you're just launching a community for colleagues or a hobby, you need to aim for 10 organic posts (i.e. not posts created by you) per month.

Communities which failed to achieve enough posts from enough members generally fell into one of two categories. They either became a ghost town devoid of any meaningful activity or they became a 'life-support community' propped up by occasional blasts of activity from an increasingly desperate community team.

The 'big bang' launch

The obvious way to reach a critical mass of activity is to do what most people hosting a party do – *tell everyone to arrive at the same time.* This is known as the 'big bang' launch. You launch the community and then try to drive as many people to it as quickly as possible. You can focus all your efforts on having the biggest launch day possible.

This approach does make sense intuitively. If you need 100 monthly participating members and you have an audience of 10,000 people (customers, employees etc.), you can probably send a mass email and reach that number in a matter of hours.

But there are two major fallacies in this approach.

1 **Members can't see each other until they participate.** The empty room analogy still holds true. Do you really want to send 10,000 people to an empty community and hope they spontaneously start participating? You only get one chance to make a good first impression and an empty community is the worst impression you can make. Visitors won't be aware of each other unless they participate and they won't participate unless they know others are there.

2 **Members don't stick around.** Even in the rare cases where you do manage to drive a huge amount of activity upon launch, this becomes a spike of activity rather than a sustained level of participation. Our data showed many communities had an initial spike of activity at their big bang launch. In almost every case, participation quickly dropped back to life-support levels.[1]

Even if your big bang launch succeeds, are you ready for that level of success?

Can you respond to hundreds of questions a day? Can you check these hundreds of posts don't contain anything abusive to other members or anything which would pose a legal risk to you? Can you deal with dozens of members asking you to reset the passwords they've forgotten (yes, even though that's a feature on the website) or resolve countless petty disputes? Going from 0 to 1000 can be as worrying as failing to gain traction at all.

Therefore, instead of launching big, I recommend launching *fast.*

The fast launch

This is an approach I've used with clients for over a decade.

Instead of sending thousands of members to your community when you launch, you stagger your promotional efforts over time, continuously improve the community, and cater to each group individually. You don't launch big, but you start small and move fast.

In this approach, you begin with a core group of founding members and grow rapidly to establish momentum. This ensures each new member has a slightly better experience than the last, but only the founding members will have the empty room experience. The difference is these founding members *want* the empty room so they can *found* the community. They are prepared for it. They want to do the work of filling the room.

When you launch fast, instead of launching big, you expect to get just a handful of contributions in the first week. But two posts soon become four, four become eight, eight become sixteen etc.

When you launch fast, you devote your resources to ensuring every single member who joins the community has the best possible experience. You have the time and resources to answer questions quickly and with empathy. When you launch fast, you can ensure your first few members feel a part of something new, exclusive, and special. You can nurture them to become top participants.

The power of existing audiences

There is a huge difference between launching a community for a hobby and launching one on behalf of an organisation.

If you're working on behalf of an organisation, you can usually invite a large group of people to join a community to get started. After all, if you didn't have any customers or employees you wouldn't be in business. This speeds up the community process considerably. It's a lot easier to launch a community and invite people who already know you than complete strangers.

If you already have thousands of people visiting your organisation's website every day, many of whom with questions they want answered, this process can be even easier. You might simply be able to redirect them to the community and get started.

However, if you can't invite a large mailing list or redirect existing website traffic, you're going to have a problem. One recent client had over a million customers but was unable to approach any of them due to the organisation's strict data privacy rules. Another client wasn't allowed to promote the community to existing customers because that mailing list was owned by the marketing team who didn't want to interrupt their communication plan to promote the community.

If you're not able to contact the people you want to join the community, you're going to struggle to get a community started. It's also going to provoke further problems down the line if two departments are competing for the attention of the same audience. In these situations, it's best to get people in the same room and figure out how to make this work for both of you. It's counterintuitive to have a large mailing list of potential members but not be allowed to invite them to join the community.

Pre-launch

There are three phases to reaching critical mass; *pre-launch, launch, and post-launch*. The pre-launch phase begins before you even begin developing your community platform and ends when the platform is live for other members to join.

The purpose of the pre-launch phase is to seed the community with the right people and activity before you launch. You want the community to look active to newcomers. If you're using tools like WhatsApp or Slack, where members might not be able to see past discussions when they join, you can simply stagger your invites over time and initiate fresh discussions each day. If you're using a white-label or enterprise-style platform, you want around 20 active discussions and a handful of founding members before inviting others to join the community.

There is a relatively simple process to reach this number:

1 **Ask (and answer) questions yourself.** Once the platform is ready, post the first questions in the community yourself (or invite colleagues to do it). The best questions are typically those which you (or your organisation) hear most often. If you can't get a list of these, you can also find relevant questions by searching on social media for terms related to your topic.

   Post a handful of questions (usually five to ten) in the community and ensure they are answered. You can answer these questions yourself if you need to (i.e. 'This is a common support question we get ... here is the answer'). Or, even better, you can rope in a few colleagues to provide them. This ensures several people show up as active in early discussions.

   It should only take a week or two to create and respond to these discussions. Once you have a few of these you can invite your founding community members.

2 **Invite and engage your founding members.** Founding members seed not just the initial activity, but also the culture for the community. Because future members are most likely to adopt the behaviour of current members, whichever behaviours and traditions you establish at the launch of your community will be perpetuated by others indefinitely. This makes selecting and working with the right founding members a critical part of the process of launching a community.

If you make it a social norm to thank those who answer a question, this norm will trickle down through each new generation of members. Likewise, if you make it a social norm for responses to questions to include screenshots and bullet points, this tradition is likely to continue as the community grows. These social norms should match the norms you created with your remarkable rules from the last chapter.

While it is possible to change the behaviour of members after you've launched, it's a lot easier to shape the behaviour of members *before* you've launched. The only way to do this is to work closely with an initial group of founding members.

Finding your founding members

Founding members aren't just going to drift in by chance. You need to go out there and find them. There are several ways to identify founding members of the community. The best methods include:

1) **Your survey and interview participants.** You can ask people who responded to your surveys or interviews if they would be interested in becoming a founding member of the community.

2) **Existing relationships.** If you have relationships with prospective members who already know and like you, they're far more likely to be willing to help you build something new.

3) **Call for founding members.** Ask who wants to become a founding member. This can be through an email newsletter, via your website, social media accounts, or any other channels. This approach doesn't tend to yield the same quality of participants, but it is useful as a last resort if the other two fail.

4) **Social media/other communities.** If none of the above works for you, this might be a sign you need to build some relationships before you launch a community. You can do this by reaching out to people talking about the topic on social media and elsewhere.

Being able to find founding members eager to help start the community is a good litmus test to reveal if the topic is engaging enough to sustain a community. If you can't get a small handful of members excited and engaged in the idea today, you're not likely to attract hundreds of people tomorrow.

Once you have identified around 30– 50 founding members of the community, it's time to invite them to your platform (already seeded with a few discussions).

It's a good idea here to start a discussion based upon topics they have already told you they're interested in and invite them to reply. Use your surveys and interviews to guide you. You can also reach out individually to your founding members and invite them to start a discussion on a challenge they're facing or something that's on their mind. You should be able to add another five to ten discussions during this process without too much difficulty.

Founding members must feel like they're founding something

It's critical founding members do genuinely feel like founding members. If you're not giving them any input or control over the decisions which are being made about the community, they will soon figure out that they are FINOs (founders in name only).

You must give founding members the ability to shape the community you're creating. They want to know they have made an impact in the community. If members have signed on to become founding members, by implication they have signed on to do actual work which helps grow the community. Give them work to do!

Unlike a marketing campaign, this audience doesn't want to be passive recipients of information, they want to be an indispensable part of the process of getting the community up and running. They can't take pride in something they haven't had any real impact in creating.

Luckily, there is plenty of work to be done when you're founding a community.

One of the easiest things to help them feel they are founding the community is to ask them questions about the kind of community they want. You can ask them what events you should host or what kind of features they're interested in.

One of the best questions you can ask your founding members, as we learned in the last chapter, is about the kind of culture they want to see within the community. You can ask whether the community should focus upon high-quality, low-noise discussions and ruthlessly moderate those which fall below the quality level. You can ask if the community should endeavour to help every member resolve their problem regardless of how noisy it gets. Every option has pros and cons and you can let your members lead the way.

You can also ask your founding members about the traditions and social norms that might be powerful within the community. Then work with them to create those traditions. You might start a tradition of showing gratitude to the person who answered the question or thanking people who ask brave questions. You might celebrate member birthdays or invite members to share their best achievement in the last month.

You can also ask what kind of content would be useful to founding members and what roles they might like to take within the community. There are an infinite number of unique roles founding members can assume within the community. You can even create a shortlist of areas where you need help and call for volunteer moderators, give someone responsibility for specific topics (initiating new discussions and events within that topic), or have people as greeters. You might also host polls and invite members to vote on issues which might be relevant to the future of the community.

As a general rule, the greater the level of ownership you can transfer to your founding members, the more they will participate.

You should also consider creating a badge (we'll cover gamification soon), solely for founding community members. As the community grows, this will be the most scarce badge in the community. No one else except founding members will ever be able to earn it. However, only award these badges to the founding members who remained active through the pre-launch spell. If you give the same badge to highly engaged founding members as you do to those who never contribute, you will completely devalue the badge.

By the end of the pre-launch stage you should be able to rely upon 15–30 weekly active participants who are excited and interested in participating in the community.

As a general rule, if you're struggling to reach at least 15 active participants in this phase, you might have to rethink the community concept before launching the community. This could be an early warning signal that either your members are very difficult to reach or the concept of the community itself isn't enticing to your target audience.

This phase should only last three to four weeks. If it's any longer, founders are likely to lose interest and drift away. By the end of this phase you should feel a sense of momentum and excitement for the community.

Launch

Congratulations! You've now got a good number of excited founding members raring to build your community. You've also got a good number of discussions. Now it's time to launch the community to the outside world.

There are some very good and some very bad ways of doing this. The best way is to promote your community to small groups of prospective members at a time. This process can last weeks, even months. Using this approach, you can give each group of members a terrific personal welcome, resolve any technical issues early, and ensure that momentum is constantly growing as more people arrive.

If you're using a tool like Slack or WhatsApp, you can directly invite people with an email link or from your phone. Add a few people to the group each day and watch it grow. As each person joins you can give them a good welcome. If you're working on behalf of an organisation or using your own mailing list, you should segment your audience into several groups and send an invitation email out to different groups over several weeks. You might even want to split-test approaches (i.e. promote different benefits or features of the community) to see which is the most effective at getting people to register. Most mailing list tools make this simple to do.

You can also drive traffic by placing a link to the community on your organisation's homepage if you have one (and are able to do so). Remember you don't want a flood of traffic at this point. So consider beginning with a small link outside of the main navigation menu and gradually increase the prominence of the community on your organisation's website as you grow. Likewise you can mention the community in more social media channels, newsletters, and any other avenue.

Should you launch a community at a big event?

There is one major downside of the fast launch approach: it lacks the definitive *'launch date'* your organisation might crave.

▶

In my experience, senior executives are typically eager to do a 'big launch' at a major company event. This helps the community gain internal support and helps set deadlines for when work needs to be completed. However, there are some downsides to this.

A major problem is many events use a specific app which members can use to talk to one another. This means you're competing with another tool for your audience on the first day you launch. Worse yet, this app is typically used intensively for a few days and then abandoned when the event is done.

If you are going to do this, make sure your community is deeply integrated into the event and adds tremendous value. For example you might ask event attendees to:

- **Create questions for speakers in the community.** Even better, ask speakers to also host a discussion on the topic the following week in the community where they will take questions from all comers. This is a far better experience than giving speakers five to ten minutes at the end of this talk to answer questions.
- **Start discussions related to sessions at your event.** It's not enough to simply receive advice if members don't know how to apply it to their situation. Why not initiate discussions in the community where members can discuss how they can apply any advice given and can ask for help from the community if they need it.
- **Arrange meetups with others.** Invite members to highlight the kind of people they would love to connect with at the event and use the community to coordinate their gatherings. Host a secret after party for your founding members and invite a few others to join.

You can also provide the right context for the community to be constantly present as people go about the event. This might include:

- **Event leaderboards.** Show the current community leaderboard on big screens during the event. Even better if you can create an event-specific leaderboard to show just the current ranking of members by points they have accumulated in the community during the event. You can have a competition during the event where people can earn points for asking and answering questions in the community. This can be mentioned in talks and prizes given to the top participant at the end of each day.
- **Challenge booths.** Have booths where members can sign up for the community and either introduce themselves or ask their first questions.

Better yet, have booths where expert members can answer questions from others and earn points for the leaderboards above.

- **Post new questions from customer support in the community.** Share the latest questions customer support teams are receiving in the community and challenge members to answer them. This creates a constant stream of questions for members to answer throughout the event and earn points if their answer is correct.

- **Share event content in the community first.** If you wish to encourage people to use the community, you can post the event recordings, information, details of the after party etc. within the community first. This provides an ideal reason for people to join and visit the community.

- **Run a live 'ideas jam' session.** If ideation is a key part of your event, you can run an ideation session during the event. Start a challenge with a few clear parameters, ask members to share their best ideas, and then vote on the ideas which they like the best.

There is no shortage of ideas to encourage members to interact with one another. However, if you can't make community both an essential and valuable part of the event you really shouldn't launch your community at an event.

Post-launch

Now that your community is live, it's time to move fast to reach critical mass.

You need to steadily ramp up the promotion to build momentum. It's critical here to have all of your promotional assets ready to go before you launch the community.

Launching Geotab's community

In 2019, I spent five months working with a fantastic team at Geotab (a telematics company) to launch their community.[2] We spent most of those months meeting with various departments, lobbying for resources, and getting people amped up and excited about what the community could do for them.

▶

> Our goal was to have all of the promotional assets ready to go before the launch. The PR team was ready to send press releases, the CEO announced it at Geotab Connect (the organisation's big annual event), the marketing team promoted it on social media and other channels, and it was promoted on the main website and integrated into the product.
>
> Even the customer success and sales staff mentioned it on calls with customers. We didn't utilise all of these assets at once, instead we staggered promotion over a series of months to build momentum.
>
> Within three months we had blitzed past our targets with over a thousand discussions from hundreds of members – but it took a huge amount of work to make that happen. The secret was to line up all the support we needed before we launched.

You probably have more methods of promoting your community than you might expect. You can divide these into two categories. Existing audiences you already have access to and external audiences you can promote the community to through specific channels.

You can see examples of these below:

Existing audiences	External audiences
• Company website (navigation tab, pop-ups etc.) • Included in product or service • Newsletter • Mailing list • Social media following • Staff (don't underestimate staff referrals and promotion of the community	• Press releases • Paid social adverts • Influencer outreach and promotion • Search engine optimisation

Using paid social ads

Paid social ads are often a good backup option if you're struggling to attract enough members to get started. However, social ads on Facebook, Twitter, and other channels come at a cost.

In the autumn of 2017, LungCancer.net sent out a series of five week-long paid Facebook announcements to increase participation.[3] The advertisements reached almost 92k people and attracted 863 new members into the community. In total, LungCancer.net paid $2.02 to acquire each new member.

The number of members you attract and the cost per member will depend upon the type of audience, the quality of the ad and the conversation rate this leads into. However, the key principles are generally clear, you can attract a large audience at high speed if you're willing to pay. If you've spent a few hundred thousand dollars on a platform, spending an additional $10k to attract 5,000 members to use it might be well worth the investment.

Promotional plan

Create a promotional plan which details every communication you will send to your audience and through which channel. You can use our template at www.feverbee.com/buildyourcommunity. A typical promotional plan might look like the below:

Week	Actions
Week 1	• Promotion to event attendees • Reminder to founder members of launch date • Invite for the staff to join and participate
Week 2	• Promotion to segment 1 of 4 of mailing list
Week 3	• Addition of community navigation tab to homepage • Promotion to segment 2 of 4 of mailing list • Reminder to segment 1 • Reminder for staff to join and participate
Week 4	• Promotion to segment 3 of 4 of mailing list • Reminder to segment 1 • Reminder to segment 2 • Addition in the customer onboarding process • Promotion to segment 4 of 4 of the mailing list • Reminder to segment 2 • Reminder to segment 3
Week 5	• Mention in company newsletters • Reminder to segment 3 • Reminder to segment 4

Week	Actions
Week 6	• Navigation banner announcement • Social ads to attract 1000 visitors • Reminder to segment 4
Week 7	• Social ads to attract 1000 visitors • Pop-up on company website • Mention in press releases • Inclusion in staff signatures
Weeks 8–12	• Social ads to attract 1000 visitors • Pop-up on company website • Influencer outreach • Inclusion in product

In this phase you should see a steady increase in three metrics:

1 **Active participants.** The number of members participating in the community should rise steadily each week. You should also notice one or two top members emerging.

2 **Number of discussions.** The number of discussions initiated by members (i.e. not by you and your team) should also be steadily increasing each week.

3 **Organic search traffic.** If your community is public and searchable, you should see around a 10%–15% increase in visitors arriving by search traffic each month.

If you're not seeing growth in these metrics, it's likely you're either struggling to attract enough people to visit your community each week or you're struggling to keep them engaged.

If it's the former (look at the number of weekly visitors if you can), check if your announcements about the community are still reaching the same number of people as before. You can always target more people in your promotional messages and tweak the messaging to highlight different benefits. As a general rule, try to keep the messages as short and as direct as possible.

If it's the latter (i.e. members aren't participating), it's either because they don't have problems to solve or they don't feel confident asking questions in the community. Speak to them directly to find out which. You might need to change the concept of the community (focus on the broader industry) or create a special place for newcomers to ask their first questions.

You can see the entire process illustrated on the following page:

Timeline for a successful community launch

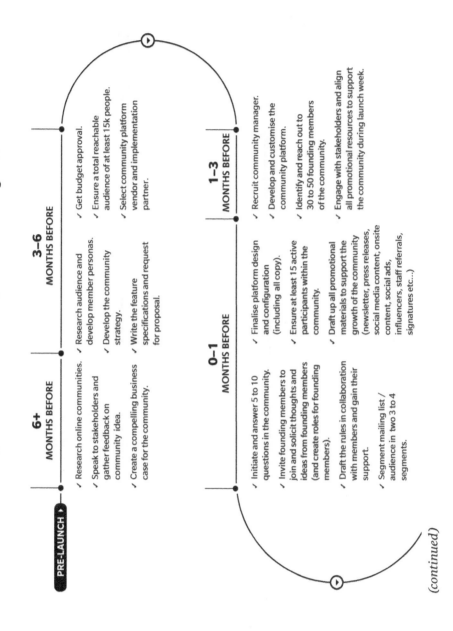

PRE-LAUNCH ▸

6+ MONTHS BEFORE

✓ Research online communities.

✓ Speak to stakeholders and gather feedback on community idea.

✓ Create a compelling business case for the community.

3–6 MONTHS BEFORE

✓ Research audience and develop member personas.

✓ Develop the community strategy.

✓ Write the feature specifications and request for proposal.

✓ Get budget approval.

✓ Ensure a total reachable audience of at least 15k people.

✓ Select community platform vendor and implementation partner.

1–3 MONTHS BEFORE

✓ Recruit community manager.

✓ Develop and customise the community platform.

✓ Identify and reach out to 30 to 50 founding members of the community.

✓ Engage with stakeholders and align all promotional resources to support the community during launch week.

0–1 MONTHS BEFORE

✓ Initiate and answer 5 to 10 questions in the community.

✓ Invite founding members to join and solicit thoughts and ideas from founding members (and create roles for founding members).

✓ Draft the rules in collaboration with members and gain their support.

✓ Segment mailing list / audience in two 3 to 4 segments.

✓ Finalise platform design and configuration (including all copy).

✓ Ensure at least 15 active participants within the community.

✓ Draft up all promotional materials to support the growth of the community (newsletter, press releases, social media content, onsite content, social ads, influencers, staff referrals, signatures etc...)

(continued)

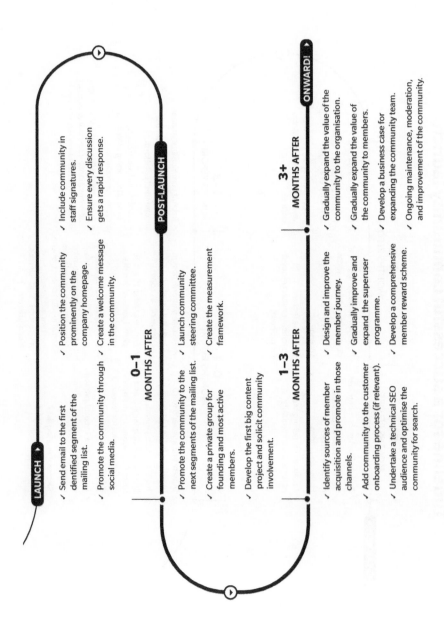

LAUNCH

✓ Send email to the first dentified segment of the mailing list.

✓ Promote the community through social media.

✓ Position the community prominently on the company homepage.

✓ Create a welcome message in the community.

✓ Include community in staff signatures.

✓ Ensure every discussion gets a rapid response.

0–1 MONTHS AFTER

✓ Promote the community to the next segments of the mailing list.

✓ Create a private group for founding and most active members.

✓ Develop the first big content project and solicit community involvement.

✓ Launch community steering committee.

✓ Create the measurement framework.

POST-LAUNCH

1–3 MONTHS AFTER

✓ Identify sources of member acquisition and promote in those channels.

✓ Add community to the customer onboarding process (if relevant).

✓ Undertake a technical SEO audience and optimise the community for search.

✓ Design and improve the member journey.

✓ Gradually improve and expand the superuser programme.

✓ Develop a comprehensive member reward scheme.

3+ MONTHS AFTER

✓ Gradually expand the value of the community to the organisation.

✓ Gradually expand the value of the community to members.

✓ Develop a business case for expanding the community team.

✓ Ongoing maintenance, moderation, and improvement of the community.

ONWARD!

Registration form errors

Don't ask members to complete too many steps to get started. The common mistake is to force members to spend far too much time completing their profile to register. This means they need to find an image of themselves they like, upload it, write their personal bio, share their work history etc. The meagre benefits of asking members to complete a long profile is far outweighed by the costly number of members who won't bother to complete the profile.

Yes, you can certainly find data that shows members who complete their bio and upload a photo participate more than those who don't. But this data confuses cause and effect. As members begin participating in a community they begin to care more about what others think of them. This in turn drives them to update and maintain their profile. Which is why the most active members also tend to have detailed profiles.

In most communities anyone can browse activity without having to register. If a member has registered, it usually means they've found something they want to do. Often they want to ask a question or reply to one. If they have to complete a profile before, most will simply give up.

You should make it as easy and as quick as possible for members to do what they came to the community to do. Fortunately, in recent years, the trend has shifted from collecting as much data as we can about members (in case some of it might be useful) to collecting as little data as needed to avoid any legal problems. This is a good thing. In the majority of cases, you don't need more than a username, password, and an email address. Often you don't even need a real name.

Every step you take to simplify the registration process will pay dividends for years to come. Increasing the conversion rate by a few percentage points right now can have a compounding effect of thousands of active members within a few years.

This explains why tools like SSO (single sign-on – where members can register and log in to a community through existing user or social media accounts) are so important. They typically reduce the process of joining a community to just a click or two.

First contribution

Once members have registered, it's critical they make their first contribution as quickly as possible. The odds on someone participating decline sharply with every passing hour between registering and making a contribution. Most newcomers either participate immediately or never at all.

However, not all contributions are equal in keeping members engaged. In our data, we discovered members who start a discussion (as opposed to replying to one) are 7% more likely to make a second post and 8% more likely to make 10 posts. A small difference like this, compounded over several years, can have a big impact upon the overall level of participation. Therefore, you should invite newcomers to start a new discussion at their first contribution as opposed to replying to an existing one. But starting a new discussion in a community isn't always an easy thing to do.

Helping newcomers ask questions

Imagine walking into a crowded room full of strangers and asking for help.

You wouldn't know if the question you're asking has been asked dozens of times before, whether you're going to sound dumb for asking an obvious question, or whether colleagues you respect are going to be in the room and suddenly realise you don't know as much as they thought you did. Worse yet, what happens if you don't get a response? What would you do if no one replies to a question?

Newcomers face this experience every day.

One way to help is to create a specific 'newcomers corner'. This is a place you direct newcomers to join (or automatically enrol them in the group) and solicit their first questions. Ideally, you want a mentor for this group who will also take the time to answer these kinds of questions. This ensures members are getting an empathetic response rather than a variation of 'read the manual!' or 'research this question before you ask it!', both of which can be common in established communities (notably more technical communities).

A huge benefit of having a newcomer or 'getting started' area is that you can separate expert-level discussions from the basics. An infamous problem with building communities is your top members will inevitably spend the majority of their time answering repetitive questions from beginners. This can get tedious for everyone pretty quickly.

Last year we had a client facing this exact challenge. Experts were becoming increasingly frustrated at repeatedly having to answer the same questions. The beginner-level questions were crowding out the advanced discussions our experts enjoyed. In turn this was causing experts to be increasingly intolerant of newcomers – often to the point of driving away new customers through their cold, rude responses.

Our solution was to create a separate place for newcomers to engage with one another. But this solution was with a twist. Instead of just asking community newcomers to join a newcomer group, we instead invited all new customers each month to join a private cohort group just for them. The magic of this approach is now newcomers no longer feel they are going through the experience of learning about a new product (or topic) alone – instead they have a safe place to ask basic questions and learn how other customers in their precise position resolved those same problems.

Each group had two volunteer mentors who were eager to help new customers get started, answer beginner-level questions, and ensure these customers had the best-possible experience. This not only resolved most of the questions newcomers had, it also kept the rest of the community from having to answer the same questions.

At the end of each month each cohort 'graduated' to the main community where they could engage fully with other members and harness the full knowledge of the community equipped with the knowledge of the product to contribute effectively and with an established group of contacts. At the time of writing, the retention rate of our cohort groups is 21% higher than those customers who were not invited to join retention groups.

What if members don't have any questions to ask?

The problem with inviting newcomers to ask a question as their first post is many simply don't have any questions to ask. It doesn't matter how nicely or persuasively you invite people to ask a question if there isn't any information they feel they need.

Many communities use welcome threads for this group. Welcome threads are more effective than you might imagine. In 2019, I looked at data from 522 welcome threads identified in 14 different communities. I then identified members who posted in one of the welcome threads within their first 30 days of becoming visible in the community and analysed how long they remained active compared with those who made their first contribution elsewhere.

The results were clear. Members who replied to a non-welcome discussion as their first contribution created an average of just two discussions in the community and posted an average of nine comments in total. Members who replied in a welcome discussion in their first action contributed an average of 7.7 discussions and created a remarkable 149 comments.

In summary, you should invite your members to do two things when they join the community:

1 **Start a discussion.** Ideally a question or challenge they could use help with. This should be the primary call to action in most communities.

2 **Reply to a welcome discussion.** Ideally a discussion which lets members share something interesting about themselves.

Both of these will help members unlock immediate informational or social value from the community on their very first visit. Use your welcome emails, direct messages, and onsite notifications (where possible) to guide members to take one of these two actions when they first join a community.

What keeps members hooked?

In the rest of this book, I'll share plenty of strategies to keep members hooked. However, for now it's important to learn *what* keeps members hooked in a community. The most obvious answer is to satisfy their motivations for participating in the community in the first place. A 2004 study examining hundreds of members from 27 unique communities found the following core reasons for people participating in a community:[4]

Reason for participating in the community	%
Information exchange	49.8%
Friendship	24%
Social support exchange	10.9%
Recreation	8.7%
Technical reasons or common interest	1.7%
Other	3.1%

While friendships and social support are important to any community, online communities are unique. Their prime value lies in providing members with access to information. The majority of people will keep coming back to the community as long as they feel they can keep gaining valuable information.

The problem with focusing too much on information, however, is the majority of members often visit only when they need information. That might not be very often. This is where we need to abide by a key principle. To keep members hooked you need to surpass their expectations by providing them with incredibly valuable information they didn't even know they needed. For example, someone that visits looking to solve a problem with their iPhone might also see related discussions and articles giving incredible iPhone productivity tricks or photo editing advice.

Likewise, an engineer visiting the community of a software product might see an opportunity to participate in an upcoming live chat with the CEO or product engineers. The more scarce and useful information is, the more members keep coming back.

You might also share resources or news in the community members are unable to get anywhere else or host live problem-solving sessions where members can engage directly with experts and one another. Some communities offer trial versions of the product to founding members. Sephora (a client) runs a large programme giving away samples of their products to top members.

You get a very short window to make a good first impression and create a sense of momentum. Don't waste this incredible opportunity. But even the information-packed communities can't retain members forever. Due to competition, changes in policies, or your members going through life changes (having children, starting a new job etc.), your community has a natural churn rate.[5]

It's perhaps best to consider community members as similar to employees in an organisation. Some will be there for a matter of months, others a handful of weeks, and a tiny number for years. The key is to extend the amount of time they spend in the community and do everything in your power to ensure they give and receive the most value to and from the community.

The longer members remain as members, the more knowledgeable they become and the less likely they are to seek information (and the more likely they are to provide information).[6] These members sometimes might visit the community less often, but contribute more posts each time they visit.[7] But length of membership alone isn't a strong predictor of whether people contribute.[8]

What truly matters in ensuring members proactively share information is (a) whether members feel they can make a unique, useful, contribution to the community and (b) whether members feel a sense of *psychological ownership* over the community. In the next chapter we will discover how to create a powerful sense of psychological ownership amongst your community members.

Summary

Your community needs to launch fast and quickly reach a critical mass of activity. You don't need thousands of members to do this, often just a few dozen active founding members is enough to get things started. Try not to have a 'big-bang' launch. This typically gives you an impressive-looking spike of activity at the beginning, but it never fades. Instead aim to launch small and grow fast. There are three steps here:

i First, have a pre-launch period to have a number of questions in the community and some answers which your first founding members will see.

ii Second, stagger your invites and promotion to and of the community over a series of weeks rather than promoting the community to everyone at once. This helps every member have the best first impression of the community.

iii Third, as your community grows, ensure your beginner members have a place where they can ask questions without being abused or feeling they don't belong within the group. A simple method for doing this is to have a separate getting started area or a cohort group for these kinds of questions. This can prevent veterans from becoming frustrated by having to answer the same questions and drive more activity from newcomers.

Once you have reached the critical mass stage you have to excel at keeping members hooked. This means surpassing their expectations which first brought them to the community, most notably the need for information.

Checklist

1 Ensure you have a few answered questions in the community.

2 Create a list of up to 50 founding members.

3 Invite founding members to join the community and offer them unique roles and benefits within the community.

4 Create your 12-week promotional plan and ensure you have everyone aligned to it.

5 Invite your early members to ask questions or introduce themselves to the community.

6 Deliver unexpected value from the community to keep members coming back.

Tools of the trade
(available from: www.feverbee.com/ buildyourcommunity)

• FeverBee Promotional Plan

• FeverBee Founding Member List Template

• FeverBee List of Activities

• FeverBee Template Messages Kit

chapter 6

Nurturing superusers in your community

In September 2019 alone, Airgetlam contributed 657 responses to the Sonos community.[1]

Take a second to think about how much time this took. Airgetlam would've had to have read each question before giving an answer. Let's conservatively estimate it takes two minutes to read the question and another two minutes to come up with an answer. This means Airgetlam would have spent around 44 hours of his spare time that September (more than a typical working week) doing voluntary customer support for a manufacturer of audio systems.

This wasn't even an exceptional month for Airgetlam. Since joining the community in November 2015, Airgetlam has contributed more than 20,000 responses to the community – that's about 166+ days of full-time labour. This kind of extreme volunteering is a common (and yet still strange) phenomenon in communities.

No one shopping at their local supermarket offers to help stock the shelves, sweep the floors, or approach other customers to see if they have questions or need help. But that's in effect what people like Airgetlam are doing every day. And it's happening in almost every community (and in every industry) you can imagine.

It's happening in the communities of high-tech brands like Apple, SAP, and Google. It's happening in retail with brands like Sephora, Debenhams, and Best Buy. It's happening at banks (Wells Fargo, Bank of America, Monzo), telecom companies (Verizon, AT&T, BT), travel companies (Southwest Airlines) and many, many more.

It's happening in non-brand communities too. In any group of colleagues and friends, there will be a handful of people taking on the role of responding to most questions, organising most activities, and driving progress forward. No matter what kind of community you're building, your success is likely to hang upon a few highly motivated members.

The awkward truth about communities

This is the awkward truth at the heart of online community building. Online communities are far from the egalitarian digital utopias we often presume them to be. Sure, there are some communities out there where members contribute equally and benefit from the collective good they create. But almost every other community owes its success to a tiny handful of highly motivated members.

In this chapter I'm going to explain why the success of your community depends far less upon the number of members you attract and far more upon the quality of members you nurture. You're going to learn how to identify potential superusers like Airgetlam and how to nurture them into top participants.

How big are most communities?

To understand why a handful of top members are critical, we first need to understand how many members typically participate in a community.

For a long time, I felt most organisations were fibbing about the size of their communities. Sure, they might boast about having hundreds of thousands, even millions, of members who at some point had completed a registration form. But how many of them were still active? Activity is a far better barometer of a community's success.

In 2019, I decided to get to the bottom of this. A colleague and I scraped data (copied into a format which is easy to analyse) from over 38 large brand communities to determine how many people were actively participating in the community in any given month.

We discovered something surprising. The number of participants in most brand communities was *drastically* lower than most companies were claiming. Our research showed the median number of active contributors for a firm-hosted community in any given month was just 355[2] (or about 12 unique contributors per day).[3]

Even the very largest companies in our data set had far fewer active participants than we expected. EA Games, one of the largest communities we studied, has 300 million customers but only 51,000 unique community contributors per month. That's less than 2% of their customer base actively engaged in their community in any given month. And playing games is one of the most sociable things people can do online. Most brands have a far smaller percentage of their audience participating in their community.

Drop in the bucket

In most cases, the number of members participating in their community is just a *drop in the bucket* compared to the total size of their audience and the activity they generate. Five hundred active contributors is just a drop in the bucket if your organisation has 500,000 customers. Fifty questions per day is just a drop in the bucket if customer support is receiving 5,000. Likewise, your community might generate 10 ideas from the community, but product engineers already have a roadmap filled with ideas from support staff and others. And, sure, a community might increase customer loyalty, but so does creating better products, improving the support, better marketing, and reducing prices.

Even if you perform above average in almost every conceivable measure compared to other communities, your community is still likely to be just a drop in the bucket compared to the rest of the organisation.

This is also true if you're building a community for a local club, activity, or for employees of an organisation. The total number of people who participate and their level of activity is just a drop in the bucket compared to the total size of the audience you could feasibly reach. Fifty people participating in a community of employees is a drop in the bucket compared to the number of employees sending emails to each other every day.

However, as we're about to discover, it doesn't matter if your community is a drop in the bucket as long if it's making waves.

How many members do most communities need?

Ask anyone managing communities how many members they want in a community and the answer will usually be the same; they want 'more'.

This is a mistake.

When more is your goal your community becomes about size. But have you even been in a successful group and wished it was bigger? Have you spent time in a local community you enjoyed and wished there were more people in it? People in a successful community don't want the community to grow bigger, they want the community to grow better. They want to feel better listened to, better connected to one another, and have better access to information.

When your goal becomes solely about size your objectives and those of your members become misaligned. This is going to lead to plenty of problems later. Worse yet, communities will *never* have the same reach as your email list or be able to provide the kind of direct one to one support that a customer support team might be able to. When your community is defined by the level of engagement, you're inevitably going to be compared against other channels which naturally drive a lot more of it. This isn't good for you and isn't good for your community.

Worse yet, if you try to drive an exponential increase in engagement, you're inevitably going to end up doing things which are going to hurt the community in the long run. You might host fun, engaging challenges which attract a lot of participation in the short term instead of starting serious discussions which help members over the long term. You might go for big promotional swings, even if the flood of new members overwhelms the careful culture you've nurtured in the community over the past few years.

Beyond the level required to reach critical mass, the number of people participating in the community really doesn't matter. What does matter is nurturing a tiny group of top members who will generate most of the value in a community. Whether you envision your community being big or small, it's the tiny group of top members who will truly drive you forward.

Communities thrive because of participation inequality

Almost every community shares the same dynamic.

First, you have a relatively tiny top tier of members providing the majority of contributions. Next, you have a small group of irregulars who dip in and out.

Then you have a bunch of newcomers coming to ask questions. Finally, you have a mass of learners (or lurkers) who consume information without ever contributing.

This also shows up clearly in our data. We segmented active members (at least one contribution in the past 30 days) into categories by their relative level of participation. Then we looked at what percentage of posts each group contributes to the community. You can see the results below.

Category	Mean % of posts contributed	High	Low
Top 0.01%	10%	29%	2%
Top 0.1%	13%	29%	2%
Top 1%	28%	61%	11%
Top 10%	56%	91%	38%
Top 50%	85%	97%	72%

As you can see, in brand-hosted communities, the top 10% typically contribute the majority of posts in a community. This isn't a surprise. The majority of people come only to ask one question and leave when they get a response. What's more interesting is the top 1% who contribute almost 30% of all posts in the community.

Almost every community has a top 1% of members who create a majority of the activity in the community. But even this hides the true value of the top 1%.

When we looked deeper at the *types* of contributions this top 1% make, we discovered they don't participate the same way as everyone else. For starters, they typically spend a lot more time creating higher-value content – such as replying to questions from other members. Airgetlam, for example, has responded to 20,000+ questions in the Sonos community but created just 22 of his own in the 4.5 years he's been a member of the community.[4] He's a value-generating machine.

The top 1% of members are also usually the ones who create blog posts, testimonials, and take volunteer roles to help the community. It's the top 1% you need to work most closely with to achieve your community goals.

Think back to the types of impact I asked you to identify when setting your goals. My bet is the majority (if not all of them) don't require the masses but a tiny group of committed members to achieve. For example:

• A tiny number of committed, active members can answer hundreds, even thousands, of questions in a community every month.

- A tiny number of committed, active members can create hundreds, even thousands, of articles sharing excellent advice on the topic, your organisation, or your products. This directly increases member retention and satisfaction.
- A tiny number of committed, active members can create enough reviews to make you the leading product in whatever category you're in and generate millions of dollars in sales.
- A tiny number of committed, active members can give you feedback on all of your marketing efforts and ensure your next campaign is a smash hit.
- A tiny number of committed, active members can generate hundreds of sales leads for your business through referrals.

The critical step to achieving almost any goal you want to achieve in your community lies not in driving as much participation as possible but in working with a tiny group of committed members.

Who is in your community really?

When we think of community, we think of people coming together with a strong sense of belonging, rituals, and a desire to help one another. This is close to how dictionaries define communities. Yet, on almost every survey we've undertaken, the majority of respondents are simply looking for information, answers to questions, or the latest news. As tragic as it sounds, very few are looking to become part of a community of like-minded people.

So are these people really a community if they're just looking for information right now? Perhaps not.

However, in almost every community there are also a small group of superusers who are interested in connecting with and helping one another. They do feel a part of a group identity with one another. They do feel the sense of psychological ownership we mentioned before.

And it's this group of top 1% of members who are the true members of a community. These are the people you need to turn into superusers.

What is a superuser programme?

Let's begin with a definition.

A superuser programme is an exclusive programme that aims to motivate and rewards members for undertaking the most valuable contributions in the community.

Every community is going to have top members. In a community of 100 people, someone is going to be the top participant – the top 1%. But a top participant is not necessarily a superuser.

A superuser is someone who has specifically opted into and been accepted into a dedicated programme you run to support and reward members for making unique, useful contributions to the community. You might find many top members are perfectly happy continuing to contribute at the level they do today without any additional access or rewards. They're just happy and eager to help. They don't need any additional incentives or processes.

Superusers are different. They have a thirst for something more. They might join a superuser programme to increase the impact and value of their contributions both to themselves and to others. They might join a superuser programme for special access or rewards. They might join a superuser programme simply because one exists and they feel the need to be a part of it.

A superuser doesn't have to have the highest quantity of contributions. Some are simply those with unique insight or expertise. However, typically, they are drawn from a pool of members who have made a high quantity of contributions or made unique quality contributions. The only real dividing line, however, is they have been accepted into a superuser programme you are running.

What should you call your superuser programme?

Sometimes a superuser programme is simply called the superuser programme.

Other communities are more creative. Some communities call their superusers Experts, others call them Insiders, and some the MVPs (most valuable persons).

Some, like Spotify, go a step further and call it their RockStar programme. It helps if the name reflects the organisation, but if you're stuck simply go with Insiders or Superusers.

Starting a superuser programme

A superuser programme doesn't have to be a formal programme.

If you've managed any sort of group before, you've probably had some sort of unofficial process where you get to know and support some of your top participants better than others. Local community leaders, for example, typically know and spend more time with those willing to help out in areas of the community than those who aren't.

Even for a community of colleagues or acquaintances, you can make the top members feel uniquely appreciated for their above-average level of contributions to the group.

For groups that exceed a few hundred members however, you will usually want to have some sort of superuser programme to motivate people to make their best contributions to the group. The rest of this chapter will explain how to set this programme up.

Step 1: Decide what superusers will do

The first step is to decide what you need superusers to do.

If you're inviting people into a superuser programme to do what they're already doing, why bother? They're already happily motivated to do those things. You're likely to do more harm than good. If the only thing you want from them is to continue answering questions, there's no point in having a superuser programme in the first place. Superuser programmes are designed to change behaviour in a way that's valuable to superusers and the community at large.

You need to have a good idea of your superuser's motivations here. Superusers want to feel connected to you and your mission, they want to feel like they matter to you and the community, they want to feel connected to others like themselves. Your superuser programme should nudge members to do things which are aligned with these motivations.

Sure, you might want members to answer as many questions as possible. But that's just a fraction of the things your superusers can do which will make them feel valuable and important. You should also ask for their feedback and ideas, invite them to share community case studies, and maybe to create documents and resources that will benefit the community. As Jono Bacon mentions in his terrific book, *People Powered*, you should be asking members to do things which benefit the community far more than they benefit you.[5]

You might also offer superusers leadership roles within the community – perhaps writing a weekly column, helping moderate areas of the site, or writing regular news posts. There isn't a shortage of ideas here. You can even help them grow their reputation and help them become leaders in their field.

Some communities we've worked with (like Claris, formerly Filemaker) invite their superuser to speak on stage at their annual events, meet with senior staff members, and perhaps even start and run their own groups within the

community. A few even give superusers beta or trial versions of upcoming pro-
ductions to review and the opportunity to give feedback on upcoming marketing
campaigns. This will give superusers an incredible sense of importance.

The superusers are also the same group you want to support your community
initiatives. If you're launching a new event or trying to get a new discussion
series started, you should reach out to this group first, get their opinions and
feedback, and ask if they can get the initiative started. If you're looking to create
a certain culture within the community, it's going to be the superusers who will
make it happen.

Make a list of what you want superusers to do. You might want to refer to your
answers from the first chapter here when we discussed community goals. You
can find examples below:

Community goals	Superuser behaviours
Resolve 25% of customer support questions via the community.	Answer the majority of questions that are created by the community within 24 hours.
Increase the expertise and abilities of members (possibly customer success).	Create their own best resources for other members. Find the best resources on the web and share them in the community.
Increase loyalty and retention rates.	Facilitate connections between members. Welcome newcomers and reach out to members. Remove bad content.

Remember, your superusers want to do things that matter. They want to see the
impact of what they do. They want to know their contributions are helping you
and your community. It's hard to overstate the extent to which the success of
your community hangs upon your ability to motivate and persuade superusers to
do things that matter.

How many superusers do you need?

You probably need fewer superusers than you imagine – especially when
you're just getting started. One client at the moment has just two superusers for a community which is getting around 10–15 questions per day.

While it might be tempting to recruit a large number of superusers in one
batch, you don't want to flood the community with superusers to answer

▶

only a trickle of questions. If the current questions in the community are getting good, quick responses, you don't need more superusers – you need more questions (this is a different challenge altogether).

But if you're not getting good, quick answers to questions you might need more superusers. The number of superusers you need is largely determined by the size of your community. We generally aim for a 1% ratio of active participants (people who have made a contribution in the past month).

Monthly participants	No. of superusers
1–100	0–3
100–500	3–5
500–1000	5– 10
1000–5000	10–50
5000+	50+

Another way to calculate this is by the number of questions you're getting per week. A typical superuser can answer 30–50 questions per week (some can do a lot more, others a little less). You can use this to make a broad estimate of how many superusers you might need in your community (as shown below).

No. of questions	No. of superusers
0–150	2–3
150–250	3–5
250–500	5–10
500–2500	10–50
2500+	50+

Remember that each member is going to require a lot of personal attention. They need to feel connected to other superusers. It's hard to do that if you're the only person running the show. As your superuser programme grows, so does the number of staff you need to manage it. Remember that a big part of a superuser programme is making members feel special. The more people you have in your superuser programme, the harder it is to make it feel exclusive.

Step 2: Decide who to accept as a superuser

Would you want to join a volunteer programme that seemed desperate for members? Probably not. Neither would most of us. It's important that your superuser programme is perceived as something exclusive and reflects a high standard of ability. The obvious way to do that is to make it exclusive and reflect a high standard of ability. As a general rule, the more exclusive it seems to be, the more motivated members may be to join.

This means you need criteria for determining who is able to become a superuser.

One approach is to select members by their level of activity. Once you notice members are making a high number of contributions each month you might reach out and invite them to join the programme. However, make sure you average the contributions over the past few months instead of the total contributions a member has ever made in the community. You want the most active members in the present as opposed to members who were highly active several years ago.

An even better approach is to look for the specific skills and activities that match what you need members to do. If you notice members who seem to be participating with passion, are especially helpful, or have demonstrated a high degree of expertise you might want to reach out and invite them to join the programme. Try to ensure a diverse set of skills and experiences in the programme. You might want people who are super-active, but you might also want people who can answer the types of questions and create the kind of resources no one else can.

I'd recommend the following criteria for most superuser programmes.

1 Level of participation

2 Character traits

3 Interest in participating in a programme

4 Unique skills

You can see a simple example below:

	Requirement
Level of activity	Min. 30 posts per month
Passion, helpfulness, or expertise	Polite, clear, helpful
Interest	Can answer questions
Unique skills	High expertise in [widget]

Recruiting superusers

Once you have decided your criteria, you need to decide precisely how members can join. You have three approaches here:

1 **Direct outreach.** At select periods you can reach out to members who meet the criteria above and with a personal message to invite them to join.

2 **Create an application form.** You can create an application form interested members can complete to apply for the programme.

3 **Create a nomination process.** Instead of an application form, you might create a nomination form. This is where you can't apply yourself but you can only nominate other members.

When you're just getting started, you will typically reach out to members individually. But as you grow, you will usually create an application form interested members can complete to join.

Recruitment windows

Whichever method you choose, be clear about the requirements to join the programme. Many programmes have set recruitment windows (i.e. once or twice per year) where members can apply to join the programme. This creates a sense of scarcity, which encourages more people to apply.

Step 3: How will you reward superusers?

Now we get to the really critical piece of the puzzle. What's the benefit of someone to become a superuser? Why would anyone spend so much time and energy helping other people for free?

The answer is you're going to pay them in a currency they value even more than money! You're paying them in positive emotions – the feeling of being useful, recognised, respected, and connected to people like themselves.

Try to avoid rewarding superusers with tangible goods or, god forbid, money. The occasional '*thank you*' surprise gift isn't a terrible thing, but they should never expect a specific gift for performing a specific action. That's not gratitude for their contributions, that's payment – and payment not only undermines their motivation it comes complete with a wonderful collection of legal responsibilities.

Your rewards fall into one of five categories:

Reward	Explanation
Status	Actions which enable members to gain a level of prestige in the eyes of other members.
Access	Actions which afford members with unique access to people or opportunities which other members don't receive.
Influence	Actions which provide members with the ability to have a unique impact or sense of control over the community.
Connection	Actions which help members feel connected to a unique, special group.
Challenge	Actions which enable members to participate in unique challenges.

Let's go through each of these in turn.

1 Access

Access is the most common and powerful type of reward you can offer most superusers.

Superusers love getting access to things which other members don't get. Sometimes, as we'll cover in Chapter 8 Rewarding your members, this is access to a private group, the ability to create groups, or unique powers within the platform.

But most often, it's access to things only your organisation can provide. This might include access to exclusive news and information that other members don't receive. A few of our clients have revealed their upcoming product lines and roadmap to their superusers and solicited feedback. This makes superusers feel uniquely powerful and appreciated.

Another common type of access is the ability to directly contact people that work at the organisation. Knowing people who work at the brands of top companies is a powerful motivator for superusers. It helps superusers share a part of your mission.

Another type of access is the ability to attend events that the rest of the community can't. Some communities treat their superusers as VIPs at their annual events with limo rides, front row seats, and access to private areas at the after party.

Others have separate meetup events only superusers can attend. A few programmes (Spotify Rock Stars, SAP Mentors, and Eve Online) are famous for flying their superusers to meet with the product developers or chat with the CEO about the products and services they use. This is incredibly rewarding. One of my clients, Sephora, has hosted countless private events just for a select group of superusers to attend and give private feedback.

The best rewards are not what you expect

I once had a client where members often shared video tutorials and images with one another. The client wanted to reward them with free products, but I felt there was a better approach. Instead of rewarding them with free products, we hired a video expert to provide training and resources to help them create higher-quality videos.

Only participants in our superuser programme received access to the training. The feedback was overwhelmingly positive and the quantity (and quality) of videos immediately improved.

This worked because we helped them do the things they were already doing even better. This increased their status in the community and provided better content to members outside of the programme.

---

2 Status and recognition

The second most powerful motivator is status and recognition within the community.

Your superusers probably don't just want to participate, they want to lead. They want to cultivate and build a reputation within the community. They want validation from other members and from the organisation. You have some inexpensive tools you can use to engender these feelings in superusers.

For example, if you name-check your top community members on stage at a big event – this shows a huge appreciation for members. At Geotab, I worked to ensure the top members of the community received a personal note from the CEO (from the CEO's email address). This was a huge reward for members and it also gave them a direct line to the CEO. I wouldn't recommend this for more than a handful of the very top members, but it was transformative in how members felt about their contributions to the community and they became the top members going forward.

You might also give your superusers a badge or tag which appears next to their name alongside every contribution they make. Some brands make custom versions of their products just for top members of the community. The more you can provide members with a high sense of status in the community, the more likely they are to keep contributing to the community.

Thinking beyond just the community

One software client was struggling to find ways to help members demonstrate their status in the community. My surveys and interviews showed members really didn't give a damn about a badge on their community profile. However, when researching our client's top members, I noticed several were updating their Twitter and LinkedIn bios with their veteran status within the field (i.e. 10+ years in [topic]).

Instead of just giving them a badge to be displayed in the community, we created a verified list of our members' status displayed in the community (superuser, VIP, veteran etc.) and created custom headers/avatars featuring their profile they could display if they wished.

Over half of our superusers used them and most even updated their social media bio with a link to their 'verified' status in the community. Later we began taking photos of them meeting with the CEO and attending events and shared them for free. Just under half the superusers featured in the photos shared them on their profiles with my client's branding.

Social media has become our main tool of self-expression. Make sure you help members show off their successes outside of the community as much as inside of it.

3 Influence

The third biggest motivator is influence. Your superusers want to feel like they've had a big impact upon the community. They might see this in the total reach of their contributions, the gratitude they receive, or seeing the outcome of things they have participated in.

You can give superusers influence in three ways.

1 **Give superusers input on key decisions.** The easiest form of influence to offer members is the ability to give input on key decisions – especially those concerning the community. You should be constantly seeking their ideas and opinions for what they want to see within the community. Another is feedback on what you do. For example, you might want to solicit feedback on upcoming products, marketing campaigns, or major decisions before announcing them to the community.

2 **Make their statistics visible to them.** Some community platforms show superusers the number of people their contributions in the community have reached. Once superusers can see the number of people they've helped, they're motivated to increase the number. A top tip here, monthly reports sent

to superusers showing their impact and comparisons with the average can also motivate superusers to participate more.

3 **Unique powers.** As we'll see in the gamification chapter, you can also equip superusers with unique powers and abilities to do things other members don't get to do. This might include moderation, creating certain types of content, or editing parts of the site (like a FAQ, documentation, or knowledge base).

Influence is about helping superusers see their impact. The more you can provide superusers with opportunities to have and see the impact they've made, the more motivated they will become to have an even bigger impact.

4 Connection

A major benefit of a superuser programme is the feeling of connection and identity it provides to members. Your superusers get to feel they are part of a unique, exclusive, group of insiders. This might be one of the few places where they feel they truly belong and with like-minded souls. This might be the only part of your community where a true sense of community exists.

You will notice that many of the ideas from above also help foster a strong sense of community between superusers. One of my clients had a core group of a dozen superusers who spent hours every day talking to one another in a private area of a community set up just for them. They wished each other good morning when they woke up and goodnight when they went to bed. They still answered plenty of questions and helped out on a bunch of projects in between, but that sense of unique connection was the glue which made it all work.

Don't underestimate the potential power of creating a sense of belonging, identity, and connection between members. It's a powerful motivator for many superusers. You can even highlight the ability to connect and collaborate with people as smart and as passionate as they are as a major benefit of joining the programme.

Be aware, however, that this requires work and it's not always smooth sailing. You need to establish traditions and invite members to openly discuss their thoughts and feelings with one another. You have to allow off-topic discussions and the ability for members to share things which might otherwise make a brand uncomfortable (such as talking positively about competitors for example or sharing difficult situations in their own lives).

You may also have to deal with conflicts or disputes between this group – perhaps even a split into two or more 'factions'. It's not uncommon for rival factions to form and one to eventually split off and try and form their own community.

5 Challenges

The least used reward (and potentially the most interesting) is the ability to work on exciting projects together. Not every superuser needs to feel influential or recognised, but many will find it alluring to tackle an exciting challenge with other superusers.

This ties back the tasks to what you ask superusers to do. Sometimes simply setting an exciting challenge or problem for superusers to work on can be a big enough reward in itself.

For example, you might set superusers a challenge that your organisation or the community is facing and see if your superusers can come up with good solutions. Some superusers just want to tackle the hardest problems they can. Simply getting the ability (or the tools) to tackle harder challenges can be motivating. This is where rewards like training (see earlier box) and being able to learn more about the products can help. As a result of this training members can tackle more difficult problems than they otherwise would've been able to.

WARNING – Superuser programmes require resources!

Superuser programmes need to be properly resourced to succeed.

If your superusers are responsible for 30% of your content, you should be investing 30% of your resources on the programme.

This can seem like a ridiculous amount of money to be spending on such a tiny group of members, but this tiny group of members will be creating most of the value in your community.

It's a huge mistake to create a superuser programme without the resources to run it properly. You're going to risk upsetting your top members and turning them against you.

You can see a list of possible rewards on the following page. This isn't a comprehensive list. However, it does provide many of the most common perks you can offer superusers.

Feeling	Perks
Access	• Exclusive news and information (product information/roadmaps etc.) • Direct access to you and company staff • Access to training and expertise • Attending events
Status	• VIP treatment at events • Mentioned and recognised in newsletters and on stage at events • Badges for member profiles and social media • Special SWAG for members
Influence	• Giving feedback on key decisions • Getting early access and being able to give feedback on the products • Unique powers to control parts of the community
Connection	• Sense of exclusivity • Participating in a private group just for superusers • Feeling a sense of belonging with other top members
Challenges	• Working on exciting projects with similarly minded members • Trying to solve problems no one is able to solve

Growing a superuser programme

A superuser programme will go through several distinct phases as you grow. Initially it will be informal and ad hoc. Over time, it will have a more formalised structure with clear activities and investment. We can divide the development of a superuser programme into three broad stages.

Stage 1: Formation

In the early stages of a superuser programme, you don't need to create detailed documentation for the handful of superusers you're going to approach. Instead, you should reach out to some of the early top members in the community (often likely to be amongst the founding members group) and see if they want to join a private group just for top members like themselves. This group can be hosted within the community or on a tool your top members use every day like Facebook Groups, WhatsApp, or Slack.

In this group, you might ask for their ideas and opinions on relevant issues, invite them to attend monthly product or roadmap calls, and maybe supply them with a thank you note from senior executives within the organisation.

This works well for the first three to five members. Once you begin to expand beyond this, you probably want to formalise the process and structure things a little better. Even here you can solicit the feedback of your first few members and see what kind of processes and structure they want. This ensures you're designing a programme 'with them' and not 'for them'.

This phase is a good time for experimenting with what members do and don't want to do. You can also test out different types of benefits and see how members respond. You can try inviting members to perform different tasks and see which are most popular. It's a lot easier to test things when only a handful of people are going to see the results.

Stage 2: Formalising processes

During the second stage, you start to formalise the processes for joining the community, the benefits members get, and how the programme is run. You probably want to create a page, or at the very least a discussion thread, which shows information about the programme. This should include its goals, the criteria for accepting members, and the benefits that superusers receive.

In this phase, you also change your recruitment from hoping you notice potentially good members to a clear application form members can complete. It's best to use recruitment windows (typically every three to six months) to create a sense of scarcity here. During this window you announce the programme and invite people to complete the application form to join. You may also want to remove superusers who haven't been contributing much to the community during this phase.

At this point, you need to work internally to ensure senior people are paying attention to and support the programme. For example, there is no point in superusers giving you feedback if no one is willing to use it. Likewise, it's hard to provide superusers with exclusive access without internal support to give them exclusive news, information, or free products to try and give feedback on.

You should also move your discussion area for superusers onto the main community website at this stage. This both encourages superusers to visit the community more frequently *and* enables you to scale the programme later.

Stage 3: Fully developed programme

If your community never expands past 100 questions per day, you probably don't need to go this far. However, if it does, you're going to need a fully developed programme in place to help the superuser programme grow without any major issues.

The cardinal rule at this phase is to remove any ambiguity about what the programme is and how it works. This means documentation – a lot of documentation! Most of the largest communities with superuser programmes create a dedicated microsite that might be connected to the community but live outside of it. Microsoft, SAP, Autodesk and others are terrific examples of how this can work in practice.

Develop your documentation in partnership with your superusers. Your documentation should outline who the programme is for, what members get from it, and what kind of behaviour is expected. You can also outline specifically who is recruited and why. You should list the current members of the programme too. It's a good idea at this stage to feature the achievements of the programme too and discuss what members have been up to. Some programmes even feature case studies and testimonials.

You should also switch from an application form to a nomination form. Members can only be nominated by other members. This should only be undertaken during limited recruitment windows of once or twice a year. Once superusers join, you can guide them through a specific series of onboarding and training activities designed to help them get rapidly up to speed.

At this point you might also distinguish between superusers who have been members of the group for a long period of time and complete newcomers. Some programmes divide this over three levels from Rising Stars, Top Contributors, to Mentors. This provides additional recognition to members who have been in the superuser programme for a while.

During each recruitment window you can review the contributions from members over the past 6–12 months and decide whether to invite them back into the programme or not. This encourages all superusers to continue participating in the programme. Create a 'thank you' page for members who have helped the programme in the past but are no longer a part of it.

By this point, the superuser programme should also be widely supported internally. You often want to have up to $25k–$50k in discretionary expenses you can use to reward members, fly them in to meet your team, to send out items, or host events etc.

Remember not to expand this programme too fast. Superusers need to have real work to do. If there aren't enough questions to answer or no clear place where superusers can help, you're going to lose some prospective superusers quickly. Also remember that superusers are an investment in time, energy, and resources. So don't recruit more superusers simply because you can, recruit them because you need them to perform clear and specific activities.

Finally, remember superusers want to feel unique and valued. The more people there are in the superuser programme, the harder it is for any one of them to feel special. If it gets too big you might find some of your top superusers get frustrated or they no longer feel as unique or special as they once did.

Breakdown of different phases of a superuser programme

You can see a broad breakdown of the different phases a superuser programme might go through below. Note, you don't need to go through every phase. Smaller communities might not reach the full programme stage. If you're running a smaller community for a hobby, employees, or non-profit, you may only need a few superusers in an unofficial programme to make this work.

	Formation	Development	Full programme
No. of superusers	2–5	5–50	50+
Resources	25% of community leader's time	50%–100% of a community leader's time	Several staff responsible for the programme
Application	Head-hunted	Application form Application window	Nomination form Nomination window
Tiers	None	Two tiers	Rising stars Top contributors Mentors
Rewards	Access Status SWAG	Access Status Connection SWAG	Access Status SWAG Influence Challenges

▶

	Formation	Development	Full programme
Internal work	Experimenting and gaining permissions to provide some levels of access	Lobbying to better connect superusers with employees	Fully established processes for treating members properly

Summary

Your community probably isn't going to be an egalitarian utopia. The success of your community hangs upon your ability to identify, nurture, and motivate a tiny group of superusers who generate the majority of the value your community produces. To achieve this, you need to create a dedicated superuser programme which expands as your community grows.

If your community is small and private you can do this unofficially just by regularly reaching out to and checking in on your top members. You might connect them to one another and get their ideas.

However, in a larger community, you want to develop a superuser programme which will encourage members to perform high-impact behaviours to gain rewards they value. The best rewards are intangible. They include things like unique access, increasing their status, influence, a sense of identity, and the ability to tackle interesting challenges.

You only need two to three superusers to get started, and your superuser programme will probably be limited and informal at first. You can simply invite some top members to a private group and go from there. However, as you grow you will want to expand the scope of the programme and minimise any ambiguity. Make sure you have a clearly appointed person responsible for managing the programme and create a series of tiers for members based upon how long they have been a member.

The key is collaboration. You should be constantly engaging with your superusers to ensure you're not just building a programme for them, but you're building a programme *with* them. Give your superusers the tools and rewards they need and let them lead the way.

Checklist

- -

1 Decide what you need superusers to do – this should match your goals.

2 Decide your criteria for superusers. How will you find people and how will you recruit them?

3 Decide the rewards they will get. What special access, status, influence, connections, or challenges will they get or be able to participate in?

4 Begin reaching out to your first members and introducing them to one another.

Tools of the trade
(available from: www.feverbee.com/ buildyourcommunity)

- -

- FeverBee Superuser Reward Scheme Template

chapter 7

Keeping members engaged

A few years ago, my colleague and I flew into a New York blizzard to meet with a prospect in the publishing industry. They were about to launch a brand new community and wanted a community strategy.

As we went through our usual list of questions, we noticed something strange. They had invested a six-figure sum into the community platform and *still hadn't decided who would be managing the community*. Their plan was to dragoon someone from marketing into the project once they were ready to launch.

Needless to say, we thought this was a really terrible plan. It's nuts to make a huge investment in a community and have an untrained rookie at the helm. All the money in the world won't make a community thrive if you don't have a talented community professional to hook members in, keep them engaged, and ensure their needs are satisfied.

Tragically, this isn't an isolated occurrence. Far too many companies have invested small fortunes into developing their community website and barely given a thought to who would be running the community. Many aren't even sure what the day-to-day work of a community leader looks like.

Whether you are creating a simple WhatsApp group for a few buddies or trying to build the next Facebook, you need to master a core set of skills to drive engagement and participation. Too often this is perceived as a job anybody can do. After all, it's just *'chatting to people on the internet'* isn't it?

Leading a community is a completely different ball game. It requires empathy for what's really driving your members, an understanding of what kinds of discussions do or don't work, and an appreciation that every single word you use to communicate will have a big impact upon someone's likelihood of participation. If you're leading a community, you need to be able to sell the vision of the community's future, get people excited about participating, and persuade them to share their expertise (often with their biggest rivals).

This is less like talking to your buddies on Facebook and more like going to a conference filled with strangers and trying to host an afterparty for them. How would you get people to show up, participate, and contribute? How would you make sure everyone had a good time? How would you get people to open up and talk honestly about their problems?

In this chapter, I'm going to outline the skills you must acquire to lead your community and give a step-by-step breakdown of what these skills look like at beginner, intermediate, and world-class levels.

Do you need a full-time community leader?

If you're leading a community as a hobby or side project, perhaps not. There are plenty of communities which have succeeded, even thrived, without having someone full time to manage them. Sometimes your passion and whatever hours you can spare can be enough.

However, if you're building a community for professional reasons and working on behalf of a business, then *yes*. You almost certainly do. Sometimes organisations ask me at what stage in the community lifecycle should they hire a community leader. The answer is *right at the beginning!* You can't wait for a community to be a success before hiring someone to lead it. Without a leader, a group won't ever become a success.

As a general rule of thumb, you should be investing at least as much in the community team to manage the project as on the technology itself. If you need to reduce your spending on technology to make that happen, then do that. The value of a great community leader can't be overstated.

Here are two graphs. The first shows what happened to the Mayo Clinic community after they hired a top-tier community manager. The second shows what happened to my very own FeverBee community after I stupidly decided not to replace the community manager.

The value of a full-time community leader really couldn't be more apparent.

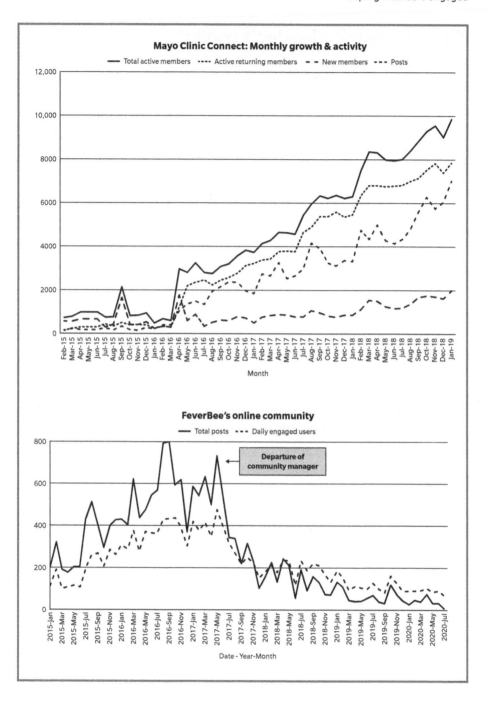

Mayo Clinic Connect: Monthly growth & activity

—— Total active members ···· Active returning members – – New members --- Posts

Month

FeverBee's online community

—— Total posts --- Daily engaged users

Departure of community manager

Date - Year-Month

The community leader's toolkit

The community's leader's toolkit is more limited than you might imagine.

In most communities, there aren't many things you can do that your members can't.

Sure, you can tweak the website design, remove or reward members, and publish content and newsletters, but that's about it. If you work for an organisation, you might also be able to leverage your role to influence members with exclusive information or benefits.

The real work of leading a community is less about exercising unique administrative powers and more about subtly influencing and persuading members to do the things which are best for them and for you. And, for the best part, you're going to be using the exact same tools your members do every day. The only difference is you're going to use those tools at a far more advanced level.

Breaking down engagement skills

Let's break down the core community engagement skills into five categories.

1 **Starting interesting discussions.** This is the core work of asking questions and starting discussions members want to participate in.

2 **Keeping conversations going.** This is being able to reply to discussions, keep them going, and ensure members feel better for the contributions they've made to the discussion.

3 **Creating content.** This is your ability to create content (which members love) and solicit and curate content from others.

4 **Hosting and facilitating events.** This is hosting events members enjoy attending and helping them host their own events.

5 **Engaging directly with members.** This is how you privately engage and interact with members of your community in direct messages.

This sounds rather simple doesn't it? But then so is a paintbrush. It's mastering how to use the paintbrush which really sets the great artists apart. Each of these five skills have hidden techniques you should master to properly lead your community.

The art of asking a question

It really doesn't take too much skill to ask a question or start a discussion. Your members are doing it every day. You've probably asked a few questions already today. Did it feel difficult? (See, I asked a question right there!)

However, in most communities you will notice there are questions which seem to start a fire of endless debate and those which flicker without ever really catching on. The exact words you use and context you establish in your question will determine how many responses you receive.

Asking a question vs starting a discussion

Let's clarify some terminology. There's a difference between asking a question and starting a discussion. Asking a question refers to a specific problem that someone wants help with. When you ask a question, you want the best answer that solves the problem (not as many answers as possible). Some platforms even have a specific Q&A functionality which allows members to select the best answer from those posted.

Starting a discussion is different. When you start a discussion you're starting an open-ended debate on a topic without a specific answer. If I'm asking you what time it is, I'm asking a question. If I'm asking you what you think about Russian poetry, I'm starting a discussion.

Six rules for asking popular questions

If you're running a large community already, you probably don't need to ask too many questions or start too many discussions yourself. Your members should be doing this for you. But it can still be handy to edit and guide their questions.

However, if you're launching a new community or managing a small community, you're going to spend a lot of time asking questions and initiating discussions. And if you want to receive a good number of quality responses, there are some clear principles to follow:

1 If you want an answer, ask a question

If you want an answer, ask a question. This sounds simple, but you might be surprised how often people don't do this. More importantly, if you're using a forum-based platform, put the question in the subject line so people can quickly scan and visit if they know the answer. If you're using a group messaging tool, put the question right at the beginning and then provide the context later.

2 Be specific in the topic

Reviewing the community of Geotab right now, I can see two discussions. One has the subject line of 'Idling Report' the other has 'I'm trying to run unverified logs report. I don't have the option to select all of my drivers. Is this an option or is it a setting issue?'

Which topic do you think gets the most responses? The short or the longer discussion?

The longer topic. It's specific and clear. Any casual browser who feels they know the answer is more likely to provide it. The subject line of 'idling report' doesn't tell us much. Is it a problem with the report? Can they not access the report? Are they sharing how much they love it? Are they just keen to talk about idling reports? Heck, what even is an idling report?

Equally important, when you make your subject line specific you're more likely to attract search traffic from people searching for that question. This search traffic is important. It drives most of the growth in most communities. In addition to asking questions, you should spend time tweaking the subject lines of questions from members to be more specific and aligned to search traffic.

The bane of many community leaders' existence is dealing with countless members who ask questions with subjects like 'What do you think about this?', 'Need help!', or 'Urgent problem!' After a few months, it's likely that most of the new visitors to your community will arrive through search so optimising these titles is critical. Go through questions from a couple of months ago and tweak them for better search visibility.

3 Use multiple types of discussions

Can you imagine going to a party where the host constantly asked 'What do you think about [topic]?'

After a few questions, you wouldn't only get bored, you would get suspicious too. The same is true in online communities. I've worked with some community leaders who thought simply asking members what they thought about a different topic each week was enough. Members can quickly sense if you're trying to drive engagement just for the sake of engagement. It just feels phony.

It's a good idea to have a genuine reason for asking a question (i.e. you should genuinely want to know the answer) and not just hope to count a large quantity of answers. The answers should have some practical value for you as a person or an organisation.

Three types of questions

There are broadly three types of questions you can ask members. These are:

1 **Open questions.** These are questions with no clearly defined type or length of answer. A good example might be: 'What has been your best memory of (topic)?' or 'What is the best way to solve [problem]?' They're good for helping members connect and bond with one another. If you want members to share emotional states, ask these kinds of questions.

2 **Closed/specific questions.** These are questions with a limited range of responses. These often relate to answers involving a number: 'How old were you when you became interested in [topic]?' or 'Which of these is better (x) or (y)?' Closed questions are less intimidating for members to answer and can yield really useful answers to attract search traffic or yield valuable information for members. Comparative questions (especially relating to products/purchases) are especially valuable.

3 **Hypothetical questions.** These questions are technically open questions but allow members to have some fun and reveal a little more about themselves. Predictions, especially, seem to be popular in many communities. You can ask questions such as 'What would you do if …?' or 'What do you think will happen when. … ?' Hypothetical questions don't require a lot of expertise to answer and are therefore easier for newcomers to participate in.

Make sure you use different types of questions to drive different types of conversations. Over time you should see a rising number of your members asking questions and starting discussions. This is the moment you can gradually begin easing off starting discussions and asking questions yourself.

4 Create questions with high emotional rewards for answering

Compare these two questions below:

Question 1: *'I can't get my printer to work, it says I have the wrong driver installed. Can anyone help?'*

Question 2: *'Hi everyone, I'm looking for a few printer experts out there. I've tried installing [type] of driver but it keeps coming up with [type of error]. I also tried [x], [y], and [z], but still nothing?*

'I would call customer support but it's not open until tomorrow and I need to print this out tonight and take it to the passport office tomorrow to get my new passport in time for my honeymoon to Barbados.

'Can anyone else? I'm getting scared I can't fix this in time!'

As someone with the answer, would you feel better about answering the first question or the second?

It's not even close, the answer is obviously the second. This isn't just because you know what the original poster has already tried and can give more precise advice, but also you can see what answering the question means to them – which in turn makes you feel a lot better about answering the question.

Remember the motivations of members you read about in Chapter 2? One of the biggest motivators is a desire to help. The bigger the payoff (feeling of helping) the more effort your members will put into their response. You might not want to help a relative move house this weekend. But if you found out they had recently broken their leg and couldn't reschedule the moving van, you probably wouldn't hesitate to help. The emotional payoff from helping is suddenly a lot bigger.

The best thing you can do to increase the response rate of discussions is to increase the emotional payoff from answering that question. Don't just go fishing for information, but highlight how the answer would help you both in both tangible and emotional terms.

However, you should still try to keep discussions relatively short. No one wants to read long messages online. Anything between 150 and 350 words is usually fine. Also, put the call to action as close to the top as possible. Don't make members spend a minute reading a post to find what you need from them.

Put the question near the top and then add the context and the reasoning behind it. This lets members quickly determine if it's a question they're likely to have the answer to or not. Finally, make sure you tag (@mention) in people who might have the answer. You're a lot more likely to get an answer from the crowd if you point out a few specific people from the crowd to give an answer.

5 Ask questions and start discussions at a steady cadence

If you're just getting started, you should aim to have at least one new question in the community per day. As you grow, you usually want to initiate a new discussion when activity dips. You don't need to plan these out to a specific day, but you should definitely have a few interesting questions to ask when you need them.

A quick word of warning here. If your previous discussions aren't getting many responses, asking more probably isn't the solution. Either you don't have enough members visiting to see the discussions or your discussions aren't interesting enough (sorry!).

If it's the former, you need to drive more people to see your questions before asking more. If it's the latter, you should remove discussions with no (or few) responses and replace them with fresh discussions until you find those which catch on.

As a general rule, try to keep the number of questions in your community growing at a slow, but steady cadence.

Making members feel great about themselves

We often treat community support like a customer service job. Here is a response from a post in the Yahoo community a few years ago:

From: Jaimie – ADMINISTRATIN' HOO
Re: Error 554 (sais I dont have a yahoo account!) [New]
@MartinaDavidson – Your email address ends with @yahoo.co.uk and not in the @yahoo.com email extension. That is the reason for the bounce back errors.

Do you think the person who asked the question feels better about the company or feel like they were listened to? Do you think they are going to want to regularly participate in the community again?

I doubt it.

Now compare this to the response below from Colleen Young, Director of Community at the Mayo Clinic.

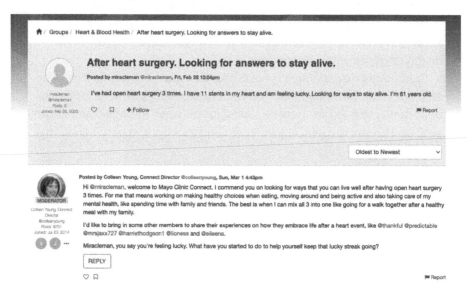

Can you see what Colleen is doing here? She noticed it's the member's first post and welcomed them to the community. She made a personal connection with her own experiences. Then she '@mentioned' six other members who she felt could also participate in the community. Finally, she asked a further question to encourage the member to come back and participate in the community a second time.

Colleen's response seems dead simple, but it showcases the amazing power of what a great community manager does. She's a community artist with a paintbrush. Not only will the recipient of her message receive useful advice, they're also more likely to connect with other members and feel better about participating in the community. Better yet, the other six members are going to feel like they can make unique, useful contributions.

Community leadership or customer support?

In my experience, online community leaders tend to fall into one of two categories.

The first group sees a long list of discussions on the website or questions in their community and lets out a silent groan before getting to work answering each of them as efficiently as possible.

They try to use an impersonal, inoffensive tone and deliver factual information as best as they can. They think they're doing community management, but they're really just doing customer support by another name.

The second group sees a long list of questions and gets excited. They see opportunities to forge new connections between members and improve how members feel about themselves and the community. They know every question is a rare chance to help a member become more deeply engaged within their community.

Community management is not customer support. The goal isn't to be efficient, it's to be empathetic. You want to see every post as an amazing opportunity to build stronger relationships between members and ensure each person you respond to feels seen, understood, and better about the community.

You want to bring your empathy and personality into the conversation. In our community training courses (which Colleen completed), participants often seemed surprised to learn they're allowed to show their personality. This doesn't mean you should be cracking jokes when a member discusses a recent heart attack or reaching for the right pun during a serious product complaint. But it does mean the way you behave online shouldn't be radically different from offline.

You might adjust your personality slightly to match the audience, but you shouldn't turn into a corporate drone.

Six elements to a fantastic community response

You're probably going to have three kinds of messages to respond to.

The first are those posted in your community. These will be questions or discussions that require a response as quickly as possible. The second are those that come via email or a private message. The third are in person. In each case, your response should embrace the following principles as best as you can.

1 **Speed.** You should respond as quickly as possible. Our data shows that members are 27% more likely to participate again if they receive a response to their first post within 24 hours. Any longer and they might as well search the web or go online. If you can reply quicker than this, even better!

2 **Personalisation.** Members want to feel unique. You should reference the unique aspects of their message and use the same language as they do to describe their problem. If you have shared experiences or interests, drop that into the response too. Ask further clarifying questions to sustain the discussion and gather more information.

3 **Friendliness.** You should use a warm, positive tone to reply to discussions. Apologise and acknowledge the emotional struggles they're going through. Use informal language where you can. Pick up on social cues about what the members need by the tone and language they use in their discussions.

4 **Knowledge.** Share any knowledge you have to help resolve the question. Don't just link to an FAQ or a resource, extract the information and drop that into the discussion. Add any previous insights shared in the community. If the answers require considerable detail, use bullets points, images, and videos if you can.

5 **Connection.** When possible, bring other people into the conversation. Your job is not about replying to every question yourself, but encouraging other people to answer the question. You can use @mention features or drop them a line and see if they can respond. The more you do this, the more it becomes a habit for others to participate.

6 **Resolution.** There is a big difference between providing an answer and making the member feel fantastic afterwards. Sometimes a member comes to a community with frustration and your job is to provide the answer but make sure she is no longer frustrated. You can check in and see if there is anything

else you can help them with. Try to show the member the impact they have had: 'Thanks for this. I passed it onto our engineering team who are making changes' etc.

You're not expected to master all of these skills tomorrow. But you can gradually practise them and get better at sustaining discussions and engaging with members. You don't even need to wait to have a community to begin practising it. Practise it in your responses in your emails today and in responses to your messages. You will notice a rapid improvement in the quantity and quality of responses you get from your friends and colleagues.

Creating and curating content

One of my first community roles was for the unfortunately named 'UKTerrorist' website (the name was based on a game, Counter-Strike, in which terrorists battle counter-terrorists). A couple of times a week, I would post the latest updates about the game on the community. This news would typically include the latest versions of the game to download, new maps (levels) to play, or quotes from the creators about what was coming up. I must admit, I wasn't the best 15-year-old gaming journalist out there, I simply copied content from other sites to save time.

One evening, when I was short of news, I drafted a story about a friend who had recently switched from one gaming team to another. This single story prompted more comments than any other story I had ever posted.

It turns out gamers were far more interested in others playing the game than they were about the game itself. I started regularly writing about the gamers instead of the game. Activity continued to rise. Before long, I barely bothered writing about new game updates anymore. I wrote about the achievements of the players instead. If there wasn't any news, I would publish interviews with players, survey members and post trend reports, and write opinion pieces ranking the top players.

I had stumbled upon a simple truism about community content: *members love reading about themselves and people like themselves*. People have a craving to know what people like themselves are doing.

The best content for a community is content about the community.

Pick up the local newspaper this week. What do you notice? It's filled with stories about people in the community. Editors long ago realised that people want to see if they or someone they know has been featured in the newspaper. It's what drives readership. And you can use this as the basis of the content for your community.

Tools for creating content

Technically, anything that's published on a website is content. But I'm going to adopt a slightly narrower definition for our purposes here. *Content is any static, non-discussion form of media authored by you or a member on your site.* The intent is typically to inform and entertain rather than start a discussion (although there are some exceptions).

Unless your community is on a platform which only allows discussions, like a WhatsApp group, you probably have several tools for creating community content. These might include:

- **Blogs/articles.** These are longer-form content posted by you and your members in the community.

- **Knowledge/documentation.** These are articles which are organised into documentation or knowledge shared by others.

- **Newsletters.** This is typically a curated email containing the latest news and activities in the community.

- **Digests.** This is an automated email which is sent to members who have opted in (or not opted out) of receiving it. It is typically sent on a weekly basis.

- **Automation emails.** These are emails which members *trigger* based upon actions they have performed in the community. The welcome email is the most common but other organisations have broad decision trees sending different emails to different members based upon different actions they have undertaken.

- **Video/photo galleries.** These are curated videos and photos members have contributed to the community.

- **Reviews.** These are member-generated reviews posted about products and experiences.

- **Podcasts.** These are podcasts created for the community containing discussions about what content is most popular.

- **Static copy.** This is the text written on your community website and in any notifications which pop up to members within the community.

If you want your content to be read, watched, and heard, you have to make it worthwhile to your audience. This is such a simple rule, but it's staggering how often it's ignored.

A common mistake is to publish the same repetitive content on a weekly basis whether members are engaging with the content or not.

For example, one community I'm following recently posted a full long news post to announce episode 55 of their podcast. Skimming through the site, it's clear these weekly announcements have the fewest number of views, likes, and comments of any content posted in the community. It's a repetitive release of show notes each week. If members want to subscribe to the podcast, ask them to do that. By episode 55, I'm betting most members have already decided whether to do that. Don't post repetitive announcements in the community.

I raise my hand and take some responsibility for repetitive content.

In my first book, *Buzzing Communities*, I advocated that community leaders should create a content calendar with repetitive content each week. This meant you might have a member interview on Monday, product announcements on Tuesday, and new product reviews on Wednesday etc.

Over the past decade, I've realised this often didn't work as well as I thought. After the first few weeks, the metrics on repetitive content drop sharply as the novelty factor wears off. This is the same for weekly discussions such as 'What are you working on?'. After a few weeks, the number of people participating tends to dwindle to a handful of superusers.

The problem is largely one of quality and value. Once you have a content calendar in place you have to fill the empty spots with content. Alas, ideas that sound great on paper (like member interviews) often don't work as well in practice. Sometimes the member isn't well known or doesn't say anything which is especially unique, useful, or interesting to other members. Once you've got through the top few members in the community, it's hard to find known members with especially unique or powerful advice for other members.

A much better approach is to keep content unexpected, exciting, and incredibly valuable to members. The advice I'll recommend here is based upon an additional eight years of experience since publishing my first book and a far better understanding of what your members are actually looking for within the community.

There are generally six types of content which work well in most types of communities:

1 **Case studies/interesting experiences.** Instead of interviews, post case studies with members. Case studies encourage members to share something

interesting they have done which could be valuable for other members. Any videos or long-form advice articles which highlight specifically how members resolved a common challenge or improved their results are usually popular within the community.

2 **Analysis and breakdowns.** Do a detailed breakdown or analysis of common situations members face. Be as specific as possible. Take what members are doing and do a detailed breakdown of it (what's working well and not well?). This is similar to case studies but highlights areas of improvement as well as what's not going well. Almost every community lends itself to breakdowns of situations members face.

3 **Templates and resources.** Create templates members can use. For example, templates that help them structure their work, plan out a project, or evaluate their success can save members a lot of time. Likewise, resources on topical issues can also be very useful.

4 **Surveys and data.** Your members will probably enjoy seeing how they compare to other members. A survey is a useful way to collect data and get the current pulse of your members on a wide array of topical issues. This might include time spent on a project, current level, salary level, or anything that might be interesting. You can then publish the results. This works well when members can compare themselves to the average or use the data to support their own work.

5 **Interviews with a VIP.** Better than an interview with a member is an interview with a VIP in your sector. These work best when the person is well-known and respected by most of the audience. If you wouldn't invite this person on stage at a major conference, they're probably not a good match. Aim high for these interviews. You might be surprised how many book authors are keen to talk to community members.

6 **Adapting existing content.** If you're short on ideas, the easiest thing to do is to communify your existing content. This isn't a real word, but let's pretend it is. And let's pretend it means adapting your content to make it socially engaging. Here are some examples:

Traditional content	Community content
News announcement	Get the opinions of 10 members on the announcement and post them for others to read.

▶

Traditional content	Community content
Announcement of the new CEO	A live community discussion with the CEO. Summarise the major questions and answers in the newsletter for the community.
Guide to solving a technical problem	Live demonstration as an engineer solves the problem and takes questions from other members. Record the video and publish the results to the community.
Product release notes	Let the community guess what's coming in the product next and give rewards for the right answer. Take suggestions for the next product releases.
Optimisation tactics	Invite the top 10 members to share their best tips for getting more out of the product and post this as an article in the community.

You get the idea. Almost every type of news or announcement content can *communified*. If you're just starting out and looking for some interesting content ideas, communifying your existing content is usually a good way to start. It's relatively easy to get the opinions of a few members on a topical issue and publish the results.

WARNING – Don't create a notice board!

If you treat your community like a notice board, your members will ignore it like a notice board.

I frequently encountered this problem while working at The World Bank. Communities were little more than a notice board of new articles with no debate, discussions, or any exciting activities. You shouldn't post the same content in the community as you would anywhere else. I've seen press releases posted in some communities, it's a terrible waste of the community's attention.

Whatever kind of content you create, be ruthless about measuring and honestly assessing its impact. Far too many community leaders persist in creating content which is not widely viewed, shared, or appreciated by the community – yet still takes them time to create and produce. Good content takes a long time to create. Make sure you're spending the right amount of time creating each content.

Big win content

In almost every sector there is the opportunity for 'big win' content (sometimes known as 10x content).[1] This is content so unique and so valuable that it moves the needle for the entire sector and provides enduring value to your members.

Sometimes this is a detailed guide or comparison tool based around equipment or software your members might use within the topic. Other times it's a definitive ranking of the top people in your sector. It might also simply be something completely unique to your sector.

Backpacking communities might create an interactive to compare backpack techniques, sports communities might create a place for members to share their best highlights, software-based communities might create a knowledge base all members can contribute to.

Soliciting and curating content

It's one thing to create content yourself, it's another challenge entirely to get members to create and share their own content. In the past, I recommended all communities should encourage members to create and share their own content.

In practice, this doesn't always work so well. Your community might soon become flooded by poor-quality contributions from self-promoting members. If you've visited LinkedIn recently, you know what I mean. Poor-quality and self-promotional content is the easiest way to drive members away. A much better approach is to flip the dynamic. Make posting content a scarce activity which members *get* to do if they meet certain criteria.

You can do this in one of three ways.

1 **Restrict who can post content.** You can limit *who* can publish content. If you limit who can publish content, you might only give the ability to post content to members who have shown a high level of expertise within the community and a commitment to post high-quality content.

   You might also create roles within the community (i.e. [topic] expert) and invite members to apply for it. Members get to feel a unique sense of value (and perhaps a sense of superiority). They also know if they don't produce high-quality content on a regular basis, they might have to relinquish their position.

2   **Restrict how much content (or when) can be posted.** A second approach is to restrict how much content can be posted at any given time. This creates a sense of competition for members to submit the best content during a given time. For example, if you only feature one member-submitted post per week, members might compete to create the best post this week.

   However, be aware this approach only works when there is a high demand to be featured within your community.

   If you're just getting started, there isn't much incentive to have a featured content article within your community. But if you run a large community, where a featured contribution can attract a large amount of attention and help a member build a good reputation, this can be the perfect approach (academic journals, for example, are a classic example).

3   **Restrict what type of content can be posted.** You can place limits and set high standards on the kind of content you would accept. Not all types of community content are created equal. As a general rule, I'd try to limit members from posting opinion pieces or basic advice articles. Basic expertise can be useful but too often veers into self-promotion.

   In most cases, the best content your members can create is sharing their own experiences from which others can learn. You usually want your members to share their case studies, their breakdowns of their creations, or reviews of what they have been doing, trying, and using. This kind of content is typically much better for members.

A simple way to measure content

You can measure the value of content to members simply by asking them what they value.

Create a poll, survey, or even a simple discussion post and ask members what content they liked the most and which they gained the most value from.

You can stop spending time on the less appreciated items and focus on making the more appreciated items even better.

Newsletters

If your community platform lets you send newsletters, use them wisely. Unfortunately the bar for community newsletters has been set low. Too many communities send newsletters filled with content which isn't relevant enough to most members. The best newsletters are short and filled only with the highest-quality contributions. If you don't have enough high-quality material, don't send the newsletter.

The single purpose of the newsletter is to bring members (especially fringe members who aren't deeply engaged) back into the community. This means you need to include links to the kind of content these members might find interesting and useful.

One of my favourite examples of this is The Overflow newsletter published by the Stack Overflow community.[2] The Overflow newsletter typically contains around a dozen links – each with a small snippet, nicely formatted, for members to see. The newsletter is divided into three areas:

1 Best of the blogs (notice the scarcity factor at work here).

2 Most interesting questions.

3 Links from around the web.

By including links from around the web, Stack Overflow is positioning itself as not only a community for its members, but for everyone interested in the topic. It also provides regular members a reason to see a curated list of content from around the web that they might otherwise have missed.

A second interesting approach is to simplify the content to the top five items shared in the community each week. If you don't have five good enough items, then shorten it to the top three.

Even if your platform doesn't allow you to send out newsletters, you can still gather the email addresses of members and send an email roundup. Or even share a simple Word or Google document with the latest news via whatever tool you're using.

Digests

Many community platforms might send out automated digests to community members. Digests are not the same as newsletters. Newsletters have a gatekeeper who determines the content which should appear. Digests are typically an automatically generated list of the latest or most popular content within the community. On some platforms (i.e. Salesforce), members receive a digest based upon what groups they have joined. Others send the same digest out to all registered members.

Digests serve a similar purpose as newsletters – they bring people back to the community. They also let members scan the latest questions and discussion topics and see if they want to participate. In your digests you usually have some key decisions to make.

Do you want members to see what's new, what's unanswered, or what's most popular?

The problem with sending digests filled with new or unanswered questions is the content might not be engaging enough for most members or might prove too difficult to answer (there's a reason these questions don't have an answer yet after all!). However, the problem with sending digests filled with the most popular content is the majority of recipients might have already seen it.

The simple option is to show what's most popular, new, and unanswered in a single email. However, not many platforms let you do that. An alternative approach is to send members a monthly digest with a limited number of posts so those who don't visit often can quickly get back up to speed.

The best option, however, is to send two digests. Your top 10% of members get a list of new and unanswered posts they're likely to have the expertise to tackle. Everyone else gets to see what was popular last month.

Activities and events

An activity is any time-limited engagement hosted by or within your community. These complement your content efforts and let members participate in a shared experience. This helps both drive activity and unite members.

Some common types of activities include:

- **A sprint/hackathon.** Amongst the most famous kinds of events are *sprints* or *hackathons*. This is where a group of people work rapidly over a limited amount of time (often 24 hours to 1 week) to create something of value. For example, you might set members a challenge to post their definitive list of newcomer resources, create a guide to a resource, tag or update a large amount of content, or simply develop their first app/story/project using your software/tools/advice. These tend to be the most valuable.

- **Quiz.** Live quizzes can be fun. The key is to set the question and give awards to the member who can post the answer first. Members get their ranking at the end. These should increase the knowledge and expertise of members.

- **Mentoring groups.** Create a time-limited mentoring group where people can put themselves forward to mentor other members. Make sure you have members who want to be mentored too.

- **Live webinars.** Host live webinars tackling a definitive topic. You can even invite members to put themselves forward to host a webinar for other members. During this webinar they can do a breakdown of what they're working on. Keep the recording and share it within the community.

- **Offline gatherings.** Members can put themselves forward to host an offline event for people in their area. You can promote events to other members. Even better, you can set a specific day for them to do this.

- **Conferences.** We have already covered how best to connect offline events with the community; just remember to facilitate plenty of time for community members to meet and connect with other community members.

You don't have any shortage of possible events you can host here. The best events are those which help members feel like they can make a useful contribution, are exciting and engaging to participate in, and leave behind a valuable asset for other members.

However, similar to content, regularly scheduled activities like webinars, live chats, and guest speakers tend to prove popular at first – but their novelty soon fades and participation dwindles. There are some exceptions – but finding those exceptions is like finding the winning lottery numbers – it could happen, but you probably shouldn't keep buying tickets until it does.

Don't plan activities on a weekly calendar, but space them apart. Ensure each is closely aligned to a particular goal members have. It's a lot easier to have three to five big activities than try to do one every other week. The purpose of activities is to increase engagement, build a stronger sense of community amongst members, and try to create or do something most members find valuable.

For this reason, I'd recommend staying away from the frivolous events. A secret Santa might be fun, but it's probably not going to resonate for members a year from now. Any event you want to host should benefit the entire community and be valuable over the long term.

Summary

- -

Talented community leaders are critical to the success of any community.

It doesn't matter how much an organisation invests in community technology if they don't also invest in recruiting a skilled community leader or training one to an advanced level. Community leaders perform many of the roles we mention in this book. Critical amongst them is directly initiating and sustaining discussions, hosting events and activities, creating and curating content, and engaging with dozens of members every single day.

While each of these activities seem simple, there are plenty of techniques to master. First, when asking for discussions be sure to mix up different types of discussions. The words, phrases, and length of any discussion have a big impact. Make sure you're making members feel as good as possible about every single interaction they have with you and with your community.

Second, don't just recycle the same types of content endlessly on a calendar. Members get tired of this quickly. Aim to create big-win content which clearly improves the value of the community in the eyes of your members. Now do the same for your activities too. Don't host activities for the sake of it, be clear about the amazing value of the community to members.

Don't expect to be fantastic at this on day one. Instead you can practice every day not just in your community, but in any group you participate in. With a little dedicated effort you will be a world-class community leader.

Checklist

- -

1 Use your research to identify possible popular discussion topics.

2 Practise replying to discussions using the six features shown above.

3 Identify two to three ideas for your first 'big win' content item.

4 Schedule an event which will deliver maximum value for members over the long term.

5 Gradually practise and improve your community skills.

Tools of the trade
(available from: www.feverbee.com/ buildyourcommunity)

- -

- Buzzing Communities (available on Amazon.com)
- FeverBee's Successful Community Management Course
- FeverBee's Community Management Framework
- FeverBee's Community Accelerator (www.feverbee.com/accelerator)
- FeverBee's Template Community Job Description

chapter 8

Rewarding your members

In 2018, I was hired to present to a small group of senior executives at a software company on the topic of communities. One of them wanted to start a community for the organisation but was struggling to overcome objections of other senior leaders. He was hoping an outsider could answer some of their questions.

About halfway through my presentation, I was abruptly interrupted with a dismissive question:

'So, in your world, you think our customers are just going to help each other and share their resources for free? What's in it for them?'

As I began explaining that people do things in a community for a feeling of helpfulness, belonging, and building a reputation, he interrupted me (again!). The exchange went as follows:

Him: 'I asked about communities in a WhatsApp group I'm in. A friend of mine at [big software company] said they had tried it and you have to either pay members to answer questions or give them free stuff. Eventually it became too expensive and they shut it down.'

I couldn't resist the irony of that statement:

Me: 'Did you pay your friend to give you that information?'

Him (looking confused): 'Umm, no?'

Me: 'So why did your friend at [big software company] help you?'
Him (looking more confused): 'Because he's my friend and likes to help. Why does this matter?'
I felt I might be breaking through ...
Me: 'That's the same as any other community! People like that feeling of helping each other. The more they get to know and like each other, the more they want to help. If people aren't doing that in his community, I'd guess your friend probably resorted to giving members free stuff too quickly instead of finding out what really motivates them.'

I can't say I persuaded him, but the other executives did eventually move ahead with creating the community – *and they didn't have to pay their members to participate!* Indeed the idea of members volunteering to help a brand without expectation of payment can be a powerful motivator in getting people on board.

Paying members to participate is not just a bad idea that harms their motivation, but (as we'll soon see) comes ripe with a whole host of legal problems.

Likewise, giving members free stuff (free products, services, or even SWAG) sounds like a good idea. But this is often just payment by a different name. You never want members participating in a community to get free stuff, you want members participating because they want to help others, belong to a group, and build a reputation.

This doesn't mean you can't (or shouldn't) reward members. Rewards can be a very powerful incentive to increase participation and get members to do the kinds of things you want. However, it does mean the rewards you offer members should engender the right kind of feelings in members to perform the right behaviours. More importantly, you should be offering rewards to members which are more valuable than gifts and money.

WARNING – The danger of paying members!

One of my earliest community efforts was managing a video gaming league in the UK. This required a dozen volunteer administrators to help referee matches, update scores, and keep things ticking over. This worked well for a while. Most administrators liked to help and enjoyed the feeling of power that came with the role.

Everything changed when we secured our first corporate sponsorship. I decided to use this money to pay admins who had been working so hard for free. Everything quickly went to hell. Some admins felt they should be paid more based upon their length of service while others felt slighted if they weren't paid the same as others for their work.

Worse yet, admins began treating it like an exchange. They began putting in the minimum level of work to get paid rather than trying to do their best work. To previously dedicated admins, this volunteering had become an underpaying side job.

Four types of rewards

We touched upon several types of rewards already in Chapter 6 Nurturing superusers in your community. In this chapter, I'm going to break these down into four specific categories, provide examples of each, and then a framework for when to use each type of reward.

The four categories of rewards are reputation, access, influence, and tangible goods. Each of them serves a different purpose at a different time. You can find some examples of each below:

Type	Explanation	Examples
Reputation	This is the reputation members earn and a sense of respect they achieve within the community.	• Badges • Leaderboards • Featured in content
Access	Access to information and benefits other members don't receive.	• Private groups • VIP treatment • Internal contacts • 'First look' opportunities
Influence	This is their technical permissions within the community which might rise as their ranking increases.	• Publish articles • Moderate content • Change aspects of the website
Tangible goods	These are the specific items they gain as a result of being in your community.	• SWAG • Discounts • Free training

As a general principle, the better the rewards you can offer your members the more participation you get. No, this doesn't mean you need to start handing out cash rewards or other goodies. It might instead mean offering members more access, more opportunities to have status, or more recognition for their contributions (like being featured in the newsletter).

When you're building a community for a small group it's relatively simple to offer these rewards. However, when you work for a larger organisation this becomes more difficult. You can't simply send out an email to your entire customer list celebrating the achievements of your customers. Your marketing team would (understandably) have a problem with that. Typically in a larger organisation you need to build internal support first to be able to offer great rewards. This is the hard part that makes it valuable.

For example, if I want a client to offer top members trial versions of a new product, I need to work with marketing, engineering, and legal teams to make that happen. This takes time, but it makes the community experience a lot better. Before we get to that stage, however, we need to know what rewards to offer, when to offer them, and to whom the rewards need to be offered. This is where the principles of 'gamification' come into play.

The practice of gamification

At the beginning of the last decade, some bright spark (probably) looked at how much time we spend playing games and decided to make pretty much everything we do online more like playing a game.

You've probably come across a lot of gamification over the past decade. If you've taken courses on Khan Academy, Duolingo, or Codeacademy, you might have earned 'streaks' for visiting several days in a row or 'levelled' up when you completed each chunk of the course. If you've been jogging and using Fitbit, you might get stats on how far and fast you ran and how that compares with your best times. Even Starbucks lets you earn points and level up with every purchase through the app.

Gamification isn't a new idea for communities either. Early pioneers like Amy Jo Kim have been talking about 'game mechanics' in communities since the early 2000s.[1] What's different today is the quantity and quality of tools we have available to gamify our communities.

Before the gamification craze, a member's 'post count' (total number of posts) would often appear next to a member's profile. The more posts you had, the more senior you were presumed to be. This primitive gamification system had an obvious and unfortunate side effect; it motivated members to post as many messages as possible (regardless of their quality).

Luckily, the tools and knowledge we've acquired since then mean we can develop far better reward systems. In the same way drug manufacturers can now target drugs at specific protein molecules in the body (instead of flooding the whole body with the same cure), we can now target very specific behaviours and encourage more of them in communities too. And, also like drug companies, we are getting a lot better at dealing with the potential side effects.

What is gamification?

We're going to use a lot of game terminology in this chapter. If you find this confusing simply remember that we're really just talking about a system for deciding which rewards to offer to which members (and when). While many aspects of gamification are implemented in large platforms, you can still apply these principles even in the simplest platforms to get the results you want.

Let's start by clarifying two terms: game mechanics and game dynamic.

A game mechanic is a functional element of playing a game (like points, badges, etc.).

A game dynamic is a state of mind experienced when playing the game (achievement, competition, etc.).

Gamification is the craft of using *game mechanics* to *create dynamics* that satisfy human desires and achieve your goals.

Tools for game mechanics

Some platforms let you deploy a wide array of game mechanics within your community. The most common include:

- **Points.** This is when you let your members earn points for specific behaviours (i.e. starting a discussion might be worth three points and responding to a discussion might be worth one point).

- **Levels.** Levels are rankings – typically based upon the number of points a member has earned. A newcomer might be on level 1 while a veteran might be on level 50. Levels are often connected to permissions (below).

- **Permissions.** Permissions are what members are allowed to do in a community. Once members have reached higher levels they might be allowed to help moderate discussions, join private groups, and report problems etc.

- **Badges.** Badges are visual images which can be displayed on your members' profiles. Similar to cub scout badges, they reflect achievements within the community (i.e. the 'initiator badge' for starting 20 discussions).

- **Leaderboards.** Leaderboards are a ranked list of members based upon the number of points they earn. Communities often have leaderboards of all-time rankings, based upon the previous 12 months, or within each topic within the community.

- **Challenges/missions/trophies.** These are awards (often technically badges) you can earn for completing a combined series of behaviours (i.e. if you introduce yourself, post your first discussion, *and* complete your profile, you might earn the 'rising star' award).

- **Gifting.** Gifting is where members can give each other virtual gifts (often premium accounts, points, virtual goods, or badges). Only a handful of platforms have this (i.e. Reddit).

- **Virtual goods.** Primarily used in gaming, virtual goods are assets members can collect and use within the community (i.e. a one-time ability to promote their own posts above others).

You will notice that many mechanics interplay with each other. For example, points help determine rankings which determine what rewards members earn. This also isn't an exhaustive list. Different technologies offer different game mechanics you can deploy. Broadly speaking, the more costly your platform is, the more gamification options you have. Some of the inexpensive platforms (i.e. Facebook/Mighty Networks) have very limited gamification tools available whilst others (i.e. Salesforce and Khoros) offer a more complex array of options.

However, even if game mechanics aren't built into the community platform you're using, you can still deploy primitive gamification systems the same way a teacher does in a class. You can manually give members stars and badges either in the community or in a separate system. You can create a spreadsheet and give people points for great contributions or set challenges for members to participate in. Using a low-budget platform doesn't preclude you from being able to reward your members.

Types of game dynamics

Now we know the mechanics we can deploy, we can think about the dynamics.

Don't start introducing game mechanics to a community without figuring out the dynamics you're trying to create (i.e. what do you want members to feel when they participate?). Video game designers aren't randomly dropping points or levels into any situation. They're using their mechanics carefully to create a specific feeling.

Some of the most common dynamics include:

- **Reward.** Members receive rewards based upon behaviours they've collected.
- **Status.** Members can increase their status amongst their peers for participating in the community.
- **Achievement.** Members feel a sense of achievement and accomplishment based upon their contributions and successes within the community.
- **Self-expression.** Members can customise their profiles and carefully craft their identity within the community.
- **Competition.** Members can see how they compare and try to beat other members.
- **Altruism.**[2] Members can send gifts to each other as a thank you for their contributions (or for any other reason they see fit).

Each type of mechanic can create a different type of game dynamic as you can see in the table below.

Game mechanic	Game dynamic					
	Reward	Status	Achievement	Competition	Self–expression	Altruism
Points	X	X		X		
Levels		X	X			
Badges	X	X	X		X	
Permissions	X	X	X		X	
Leaderboards		X		X		
Challenges		X	X	X	X	
Virtual goods	X				X	
Gifting		X	X		X	X

Source: Adapted from Kuo and Chuang (2016)[3]

Unless you know what drives people to participate in your community, it's impossible to determine the right mechanics. Before you select your game mechanics, you need to be clear about what kind of dynamic you're trying to create. This is why you need to do your audience research first. You need to know who the community is for and what that audience desires. This research will give you an inkling of what type of dynamic to use.

If you're leading a community for those affected by cancer, you might realise that altruism and achievement are better dynamics than competition and status. Therefore you would select mechanics such as levels, badges, and letting members award gifts to one another. However, in a customer support community, members might be more motivated to build a reputation and prove their expertise. Thus competition and status might be the ideal fit. You might thus deploy leaderboards, point systems, and create challenges for members to tackle.

Deploying the wrong game mechanic can do considerable harm to a community. If members come to the community for a sense of belonging and you suddenly make them feel like they're competing against their friends, you're going to lose a lot of them.

The most powerful rewards take longer to earn

At the core level, gamification works through prompting and reinforcing behaviour. If you take a positive action, you earn a positive reward. But the time and effort it takes to perform the action and speed at which members earn the reward matter.

At the simplest level, the longer the time between taking the action and earning the reward, the less impactful the reward is. However, this is only true with the lowest-value rewards. If the reward is perceived as especially high value, people will spend more effort and energy to achieve it.[4] The power of these rewards therefore lasts for longer.

This following table (adapted from one created by Michael Wu, a data scientist)[5] shows this well:

	Points	Badges	Leaderboards	Trophies	Ranking	Industry reputation	Team reputation
Timeframe	Immediate	Days/weeks	Week/month	Quarterly	Six months	At least a year	Several years
No. of actions	Gained after a single action		Gained after multiple actions in a short period			Gained after multiple actions over a long period	
Metrics	One-off activities		Combination of behaviours			Reciprocity and team metrics	
Ability to cheat	Easy to cheat		Harder to cheat			Almost impossible to cheat	
Public or private?	Private to the member		Public within the community			Recognised outside of the community	
Implementation	Easy to set up					Difficult to implement	
Longevity	Power fades quickly					Sustains long-term behaviours	

Build Your Community

The easiest systems to implement are points and badges. Many community platforms offer these by default. If your platform doesn't, you can set up a simple system using a spreadsheet, wall chart, or anything else to manually award members points and badges. These are usually gained after single actions in the community, i.e. a single contribution might be worth one point but a response might be worth five points.

However, the power of points and badges fades quickly. Would you really care about having 4000 points instead of 3000 points in a community? Did you really care about getting your 20th gold star in school after your 19th? This is why several studies have shown that points and badges don't usually create lasting behaviour change alone.[6, 7]

Instead these are tools to create a dynamic. A dynamic such as a sense of achievement or reaching a higher ranking. These take longer to gain, involve a combination of multiple behaviours, and have a more intangible value. They are also, as we'll see shortly, far more difficult to 'cheat'.

However, the biggest reward is usually a good reputation. A great reputation is the hardest thing to earn and yields the most benefits. There are two types of reputation here:

1 **Personal reputation.** You might earn a good reputation through positive contributions to the industry, a sector, or helping out your peers and friends. The best reputations are transferable, i.e. if you're regarded as a top community member on one platform that reputation is also respected throughout the industry or sector.

2 **Team reputation.** Team reputations are earned by a named group of people within the community (or by the community as a whole). Once a group has a powerful reputation, simply being associated with the group is highly motivating. This is perhaps the most powerful type of reputation but also the most difficult one to create.

Problems with gamification

Perhaps the real question is does gamification truly work?

In all the hype around gamification, it took years for studies to emerge which examined its impact upon behaviour. In 2014 three academics published their review of 24 empirical studies on gamification. Their findings painted a mixed picture. They discovered that while gamification can have positive effects, the effects are dependent on the context and qualities of the user.[8]

172

They uncovered two major problems with gamification, each of which you need to successfully mitigate if your gamification efforts are to succeed.

Problem 1: Undermining motivation

The first (and most common) criticism of gamification is that it can undermine your motivation. For example, imagine you have been participating in a community for years. You like the members there, enjoy the feeling of helping others, and love learning more about the topic.

One day, you suddenly find a score against your name, a collection of badges you're told to earn, and you're ranked on a leaderboard against your friends. Not only will that undermine your motivation, but it's likely to cause a whole host of new problems. Do you want the stress of competing against your friends and preserving your reputation every day?

Worse yet, you might discover this new scoring system means your peers now have the ability to edit your posts and they are in a private group you can't see or know much about. Will you want to keep participating in this kind of community?

This problem was best shown in a 2015 study of gamification in a classroom. Students exposed to gamification were less motivated, less empowered, and less satisfied. Worse yet, leaderboards and subsequent social comparisons were frequently cited for their negative consequences.[9]

You can also undermine motivation by giving members exactly what they want. When members are participating because they enjoy participating, they are usually making thoughtful, considerate posts in a tone which would most benefit other members. Their guiding star was the satisfaction of others. If you shift that guiding star to boosting their position amongst others, the quality of contributions can suffer. For example, the best way to climb the leaderboard is often to participate more, ask more questions, and pump out as much content as possible – regardless of its quality.[10]

One study in an employee community showed that while gamification did increase motivation to add more content initially, this declined over time.[11] This is also apparent in other studies of gamification.[12, 13] Scholars put this down to the *novelty* effect. Anything new is exciting at first – but once the novelty fades are members genuinely more motivated to participate in the community?[14]

In another field experiment in 2013,[15] a peer-to-peer trading service was updated with badges members can earn from performing a variety of tasks. About 3234 users were randomly assigned into two treatment groups and shown different versions of the badge system. The results showed that simply implementing a badge system did not automatically increase activity. However, those users who monitored their own badges showed increased user activity. In short, it only had an impact upon the types of people who care about things like badges.

Ultimately, gamification is highly contextual and the impact can be temporary, limited, or damaging if it's not well implemented.

WARNING – It's hard to turn gamification off!

A quick word of warning.

Once you've begun rewarding members, it's very hard to remove those rewards from members. Members feel they have earned these symbols. If you remove them, you're going to cause major problems. Even tweaking a system frequently provokes outrage. You should be extremely cautious about adding any game mechanic. You can always add new mechanics if you need them, but it's hard to take them away.

Problem 2: Cheating the system

The second common problem with gamification (and any reward schemes) is cheating.

It's pretty much impossible to design a gamification system which is impervious to cheating. Stamping out cheating is like trying to stamp out tax evasion. Almost every policy you introduce also introduces new loopholes and opportunities which are difficult to foresee in advance.

Whenever you put a score next to someone's name and show them a list of behaviours to increase the score you're going to get cheating. Cheating typically comes in one of two forms:

1 **Overposting.** The most common type of cheating is when a member contributes as many posts as possible to earn points. These might be short, quick, responses which don't significantly add anything to the discussion. For example, 'good post' or 'nice idea!'. Sometimes members initiate dozens of new discussions each week or suggest as many new ideas as possible knowing that these behaviours are perhaps more valuable than other behaviours.

   This isn't specifically against the rules, but it begins an arms race where other members have to engage in similar activities to compete. Soon your community will be flooded with low-value activity.

Luckily you have a few tools in your arsenal to fight against this. The most obvious is to tell the member to knock it off and threaten to suspend or remove the member. This can work in smaller communities, but it's harder in larger communities where you might have dozens of overposters per day and you need to systemise your response.

One approach is to add a 'downvote' option. Members who contribute low-quality posts might find they *lose* points. However, downvotes can also encourage bullying, discourage diversity of debate, and be intimidating for newcomers.[16]

The more common approach is to skew rewards towards quality over quantity. For example, a reply to a discussion is worth 1 point, but getting a response, a 'like', or having an answer marked as the 'best answer' might be worth 10 to 50 points. This requires the approval of other members to earn points. In turn, this deters members from trying to rank highly by posts alone. If reaching a new level requires 1000 points, for example, a typical member will sooner give up rather than create 1000 posts.

But this approach also introduces a new problem: *collusion*.

2 **Collusion.** Collusion is when one or more members work together to increase their standing. In early 2020, one of my clients noticed over half of the places on their leaderboard had been taken by representatives from a single company overnight.

How did they do it?

Somewhat ingeniously, they had looked at the platform we were using, discovered that being endorsed as a product expert by another member was worth a large number of points, and then all endorsed each other as experts. They had also discovered a bug where removing that endorsement didn't also subtract those points. Thus they could endorse someone, remove that endorsement, and endorse that person again.

It's relatively rare, but when the rewards for being a top member are extremely valuable (yes, a reputation can be very valuable too), you have to anticipate collusion.

Sometimes this is just a single member creating multiple accounts and rating their own answers highly. Fortunately, most modern platforms can pick up on multiple accounts using a single IP address. More likely it is a genuine collusion, i.e. a small group of members liking and voting positively on each other's activity to rise up in the rankings.

This is far harder to spot in larger communities. If my client's members hadn't got greedy and tried to take every spot in the leaderboard in the same week they might have remained undetected for a lot longer.

Preventing cheating and collusion

There are generally three approaches to prevent collusion (and most types of cheating):

1 **Don't make it worth cheating to earn the reward.** Cheating is only worthwhile when the reward is worthwhile. When the reward is tangible, such as free products, invites to events etc., then cheating might seem worthwhile to some members. Yet when the reward is intangible – such as building a reputation, getting access to staff, or having moderation powers – cheating is far less worthwhile (because it would take a sustained period of cheating to reap the reward).

   Cheating is most common when the rewards are clear and specific. Some communities, such as the Apple community, deliberately leave the rewards of achieving the highest rankings vague.[17] If you don't know what the reward is, why bother cheating? That doesn't mean they're not there – it just means you won't know what they are until you reach that level. This kind of approach inspires true fans eager to find out and deters the bad actors.

2 **Be vigilant.** If members are rising rapidly up the rankings, it's worth spending a little time checking their contributions and the reactions to their contributions to see if anything is amiss. This is easiest to do in small communities where the sudden rise of a single member is easy to identify and you have the time to investigate their work. It's far more difficult to do this in larger communities with thousands, even millions, of members climbing the ratings ladder. However, you should still keep an eye on any members rising rapidly up the rankings.

3 **Get technical.** You can develop technical solutions to spot and prevent the types of cheating above. For example, outliers can be flagged automatically for you to pay attention to. Members can be limited in the number of posts they contribute per day – or even have their scoring reduced if they post too many low-quality comments. You might even withhold awarding points if the post doesn't include enough characters or a member has posted too many times recently. Putting a daily or weekly cap on the number of points a member can earn immediately reduces cheating.

Likewise, if cheating is a serious problem, you can develop tools to prevent members from liking the contributions of the same members too often or to quickly identify reciprocal posting. Technical solutions are costly and time intensive. They best serve as last resorts rather than first options. It's rare you will need them. However, if you find cheating is undermining the contributions of other members it's worth investing time and resources into implementing a better solution.

Developing your gamification system

It's hard to design an entire gamification system from scratch.

To help you get you started, let's go through a fairly simple gamification system. For simplicity, we'll use the example of a customer support community where members have questions and people are invited to answer those questions.

Step 1: Decide behaviours to encourage

Before we begin, we need to know precisely what behaviours we wish to stimulate (this comes from the community goals we established in Chapter 1). For the purpose of this example, we have decided our primary target audience for gamification are our core group of superusers (you can just as easily use gamification to target any group, newcomers, veterans, intermediate members etc).

Target audience(s)	Superusers (top community members)
Desired behaviour	Answer the majority of questions within 24 hours

We know answering more questions is the critical behaviour and we wish to increase the number of questions answered by superusers. To do this, we need to know what game dynamic to use.

Step 2: Select your game dynamic

We use our personas to select the right dynamic. We might know from our interviews that superusers like feeling a part of our mission and they feel they are amongst the smartest members. So we will be using the achievement and competition dynamics we see below.

Target audience(s)	Superusers (top community members)	
Desired behaviour	Answer the majority of questions within 24 hours	
Persona	Like feeling part of our mission and consider themselves amongst the smartest members in the community	
Game dynamic	Competition	Achievement

Step 3: Select your game mechanics

Now we know the dynamics we're trying to create, we can start thinking about the mechanics we're going to use. This table we shared earlier is a good place to start thinking about some of the mechanics you might use to create the right dynamic. You might also want to speak to some of your target members at this stage too to get a sense of how they feel about different mechanics.

In this example, based upon our desire to create achievement and competition dynamics, we might select points, levels, badges, permissions, leaderboards, and challenges. We can add this to our table below:

Target audience(s)	Superusers (top community members)	
Desired behaviour	Answer the majority of questions within 24 hours	
Persona	Like feeling part of our mission/consider themselves amongst the smartest members in the community	
Game dynamic	Competition	Achievement
Game mechanics	• Points for answering questions • Leaderboard showing top members • Short-term challenges for members to compete in	• Levels based upon point system • Badges for unique high-value contributions • Permissions that enable members to have unique abilities

If this is your first time setting up game mechanics, it's important to have an idea of the decisions you need to make and some of the mistakes to avoid. To help you out, I'm going to dive a little deeper into the main mechanics and how they can be used effectively.

1 Points

Since many (if not most) gamification systems are based upon points, we first need to determine what behaviours are important and how valuable they are compared to one another.

Don't agonise too much over the precise values. What matters is how each behaviour relates to one another. For example, what is the value of creating a post compared with answering a question? Is answering a question more valuable than replying to one? If it is, asking a question might be worth three points and replying to a question worth just one.

Likewise, what is the value of sharing a detailed knowledge-based article or having an answer marked as an accepted solution (or best answer) compared with other behaviours?

Developing a point system is handy as it forces you to decide the value of each behaviour. At the time of writing, for example, the default gamification system from Salesforce is as follows:[18]

Action	Points
Write a post	1
Write a comment	1
Receive a comment	5
Like something	1
Receive a like	5
Share a post	1
Someone shares your post	5
Mention someone	1
Receive a mention	5
Ask a question	1
Answer a question	5
Receive an answer	5
Mark an answer as 'best'	5

Action	Points
Your answer is marked as 'best'	20
Endorsing someone for knowledge on a topic	5
Being endorsed for knowledge on a topic	20

This default point system isn't perfect, but it's a good place to start. Receiving a response to a contribution is worth five times as many points as creating a post. This encourages people to post good, interesting questions which are likely to gain more responses.

Likewise, answering a question is considered five times more valuable than asking one and having an answer marked as 'best' is worth 20 times as many points as writing a comment. This gives a good indication of the behaviours the system is trying to encourage.

WARNING – Be stingy with your points in the beginning!

A key word of warning here. You can always be more generous with points if the system isn't working, but it's hard to be less generous when you're up and running.

If members are used to earning three points for a post and now only earn one you're likely to reduce their motivation to perform that behaviour. Also if you later decide answering a question is only three times as valuable as asking a question, you can't change the system without removing points from your members.[19] This will upset members who will see their point tally plummet and will result in members losing their levels, status, and privileges.

The only alternative is to inflate points (i.e. make each post worth two points and each response worth six). This achieves the 1 to 3 ratio and will result in all members happily discovering they've earned more points. However, it also means you need to adjust the levels and rewards accordingly, which will disrupt what level or benefits members have earned.

It's far easier to begin with a conservative ratio and make it more generous over time as you know which behaviours you wish to encourage.

If you're just getting started, you can use the Salesforce system here. Your goal is to find the balance between rewarding quality over quantity – without giving away too many points too quickly.

2 Levels

Points aren't just a quick feedback system; they're also often used to assign members to levels. These levels typically confer status and rewards upon members. Levels tend to be important for two groups of members: newcomers and veterans. Newcomers need to be able to progress quickly through the early levels to feel a sense of progress, achievement, and growing influence within the community. Veterans must be able to reach levels other members can't (without ever getting to the top level).

The best way of thinking about levels is by thinking about the time it might take to progress up each new level. You typically want a newcomer to progress through the first few levels in minutes, the next few in hours, then days, and then weeks. As newcomers become increasingly invested in the community, you want each level to become increasingly difficult to reach. Thus each new level requires exponentially more points to achieve.

We've shown an example from one client below:

Level	Points	Level	Points	Level	Points	Level	Points	Level	Points
1	4	11	252	21	816	31	4160	41	28,500
2	11	12	288	22	906	32	5444	42	38,100
3	24	13	324	23	996	33	6728	43	47,700
4	42	14	360	24	1086	34	8012	44	57,300
5	64	15	396	25	1176	35	9262	45	66,900
6	88	16	462	26	1516	36	11216	46	1,05,300
7	120	17	528	27	1856	37	13136	47	1,43,700
8	153	18	594	28	2196	38	15056	48	1,82,100
9	184	19	660	29	2536	39	16976	49	2,20,500
10	216	20	726	30	2876	40	18900	50	2,58,900

In the early stages, members can progress from one level to the next in 13 days. However, at the intermediate levels (25+ points) it should take a few weeks and, at the advanced stages, it will take 1–3 months. This means that it's likely to take five years or more to reach the highest levels in this system.

Avoid these levelling mistakes

There are three common mistakes with level systems to avoid:

1 **Too few levels.** It often seems simple and even logical to have just a handful of levels which everyone can understand. You can set them up and maintain them easily. The problem is this causes members to cluster on a single level with the next level seemingly too far out of reach to be worthwhile pursuing. It takes more work to set up more levels, but it's worth the time.

2 **Unsustainable naming schemes.** Each level needs a name. You might have a naming scheme that begins easy enough. Perhaps Bronze, Silver, Gold, or newbie, regular, top members, veteran. The problem is what happens when members reach the top level. Once you've gone to Platinum and Super Platinum it's not easy to see where to go next. You can switch to animals (mole, giraffe, lion etc.) but you're still going to end up with the same confusing problem. For simplicity and sustainability, just use numbers (they scale indefinitely!). Or, if you must use names, then use numbers alongside a name (i.e. Expert (25), Expert (26) etc.

3 **Exponentially difficult to reach new levels.** The third problem is the most complicated to understand, yet also perhaps the most important. It's called the *exponential problem*. This problem occurs when you have a curvilinear point to level system. This means the point gap between each new level grows as members progress. So you might need 10 points to move up a level in the early stage, but 100 points to move up the levels in the latter stages. This creates a point curve which looks like the one following page.

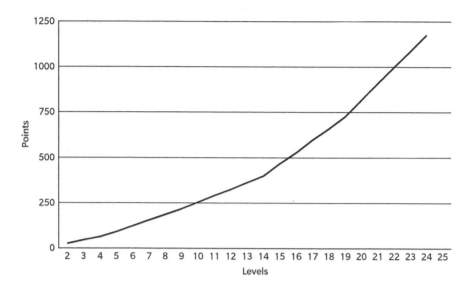

You can see now it becomes progressively more difficult to reach higher levels as each inflection point in the curve increases the number of points required to reach the next level. At the lower levels you need up to 25 points to progress. By level 20 you need 66 points to progress, which means it should take twice as long.

This allows newcomers to gain a rapid sense of progress but doesn't allow members to reach the highest levels too quickly. However, when you plot our entire point system you can see the curve begins to spike up dramatically using an exponential curve.

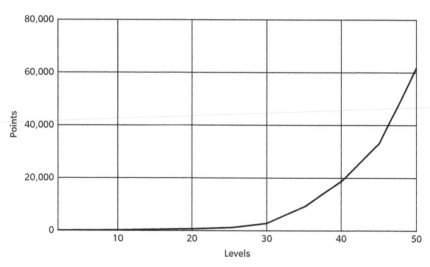

Woah! What just happened?

To progress from level 30 to 31 you would need 1284 points. But to move from 49 to 50 you would need 5732 points! This is the natural result of an exponential curve which requires progressively more points to reach the next level. The problem is members at the highest levels now have to create thousands of posts or be able to provide hundreds of right answers to move up levels. The gap soon becomes so big it demotivates members from even trying to reach the next level.

This doesn't mean creating this sort of exponential curve is a bad idea. Video games use a similar system. You do want each new level to become progressively more difficult to reach. The difference between gamification for a community and video games is video games provide you with an opportunity to earn more points as you progress.

For example, the baddies you shoot on level 1 of a video game might be worth 1 point each but on level 10 they are worth 10 points each. Now you can earn 100 points as quickly as you can earn 10 before. This system fails in a community because it doesn't have an equivalent method to let higher-ranked members earn more points than newcomers. As a general rule, you don't want to make members wait more than a few months at most to move up a level. Members should always be able to progress up a few levels a year even at the highest levels.

The challenge is to develop ways for members to earn more points as they reach higher levels. And this is where we have to borrow another concept from video games: *power ups*.

3 Power ups

Power ups are means to enable your top members to earn more points than other members can. For example, as a reward for being a member of the superuser programme, a member might earn 1000 points for every month they remain in the MVP programme. Now you can see how it becomes possible to still progress up levels – even at the highest levels – every few months without having to create thousands of additional posts.

Another option is to assign points for a combination of behaviours. This is often referred to as a 'mission' or 'challenge'. You might create a 'getting started' mission requiring members to introduce themselves, update their profile information, ask their first question, follow a few top members, and reply to their first question. If members complete all the tasks within the first week (or month), they earn an additional 500 points.

These sorts of unique challenges are very handy for members who enjoy the gamification aspects of the community – and you can design plenty of them. For example, a member who receives three 'best answers' to a question in a given month can earn an additional 500 points. Or members whose combined question views exceed 1000 points receive an additional 100 points per month etc.

You can also award additional points for members who might be nominated as 'member of the year' or 'member of the month'. This helps top members advance rapidly and keep them highly engaged within the community. Likewise, you can manually assign members additional points for remarkable or unique contributions.

In one client's community, a member shared an incredible story of her cancer journey. Our client recognised that contribution with a 'remarkable contribution' badge and a significant number of additional points. This directly rewards quality over quantity – and is almost impossible to cheat. Even the most seasoned members should still feel they can progress to new levels every couple of months.

However, power ups are not always easy to assign within a community. They often require some custom coding and development time to create. But with the right expertise and effort, you can use any activity logged about a member inside of a community to award additional points.

If you're not able to do this, then don't use an exponential point system! Stick with something simple without huge jumps and try to add as many levels as you can.

The holy grail of gamification – Universal point systems

The holy grail of gamification, 'universal points' (or unified points) is when you can integrate points earned in a community with other schemes (like your customer loyalty and reward programmes). There is just one system which combines points from actions both inside and outside of the community.

For example, you might be able to earn more frequent flyer miles for answering questions in the community or more Sephora loyalty card points (and thus discounts) for community participation. These in turn can give you access to discounts and other benefits. Any online activity which can be tracked and assigned to an individual can also be used to award them points. Instead of having two separate systems, the holy grail is to just have one.

You might also be able to assign points to members for things like the quantity of products or services they've purchased from you, how long they

▶

have been using those products, how many people they have referred to use your products etc.

This applies to training courses too. As members complete training courses they are assigned additional points in the community. This makes sense, as every training course makes a member smarter and their status in the community should naturally rise as a result. It also acts as a powerful incentive for members to complete more training courses, which might drive more revenue, increase the success of customers, or both.

You can also assign points to members for behaviours which take place offline. For example, if a member attends your conference you can award members points and badges in the community. As long as you have the email addresses of the members who attended your event, you can assign additional points to them.

This isn't easy to do. It usually requires custom development beyond what is native to any community platform. And once you've developed a system, you need to constantly maintain and update it. However, the benefits to the member and the organisation can be remarkable.

4 Roles/permissions

Roles (sometimes known as permissions) are essentially things some members are enabled to do which other versions can't. A non-technical example would be a hall monitor. Kids who are consistently well behaved in school might be assigned the role of 'hall monitor'. This is something they are uniquely allowed to do.

You can grant your members a range of technical abilities based upon their past behaviours within the community. As members increase their level, you want to give them more abilities (permissions) within your community. This increases their motivation and enables members to step forward and volunteer support for the community.

A typical approach would be to create a series of permission profiles like those on the following page:

Role	Permissions
Visitor (not logged in)	Default system capabilities
	Can read public content in the community
Newcomer	Can post three comments per day/comments are pre-moderated.
Trust level 1	Can post as often as they like
	Can send direct messages
	Can use full HTML in posts and signatures
	Can change their username
	Can publish knowledge base articles
	Can upload images
Trust level 2	Can upload file attachments
	Can mark topics as 'read only'
	Can comment on articles
	Can access private community areas
Moderation level	Can delete/remove posts from the community
	Can suspend members from the community
	Can create new topics
	Can close and lock threads
	Can pin discussions to the top of the community
Administrator	Can change member permissions
	Can change the structure of the site
	Can delete topics
	Can access the FTP server of the community
	Can customise and configure every area of the community

You can clearly see above how each role grants members a set of permissions which enable them to do different things within the community. Once they've earned a permission, they can use it to help the community.

> # WARNING – Even 45% of marriages end in divorce!
>
> Before you begin granting members immense power in your community, remember there's a high risk that at some point you might fall out with them. If almost half of marriages end in divorce the odds on you falling out with a top member at some point is pretty high.

Permissions can cause harm

Every single permission you grant to members can also be used to harm the community.

Even the most basic permissions, like the ability to post a discussion, can be used to spam the community. This is why you might want to limit the number of new discussions newcomers can create in a community (most spam comes from newcomers). You might also choose to pre-moderate their contributions (approve every post before it's made public) to prevent spam.

As members have earned higher levels of trust, you might give them the ability to do more things within the community. For example, you might enable them to send direct private messages to other members, change their username, publish long-form articles and use HTML in posts and signatures. Each of these permissions could be abused (I've ceased being surprised by how offensive people's usernames and signatures can be), yet they can also confer a sense of respect and importance upon members.

Finally, at the highest levels, you can provide members with the tools to really help (and potentially harm) the community. You might give members the ability to edit and delete the posts of other members. However, given how powerful this ability is, you should limit this permission to just a core few you really trust. No more than a handful of members should have the ability to perform a moderator role within the community. You should also reserve admin roles solely for employees of the organisation. This is for practical (as well as legal) reasons.

Regardless of how well you know and trust your top community members, you should never equip them with powers which can cause irreparable harm to the community. A member, for example, should *never* have access to any other member's private data, access to change the code of the site (FTP server access), or the ability to read a member's private messages.

It's not uncommon for a top community member to become upset at a decision or feel they are mistreated and turn rather rapidly to the dark side. In fact, once you start treating a community member like they are in charge, this outcome becomes far more likely.

Tweak your roles

As your community develops, you need to continually tweak these roles to ensure they remain well suited to the community. Roles can be fiddly and tricky to manage. Therefore, unlike levels (where you can have 50 or more), you want to limit permission profiles to just a few. Five is usually fine. Ten is okay if you have a larger community and members are rapidly progressing up to even the highest levels.

Typically each 5th to 10th increase in level also leads to an increase in roles. If you have 50 levels you might have 10 unique permission profiles. However, can you really offer 10 different website permissions to make each jump in role noticeable and worthwhile? The simple answer is no. At least not without going beyond just technical permissions and looking at rewards from a broader perspective.

The full set of rewards

The roles we've discussed so far have relied entirely upon technical permissions. These are easy to set in the community and the process then runs itself. But the number of technical permissions you can offer members is limited.

However, technical permissions are just a small part of the total rewards you can offer community members. It's likely only a handful of members truly care about uploading files, marking topics as accepted solutions, or being able to bypass the standard rules on signature size.

To really create a set of roles which motivate members you also need to consider *non-technical rewards* for participating in the community. You can do this separately, but it's better to combine roles and rewards into a single system. We've covered many of these in the previous chapter.

You can make a table like the one over the page and highlight the benefits your organisation might be able to offer to members at each role. You can now see how technical permissions are just one part of a bigger reward puzzle and it's easier to create a 'bump' in rewards at every stage of the process.

Role name	Permissions	Recognition	Access	Tangible
Newcomer (levels 0–5)	Can post up to five pre-moderated comments per day	Welcome from community manager		
Trust level 1 (levels 5–10)	Can send direct messages Can upload images	Opinion sought on how they want to engage in community		
Trust level 2 (levels 10–15)	Can use full HTML in posts and signatures Can upload a custom avatar Can change their username Can report off-topic discussions Can edit their messages	Can earn a rising star badge for their contributions to the community	Can vote on major community decisions and direction	
Trust level 3 (levels 15–20)	Can publish knowledge-base articles Can upload file attachments	Can share tips and advice for community-created eBooks	Can attend exclusive company conference calls Can apply for MVP programmes and private groups	Annual 'thank you' SWAG

Role name	Permissions	Recognition	Access	Tangible
Trust level 4 (levels 20–25)	Can mark topics as 'read only' Can comment on articles Can access private community areas	Can take responsibility for running a specific area of the community	Can attend community meetups and select company gatherings Can attend community training sessions	Discounts on products and services
Trust level 5 (levels 25–30)	Can create new topics Can close and lock threads	Can help create the community newsletter	Can email engineers directly with questions	Enrolment in a tester scheme – gets to trial latest products/ services for free
Trust level 6 (levels 30–35)	Can delete/ remove posts from the community	Chance to give a short talk at company events	Automatic acceptance into MVP programme and private group	Custom-created versions of products/ services
Trust level 7 (levels 35–40)	Can pin discussions to the top of the community Can suspend members from the community	Email and direct contact from the CEO	Invited for annual meetups Opportunity to speak at company events	Paid travel to attend company events
Trust level 8 (levels 40+)	Full moderation powers	VIP treatment at company events	Can nominate others to speak at company events	Free tickets and a small budget to attend company events/ company-sponsored events

Note how we've kept tangible benefits to a minimum. This helps to reduce cheating and reduce costs. You will also notice that this combines rising technical permissions with more recognition, access, and tangible benefits.

Even if you aren't using a platform which can grant members extra abilities or you're simply working with a small group, you can still create a system of a few levels which reward members for their past contributions to a community.

5 Badges

Badges are used in this context to refer to any visual reward you can give to members that symbolises something important. Gold stars in school, for example, are also a type of badge.

If you've been using almost any mobile app over the past few years, it's almost certain you've come across badges. They're used in most new apps which are available today. There's a simple reason for this; *they're remarkably effective.* Numerous studies show badges increase the quantity and quality of user behaviour.[20, 21, 22] Better yet, badges don't just increase the quantity of activity for which the badge was designed; they increase user engagement across multiple activities.[23]

Badges (just like symbols in the analogue world) are less about the design than what the design represents. Badges work best when they allow members to collect and display their achievements within a community. Badges become a way a member can express their identity and status to other members.

If you're using an enterprise platform, you can create and award badges to members for performing specific actions. Some, like Salesforce, even allow members to award badges to other members as a 'thank you'. If you're using something simple, like a WhatsApp or Slack group, you can either design something physical to send out to members or think of this more like earning 'gold stars' in a classroom. You can manually award them to members for great accomplishments and use a publicly viewable spreadsheet or another tool of your choice.

Some platforms enable you to automatically award badges based upon some predetermined behaviour. For example, some communities assign members badges for making their first contribution or posting their first response. Automated badges are typically earned after a member has performed a series of behaviours (i.e. starting 20 discussions might earn a member a 'conversation starter' badge – however, on the following page, I advise against this).

You can also use your discretion to award badges to members. You might award a badge to members for making unique, special, or noteworthy contributions in the community. You might not be sure right now what a note-worthy contribution is, but, believe me, you'll recognise it when a member has gone far above and beyond to create something special. These badges are highly subjective. This makes them both rare and far more impactful.

WARNING – Don't give badges away too cheaply!

Only award badges for things members are truly proud to have achieved. Many communities have a default setting for badges whereby members are awarded badges for starting conversations, replying to discussions, or other basic activities. Turn these functions off. They give badges away far too cheaply. Badges should reflect things members are genuinely proud about.

As a general rule, if a member wouldn't be proud to wear the badge at a company conference or community gathering, don't award members one. Most of us would be slightly embarrassed to walk around wearing a *conversation starter* badge for starting our first conversation. Alas, far too many badge systems do exactly this.

Trust me, members don't want to receive a badge for asking their first question, they want to get the answer to their question. Forcing members to receive and display an embarrassing badge is counterproductive. Some communities offer a shocking oversupply of badges. I've earned five badges on TripAdvisor after posting just two reviews. This undermines the value of all badges.

Good types of badges

There are three 'good' types of badges you can award in your community:

1 **Effort badges.** These badges recognise effort. Ideally members identify the badges they want and then make the necessary effort to achieve the badge. This is similar to Scout movements. For example, you might create a badge for members who create detailed guides on a topic of their choosing for the community. When a member creates a guide, they get the badge.

2 **Status badges.** These badges are awarded for a specific achievement, show-case verified expertise, or reflect a series of contributions. These are best delivered subjectively. These are similar to gold stars.

3 **Hidden badges.** These are badges no one knew it was possible to earn until they were assigned to a member for a specific contribution. You might make up a badge and award it to a member to reflect something unique and special they have done in the community.

You can create an infinite number of badges to suit your purposes and serve your needs. This also means you should use badges to help as many members as possible feel they have made unique, useful contributions to the community. A member who created a technical guide about 'widget x' can be given a 'widget x' expert badge. This is a badge they will be more likely to happily display and a badge which they would internalise.

Badges can also be awarded for participation in certain activities – such as completing training, attending events, being awarded member of the month etc. These all help members feel they have achieved something in the community. And the more that members have achieved (or feel they have achieved) within the community, the more likely they are to continue participating.

Badges shouldn't reward the same behaviours which points and levels do. Badges should recognise special, unique contributions and achievements. Badges fill the gaps in recognition systems.

If we go back to our example again, we might create a badge system to reward members at beginner, intermediate, and veteran levels. For example:

Audience	Badge	Reason and method
Newcomers	Rising star	A newcomer who has progressed quickly
	Event attendance	Given to members who attend an event
Intermediate	Special contribution	Proposed and awarded by Insiders to members who make a special, unique contribution to the community
	Special contribution – Expert in [topic]	For members who have demonstrated a consistent level of expertise in a single topic
Expert	Insider badge	Awarded to community Insiders
	Member of the month	Proposed and awarded by the community management team
	Member of the year [date]	Proposed and awarded by the community management team
	Remarkable contribution	Proposed by community manager or members and agreed by members
	Lifetime achievement	For a sustained period of participation in the community

Not every member will have the time and inclination to make it onto the community leaderboard or reach a high level, but every member should feel like they can make a useful contribution and feel recognised for it.

Step 4: Decide your rewards

Finally we need to be clear about the rewards members earn. These overlap closely with mechanics in many places.

Target audience(s)	Superusers (top community members)	
Desired behaviour	Answer the majority of questions within 24 hours	
Persona	Like feeling part of our mission/consider themselves amongst the smartest members in the community	
Game dynamic	**Competition**	**Achievement**
Game mechanics	• Points for answering questions • Leaderboard showing top members • Short-term challenges for members to compete in	• Levels based upon point system • Badges for unique high-value contributions • Permissions which enable members to have unique abilities
Rewards	**Reputation** • Given a chance to create content other members can't • Featured in newsletter and other channels • Can nominate others to speak at events • Unique achievement badges • Insider badges	**Access** • Rising levels of technical permissions up to the moderator level • Attending private community events and activities • Opinions sought on major community issues

In our example above, we're using competitive and achievement dynamics which we will create as six primary game mechanics. Our rewards clearly relate to each of the dynamics we're trying to create too. This framework is only targeting top members. We might also create frameworks to reward and encourage newcomers and intermediate members too.

If you're just getting started (or using an inexpensive platform), keep the system relatively simple for now and test your hunches. You might need to find unique and creative ways of creating the right dynamic and rewarding members. Once you're starting to see the results of your efforts, you can build a more complex system to build upon your efforts and prevent cheating.

Summary

Even on the simplest of platforms, you have a variety of tools available to encourage and reward members for participating in an online community. The best rewards are intangible. They support the reasons why members began participating in the community in the first place.

You have four broad types of rewards you can offer members. These are reputation, influence, access, and tangible goodies (but try to avoid rewarding members with tangible goods as much as possible). The process of determining when and how to reward members is known as gamification.

Gamification makes participating in the community feel a little bit more like playing a game. Within gamification there are game mechanics like points, levels, and badges etc. and game dynamics like competition, cooperation, and status.

A successful gamification system begins with first determining the dynamics you want to create, then developing a system to amplify those dynamics in the community. You will always be limited by the technology you're using but you can however still typically design a system to solve your needs.

Be warned that there are unwanted side effects to every game mechanic. So you need to be aware of what these are and design the system to reward quality of effort over quantity of effort. Create a system with an escalating series of rewards in which members can earn more points, levels, roles, and more.

Gamification won't magically transform a dying community into a hyperactive one. Gamification is better imagined as a scalpel which lets you make precise changes in member behaviour. It can however nurture members to become better contributors and change (and increase) the behaviour of people who are already participating in the community.

Checklist

- -

1 Determine what type of behaviours you wish to encourage.

2 Use your research to determine what type of dynamic you need to create.

3 Review what game mechanics are available to you on your platform.

4 Decide how important each behaviour is relative to each other to create a point scheme.

5 Create a level scheme. Make sure it's easy for newcomers to progress in days and then weeks, but veterans to progress to a new level every few months.

6 Determine what rewards you can offer and create a series of rewards based upon ranks each member reaches.

7 Monitor for cheating and adjust as you go forward.

Tools of the trade
(available from: www.feverbee.com/ buildyourcommunity)

- -

- FeverBee's Gamification Template

Resources

- Yu-Kai Chou – *Actionable Gamification: Beyond Points, Badges, and Leaderboards*

- Apple's Support Community – Gamification System

- Joel Spolsky – 'A Dusting of Gamification' (https://www.joelonsoftware. com/2018/04/13/gamification/)

- Sebastian Deterding – 'Meaningful Play: Getting Gamification Right' (https:// www.slideshare.net/dings/meaningful-play-getting-gamification-right)

- Salesforce's Trailblazer Ranks (https://trailhead.salesforce.com/en/ trailblazer-ranks)

chapter 9

Overcoming problems

Launching a community is like releasing a clowder of cats into your living room (yes, that's what a group of cats is called). It might seem fun, but it's probably going to cause a lot of stress, affect your reputation, and have some interesting legal ramifications.

In the business world, these unintended consequences are known as risk factors. And if you're not prepared for them, they can sink your community before it even has a chance to swim. Worse still, a failure to consider the risks can result in irreparable harm to your members, yourself, and your organisation.

Even if you're launching a community for a personal hobby, or a WhatsApp group for a local club or some friends, many of these risks will still apply. You should be aware of your responsibilities. So, don't skip this chapter!

We've encountered some of these risk factors already. Members might say or do something that puts you and your organisation in a legal jam or potentially cause a PR disaster. In this chapter, I'm going to go beyond just moderation issues and identify the biggest risks you're likely to face and how to mitigate each of them.

Where will the hits come from?

As Mike Tyson once said,

'Everyone has a plan until they get hit'.[1]

Managing a community at times can feel like being in the boxing ring. You're going to face dangers and get hit from some unexpected places. Some of these hits you can see coming and duck. Others are unavoidable, but you need to prepare a good defence.

I'm often stunned by how poorly prepared community leaders are for something going wrong. Many of the strategies I've reviewed over the past decade don't even consider the risk that something will go wrong. They simply assume everything will proceed without any problems. I don't know about you, but I want to be prepared for every possible problem my community faces. When something bad happens, I want to tell my boss: 'Yup, I thought that might happen ... this is the plan to deal with it.'

As the famous adage goes: 'If you fail to prepare, you are preparing to fail.'[2]

The knock-out blow

An acquaintance of mine used to run a community for a large American bank. For years she had been steadily building support from her colleagues and growing participation within the community. Then, one morning, she was called into her boss' office and given the bad news. The community had become too active and *they had decided to close it*.

The problem, as they explained, was *compliance*.

Banks must abide by strict regulations. Her bank knew from the beginning that a community was risky. Members might share bad advice with one another. However, when it was small they weren't too worried. But as the community grew bigger, so did the risk. The bank therefore decided to shut the community down; *it had become too successful!*

The five types of risk

You might be thinking risk is just your lawyer's problem. And you would be wrong ... very, very, wrong! You can't shift the risk of a community to a lawyer because (a) lawyers might not even know the full legal risks and (b) most risks aren't legal risks. Risks are your problem and you need to take steps to address them.

Before we can mitigate the risks, we need to identify them. We can separate risks into five key categories. These are shown in the table below:

Type of risk	Description
Legal	This covers every potential legal implication of launching a new community. The inherent risks here are vast, confusing, and change by sector and country (and sometimes individual states within each country). If you're launching a community in sectors like healthcare, finance, or involving minors you need to be especially careful with your legal responsibilities.
Reputation	This covers everything which could harm an organisation's reputation amongst its stakeholders (customers, employees, shareholders etc.). These risks include losing credibility with customers, losing the passion of top customers, generating negative publicity, upsetting employees, and harming (or undermining) marketing campaigns.
Risk to members	This covers all potential harm which can come to members as a result of visiting and participating in your community. If you're launching a community you have both a moral and potentially legal duty to take reasonable steps to ensure members don't come to unnecessary harm.
Risk to staff	Launching a community can potentially pose a risk to staff – especially staff managing the community. Staff who enforce the rules can also become the targets for personal abuse or unwanted solicitations. Likewise, a community may turn its wrath towards visible staff members when they feel disgruntled with the company.
Failure	This covers the risk of the community failing to gain traction, losing support, and when things simply don't work out the way you planned. This is a miscellaneous category for risks which don't fall into any of the categories above.

Let's identify the biggest risks in each category and outline the steps you can take for overcoming or mitigating each risk.

Legal risks

In the decade I've been consulting, I'm still staggered by the vast number of legal issues which can arise. These issues will likely multiply in the coming years as concerns over online privacy increase and liability for the consequences of online community behaviour remains a topic of considerable public concern.[3]

However, while the breadth of legal risks is vast, there are some that crop up more often than others. Before I begin, let me state clearly and unequivocally, I'm not qualified to provide legal advice. Make sure you consult with a lawyer before implementing or addressing any of the suggestions below. Be aware that the law often changes by country (and even by state).

Could your superusers be considered employees?

In 2011, AOL settled a lawsuit with former moderators of its chat rooms for $15m. This lawsuit emerged when a group of moderators claimed their volunteer work at AOL crossed the threshold to be considered employment.[4] Although these moderators agreed this was a volunteer position at the time, this didn't protect AOL from the lawsuit. Other groups, including contributors to *Huffington Post* (also now owned by AOL), have also tried to claim compensation for their contributions to a community with varying levels of success.

If you're running a programme to encourage and support top members, you need to be careful your superusers aren't undertaking tasks which could reasonably be considered employment. There is no definitive line here (and the law varies greatly by country on this one) but there are several areas according to my (UK-based) solicitors to be aware of.

As a good rule of thumb, the more you treat superusers the way you might treat employees, the more likely they could be deemed employees in the eyes of the law. The most common dangers include (in order of importance):

- **Replacing the work of employees.** If superusers are performing the work which was previously performed by employees, this can be considered employment. This is most likely to be a problem if paid staff are made redundant in favour of community volunteers. For example, in 2018 reports emerged Microsoft had laid off its Xbox support team in favour of unpaid volunteers.[5] This would appear to present a clear legal risk to Microsoft. However, Microsoft may have avoided the risk due to a small technicality. One commenter has claimed Microsoft hadn't technically fired paid staff but instead simply not renewed the contracts of contractors.[6]

- **Instructed what to work on (and when).** AOL's volunteer moderators famously had to work at fixed times and digitally punch in and out. This clearly closely resembled employment. If you are directing and strictly monitoring the work of volunteers, this raises the risk they may be considered employees.

- **Receiving rewards.** If superusers are rewarded with things which have tangible value, this can be considered payment for their work (and likely payment that's below minimum wage in many regions – leading to further legal problems). For example, AOL provided moderators with free internet access. This had a clear equivalent financial value.

- **Firing volunteers.** Firing volunteers for not working hard enough starts to resemble an employee relationship rather than that of a passionate volunteer.

- **Receiving training.** If your volunteers must complete a training course before being allowed to volunteer, this also starts to resemble an employment relationship.

- **Signing contracts.** Demanding volunteers sign contracts (most commonly NDAs) can seem logical, but also raises the question of why a contract is required if someone is just a volunteer.

WARNING – Volunteer agreements alone won't protect you!

Some communities attempt to resolve this legal quandary by requiring members to sign a statement agreeing that their contributions are voluntary and there is no expectation of reward.

However, just because members have agreed they're not entitled to compensation doesn't mean that courts will. This is like paying employees below minimum wage because they agreed to the contract. It might be possible (although certainly not ethical) to do it, but it still breaks the law.

You can find plenty of organisations running 'unpaid internships' who fell afoul of the law even though the interns agreed to the terms when they took the internship. Is your superuser programme really that different?

In many parts of the world (notably the USA), for-profit companies are legally prevented from accepting volunteer labour.[7] This puts community professionals in an interesting jam. Almost everyone replying to a discussion is technically a volunteer. However, there is a clear difference between someone voluntarily deciding to help out or promoting you on their own accord and running a large-scale volunteer programme in which you direct, coordinate, and reward the work of volunteers. You may wish to spend some time researching the Fair Labor Standards Act.[8]

Sometimes relatively small tweaks (such as providing volunteers with the freedom to work on areas that interest them instead of directing their work) can keep you on the right side of the law.

Are you risking your members' data and privacy?

One of my clients used to have a community of four million members. Today, they have a community of one million members.

I swear this wasn't the result of my poor advice! Instead, it was on the advice of their legal team. When the EU introduced GDPR laws on data privacy, they were advised to remove the accounts of anyone who hadn't visited the community within the past year (after a warning to members). This resulted in the removal of 80% of their members.

Interestingly, another client looked at the same regulations and simply anonymised the contributions of millions of members who didn't opt in to their new terms and conditions.

These examples highlight the challenge of new laws on privacy and the different ways companies interpret these laws. For example, I had one client who read the GDPR laws and spent several hundred thousand dollars moving their community to a USA-based provider. Another client looked at the same laws and decided it wasn't necessary.

Drastic steps like these are becoming altogether more common as companies adopt varying interpretations of new data privacy laws being introduced around the world. Mature communities with millions of posts from hundreds of thousands of members are increasingly being forced to make painful decisions to comply with the law.

Don't worry, I'm not about to bore you with the intricacies of data privacy and security laws. That's partly because I'm not qualified to do so and partly because it would take too much time. However, again, make sure you get qualified legal advice here. Given the importance of data privacy and security on the public agenda, there are some major things to consider. These are:

1 **How much data do you collect about members?** In the *beforetime* of community building, community leaders often endeavoured to collect as much data about members as possible. After all, it was free to collect and some of it was sometimes useful. You might use this data to notice interesting demographic trends or determine the kind of activities and events that might be hosted. Up until just a couple of years ago, data was considered a valuable asset and you wanted as much of it as possible.

Today, data is better seen as a costly liability. The more data you collect about members, the greater the risk of a data breach and the more severe the consequences of that breach. Most community leaders have shifted from trying to collect as much data about members as possible to trying to collect as little as needed. For example, if you don't need your members' real names, age, biographies, gender, and location, don't collect it. Often just a username and password will suffice.

2 **Have a plan for removing data you don't need.** Sit with your legal team and get definitive answers to questions such as how long you should keep members' data for – especially if they haven't visited your community in years. Develop a plan for removing a member's data from the community if a member requests it (or if you are legally compelled to do so). If you're using one of the bigger platform vendors, this should be relatively easy to do. On smaller platforms, this might involve some manual effort and cause other challenges (see box).

WARNING – Removing data causes problems!

You can't simply remove a member's data from a community without causing problems. Removing a popular member, for example, might also delete thousands of discussions they've created or responses they've given. This would hurt your search traffic and make some older, popular conversations almost impossible to follow. And don't forget removing so many discussions might affect the points members have earned for answering those questions – which in turn might affect their privileges within the community.

Most communities tackle this problem by anonymising the contributions of members who asked for their data to be removed.

---

3 **Decide whether to block access to any regions.** Data privacy laws differ by region. One client of ours, The Truth Initiative – an organisation dedicated to helping US citizens fight tobacco addiction – felt it was easier to block all visitors from countries within the EU than comply with the EU's GDPR laws on

data privacy and security. This made sense; they were a USA-based organisation targeting only people in the USA.

You might be forced to make similar decisions in the future. Even if you're not based within a country, you might still be subject to its laws if citizens from those countries are visiting. In the past we've had to make some tough judgement calls on visitors from various parts of the world.

Who owns ideas?

In 2014, I worked with a client on a community strategy which included ideation – i.e. members being able to submit and vote on ideas. Several of those ideas were adopted and one even became a primary feature of the new software product they were releasing. We were so proud of this success we even persuaded the CEO to name-check the community member who suggested the idea on stage. This backfired in a way we should've seen coming.

Instead of feeling proud to be mentioned, this member consulted a lawyer and decided he was entitled not only to the credit for the idea but also a percentage of the royalties generated from the new software product. The member eventually settled for a relatively low five-figure sum. And, despite its success, the company insisted the ideation feature be removed shortly after.

Getting product ideas from members sounds like a remarkable win for everyone. Members get to feel they are helping create the exact products they want and the company gets a list of ideas they can use to create their products. But you need to carefully peruse through the terms and conditions with a lawyer. The probability of this happening to you is low, but not so low you can ignore it.

Do members share and discuss illegal or illicit content?

Managing a community would be a whole lot easier if your members would simply stop unintentionally (and intentionally) sharing illegal or illicit content.

The most common example is copyright content – either images or videos. For example, a member might share a YouTube video featuring copyright music or movie scenes. While the person who edited and uploaded footage without permission is in the wrong – when it's shared in your community by other members it can still be a social and (in some countries) a legal problem.

This also extends to other forms of media. Members might cut and paste articles without attribution, share PDF versions of relevant books for which they do not own the copyright, and post recordings or audio clips which might support their point but are illegal to share within the community. Even stealing someone's photos and posting them in your community is a problem.

Part of the problem is your members are either unaware or ambivalent about copyright laws. If you've ever seen a YouTube video where the creator adds a note 'I do not own the copyright to this material' (essentially confessing their crime), you can appreciate the level of legal expertise amongst some of your community members.

The impact of most infringements is mild and many countries have reasonable laws in place which prevent the host of a community being responsible for the activities of its members – so long as they react quickly to remove such content when notified. However, it's still worth addressing such issues with a lawyer and developing a process for victims of copyright theft to flag potential copyright content. You should then check if the accusation is valid and quickly remove it. You might also, for example, want to check if sharing memes and gifs is ok within the community.

A more serious problem is when members share clearly illicit content – typically pornography or violent material. This is most common in communities dominated by men and, in the most serious cases, can result in your community being removed by your platform vendor. Facebook is notorious for removing Facebook groups that violate its terms and conditions without warning. Often this kind of content is either automatically flagged by the technology platform (and removed) or identified quickly by members or moderators and deleted – along with the member who posted it.

An even more pernicious problem is when sharing of this nature takes place in private messages and groups between members rather than in public. This is harder to track and stop. Private messages are, by their nature, private. You shouldn't be reading them without a clear complaint from a member. Yet, you can't ignore this potential problem.

I was shocked when one client, overwhelmed by the volume of illicit content being shared in his community, proposed creating a passworded place for *bad content* that was outside the reach of search engines.

Turning a blind eye to the problem is never the solution! It simply hides the problem until it becomes so big it can't be ignored. If you can't afford to automatically detect this kind of content sharing, at least be hypervigilant in noticing possible examples of it and offering rewards to members for reporting illicit content they see shared within the community so you can quickly remove it.

Is your competition actually gambling?

In a previous role, I wanted to host a competition for members of our community. The prize was a free trip to the company's headquarters. On paper, this sounded simple enough. Organisations do this all the time and it didn't seem too technically difficult to run.

I couldn't have been more wrong.

While competitions can be an interesting and unique way to encourage participation, they can also run headlong into a wide range of legal problems. For example, a competition will typically fall into one of three buckets:

1 **A sweepstake.** Where a prize is based upon random luck of the draw.

2 **A contest.** Where the prize is based upon skill and effort.

3 **A lottery.** Where people have to make a purchase to be in with a chance to win.

Each bucket represents very different legal obligations.

Even the type and size of the prize are important. If the prize has a conceivable cash value then it too may be subject to certain regulations (and taxes).

Also consider your own liability. If the prize is a free trip to visit your headquarters, are you prepared for someone from China to win the prize? Are you prepared to sponsor their visa, provide medical insurance, and take reasonable steps to ensure they come to no harm? What if someone from a less developed country wins, you sponsor their visa, and then they disappear after they arrive? Do you really want to wade into that legal quagmire?

The obvious solution is one taken by most hosts of competitions: limit participation just to select areas (typically just the country where the organisation is based). Yet if you limit the prize to just participants in your home country, are you prepared for the backlash from other members who wish to participate?

Also be careful how you select the winner. Is there a clear criteria you can use to determine the winner or are you subjectively making a decision?

Likewise, if you're claiming the winner will be drawn at random, you can't simply look at a list of names and pick one. That's not random. You need a defensive system for a random selection

Competitions can be fun and engaging for members, but be cautious about how you structure and implement them. If you aren't careful about the structure and terms of your competition, you might be accused of facilitating gambling. If you fail to consider the type of prize, you might find yourself saddled with enormous costs (or a member uprising).

Are you taking sufficient steps to protect minors?

In 2019, ByteDance (founders of the popular TikTok app), and YouTube (owned by Alphabet) were fined $5.7m and $170m respectively by the FTC (Federal Trade Commission) for failing to comply with COPPA (the Children's Online Privacy Protection Act).

COPPA is a United States federal law which aims to protect children in online environments. It applies to all organisations which are targeting children under 13 years of age and collects the data of minors.

You're probably not targeting minors to join your community. However, it's important you check with a lawyer and ensure you do have specific policies in place which forbid minors from joining your community and processes to prevent them from joining your community. Some organisations, such as Microsoft, have been known to require a tiny online payment for those who wish to participate. This ensures a parent is aware of their activities.

If you are encouraging (or accepting) minors as members, the broad principles of compliance include having a clear privacy policy, making a reasonable effort to provide direct notice to parents of operating practices, and obtaining parental content on any collection and disclosure of child data.

The USA is just one of many countries to enact laws to protect minors in online environments. Other countries and territories have similar laws. For example, Europe's GDPR implemented broadly similar rules for its 27 members. These have provisions for parental consent, tracking technologies, and privacy policy rules.

WARNING – Don't copy terms and conditions!

If you find yourself copying another organisation's privacy policy or terms and conditions, you should stop everything you're doing and find yourself a lawyer instead. The risks to you and to most organisations are far too high to do this on the cheap.

This doesn't mean you shouldn't review other terms and conditions, this is good practice to identify potential issues you haven't considered, but don't simply just copy them.

As a general rule, if you can't afford a lawyer, you can't afford a community.

Reputation risk

When you launch a community, you're also likely to incur a risk to your reputation (or your organisation's reputation). When you launch a community, you give every possible 'enemy' (disgruntled customer, fired staff member, or competitor) a channel to attack you in front of your biggest supporters, allies, and friends. Your community is a place where any misstep you or your organisation makes can be highlighted and amplified across the web.

Sadly, you can't (easily) prevent members from doing or saying bad things within the community, but you can plan to significantly reduce the reputational damage when it happens. In my experience, the most common risks include the following.

Bad publicity

For many organisations, the biggest risk lies not in upsetting members but in the bad publicity which can result from messages being shared elsewhere. In October 2019, messages from WeWork's private community for staff was leaked to *The Guardian*, who ran a negative story about the company at a sensitive time.[9]

Fortunately, most journalists are too busy fighting off your PR team to browse through your community looking for dirt. But any mischievous actor can initiate and feed journalists posts about members complaining about anything in your community.

If you don't think stories like 'Top customers turn on (your brand) over (issue)' are newsworthy, you haven't been in the industry for long enough. Even the smallest of community efforts should be cautious. A growing number of negative media stories highlight private group WhatsApp messages in their stories. It only takes one disgruntled member to share screenshots to cause real damage. Just because you're using a private platform, doesn't mean you're safe from any reputational harm for what happens in the community.

Beyond the obvious ethical reasons, this is also why posts which are (or could reasonably be considered) racist, sexist, transphobic, or otherwise mean and hateful should be removed quickly. It only takes a very small number of posts before *(you/your company) has a (sexism) problem*.

Once these kinds of stories take hold, it's very hard to shake off this reputational damage. Reddit, for example, is still (gradually) cleaning up its image for decisions taken almost a decade ago. In an age where people increasingly buy products and support organisations which align with their values, a small number of offensive community posts can be crippling.

Angry customers

One of my favourite moments in every consultancy project is when someone in marketing (and it typically is marketing, sorry folks!) suddenly realises that their beloved audience might say something mean about them in the community. This is followed by a seemingly reasonable request of *let's approve all posts before they appear in our community.*

My response to this is usually the same:

Customers are going to say bad things whether you launch a community or not. And if they're going to do it, we want them to do it in our community. We can provide a response, give them support, and turn them into loyal advocates.

I've lost track of the number of times a disgruntled customer has turned into an enthusiastic supporter after having a terrific, empathetic experience with the community team. Instead of trying to stop members from highlighting their frustrations in the community, you should be encouraging them to do it. Every complaint provides an incredible opportunity to keep a customer and address the concerns that they (and others) might have. Usually, the problem isn't members voicing complaints, it's when you're not able to do anything about the complaints.

In a perfect world, the organisation would acknowledge and respond to every complaint with a kind, friendly tone and resolve the issue speedily. The reality is often a lot more complex.

Sometimes the organisation isn't able to respond for legal reasons. For example, the organisation might not want the community manager providing advice on matters of the law. Other times the organisation can't respond because they don't want to reveal some confidential information about the member or themselves. For example, a company might not be able to respond to a complaint about a product that's being quietly tested amongst a handful of customers. Occasionally, the problem is simply not one which can be resolved.

In these situations, it's worthwhile putting together a list of issues the community team might not be able to resolve and sharing them within the community. This provides members with at least a minimum level of information to understand why they're not receiving the response they might want.

Should you remove criticism and negative reviews?

In early 2020, I was looking to buy a lightweight tent. I visited two communities from distributors to see what customers were saying about different brands. One community was filled with positive comments about their products. The other had both the good and the typical mixture of bad comments.

Out of curiosity, I sent an email to the community manager at the former to find out why there were no negative posts (not a single complaint) about their products in the community.

He gave me a remarkably honest answer:

'If people post a criticism about our products we try to contact them directly and remove the negative post from the community.'

At first, you can see why this sounds smart. You don't want potential customers like me seeing negative posts about your products. It might cost your business! But this approach is already incredibly short-sighted. The community which featured only positive posts didn't feel authentic. Imagine an influencer who only posts positive reviews. After a while you would become suspicious. People need to see the good and the bad reviews to make decisions.

Without negative posts and reviews, people trust positive posts less. This means you can't remove the negative comments without also removing the authenticity of the community.

Disappointed members

Customer complaints are just one reason why members get angry. You might not have much control over that. You do have a lot more control when members are critical of the community experience.

Community members are often the most passionate about the topic. For brands, they're often the organisation's best customers or most loyal supporters. They expect a high level of support from you in a community. If you fail to respond quickly to their concerns, acknowledge their contributions, and solicit their feedback in decisions, they will quickly turn against you. Worse yet, you've given them the very tool they can use to organise their efforts against you.

I've seen disgruntled members start advocating for competitor brands within the organisation's own community. If you can't provide a high level of support to members, small grumbles can quickly escalate into devastating collective action.

Another problem is unintentional leaks of confidential information. For example, someone might reveal information about an upcoming product which was supposed to be announced at an upcoming conference. As we've seen, it's fairly common for posts in a community (even a private community) to find their way into more mainstream media.

The best approach to preventing accidental leaks of information is training. Every staff member who participates in your community should receive training, which encourages them to participate and equips them with the guardrails to do it well and without problems. And while you can't prevent disgruntled former staff members from sharing private information, you can stay vigilant on posts from newcomers to quickly remove confidential information.

Risk to members

Regardless of what the law in your jurisdiction says, you have a moral duty of care to the people who have decided to participate in your community. This means you need to identify and mitigate most of the risk they face. These risks come in three forms: harassment conflicts between members and spreading false information.

1 Harassment

If you're managing a community, you need a clear policy in place which both forbids sexual advances and provides all members of your community with a simple mechanism to report cases of harassment and unwanted attention by other members. This should be shown within the contact form and included in your welcome and onboarding information.

When you do receive a report of harassment, you should take it seriously and you may wish to remove the perpetrator from the community (or advise the accused member to cease any further contact with the recipient). If the perpetrator does not abide by this instruction, you should remove the member immediately.

If you're looking for help with your code of conduct, look at events like CMX (a summit for community managers), which has excellent policies in place for dealing with harassment. You can adapt most of this to an online community too.[10]

2 Conflicts between members

In any group of people, you're going to experience minor personality disagreements. However, if these aren't dealt with they can escalate into serious conflict.

In December 2017, two gamers 'swatted' another gamer after a heated argument over a $1.50 bet. Swatting is the act of calling in a fake crime report to someone's address, which will merit the response of a SWAT team. In a tragic twist of fate, the perpetrators gave the police the wrong address and the SWAT team shot and killed an innocent stranger.[11]

Thankfully swatting is rare outside of communities targeted at young male audiences. A more common problem is 'doxing'. Doxing is the act of researching and publishing someone's private information (typically address or phone number) online. Any act of swatting or doxing should result in the immediate removal of the member and a community-wide warning that such behaviour is not tolerated.

However, it is also useful to pre-emptively try to prevent such situations by addressing conflicts before they step beyond the realm of genuine topical debate and into personal insults. Often a simple *knock it off now* style email (along with locking the discussion so others can't participate) can resolve the issue.

3 Spreading false information

In many industries, the challenge isn't persuading members to share information, but getting members to share good, accurate information. In sectors such as healthcare and banking, organisations are prohibited from sharing information which is false and can lead to harm. Even hosting such content can cause problems.

As mentioned, while many countries have laws (such as Section 230 of the Communications Decency Act) which generally protect communities as long as they abide by specific conditions, there are several exceptions in the applications in these rules which could make you responsible for any information published which causes members harm. You should research and be aware of these exceptions.

You should also consider the ramifications to members if false information is shared within the community. There are levels to false (or bad) information which range from life threatening to mild annoyances. However, bad community advice which ends up ruining a member's favourite shirt in the wash is very different from advice which results in a member getting a terrible mortgage deal, going bankrupt, or destroying a close personal relationship.

Most of the time false information causes great annoyance rather than election-changing outcomes. In one of my earliest gaming communities, one member suggested you could improve gaming performance by overclocking the monitor (essentially making it refresh the screen faster than it was designed to). About a dozen members blew up their computer monitors following this advice.

Just because you have no legal liability for these outcomes doesn't mean you have no moral liability for protecting members to the best of your abilities. You should endeavour to warn members about the risk of following unverified advice and quickly clear bad information.

Are you the arbiter of truth?

The problem with removing false information is you immediately position yourself as the arbiter of truth within the community. That might sound fun, but do you really want to get sucked into endless semantic debates about what is and isn't true?

In most cases, the consensus of the community performs this role – you would do better to rely upon the outcome of passionate (and informed) debates while pruning statements which can't be sourced and could do harm.

An even better approach is to identify 'risky' topics and either pre-approve these responses or check them for accuracy. Wikipedia follows this approach in its community. There are plenty of articles only members with a good reputation are allowed to edit. You can do the same with any topics which may significantly affect your members' health, wealth, or relationships.

Risk to staff

In most communities, activity can happen at any hour of the day. Members are demanding and want answers quickly. You (and potentially your team) are the focal point for your community – especially disgruntled members. This creates two acute risks to the community team (i.e. you) in managing the community. The first is 'burn out' or mental health problems caused by the nature of managing an online community. The second is the risk of being targeted by vengeful members of the community.

Larger communities typically have a paid moderation team to provide quick responses 24 hours a day, 7 days a week. However in smaller communities there isn't the need, nor the budget, for moderation teams. Instead community managers are implicitly expected to *keep an eye* on the community over the evenings and weekends to ensure nothing *blows up*.

If you agree to this implicit understanding, you will never be able to relax. This is like being told you can go on vacation, but every three hours you need to push a button or some terrible unspecified harm might happen (fans of the TV show *Lost* might rejoice). Sure, it doesn't take long to check the community, but it's psychologically damaging.

Worse yet, you're probably not going to just skim the community for problems. While you're there you might as well check your emails, respond to other questions, and see if anyone else needs help. It's not surprising that the topics of burnout and self-care are some of the most frequently discussed topics in community management today.[12]

The solution here is a healthy dose of realism. Very few problems are show-stoppers – especially in small- to mid-level communities. Sure, it is *theoretically possible* that someone might post a problem in your community so serious that it needs urgent attention before it becomes a major threat to the company (or the member). This is especially true in larger online communities where members have been known to post threats of violence to themselves or others. Swift action in these communities can quite literally save lives.

But, as tragic as these situations are, they are incredibly rare and I can't remember any community manager outside of a one million plus member site who has ever had to deal with it. Few (if any) community leaders can seriously claim to have prevented a crisis – despite checking their community every few hours. The largest communities have a moral obligation to hire paid moderation teams specifically for these challenges.

It's not likely that the community will implode because you're not checking it every few hours. It is, however, extremely likely that checking the community every few hours will harm your mental health and leave you unable to support the community at the level it needs. Give yourself and the community a break outside of working hours. Very few things can't wait until the morning to be dealt with.

The second type of problem is harassment and personal attacks from community members. This is sadly as common as experiencing burnout and often more consequential.

The bad apples in the big forest

In February 2020, author Tim Ferriss warned of the dangers of having a large audience by comparing them to the size of cities:

'Let's assume you only have 100 or 1000 followers. You should still wonder: At any given time, how many of these people might go off of their meds? And how many of the remaining folks will simply wake up on the wrong side of the bed today, feeling the need to lash out at someone? The answer will never be zero.'[13]

Once you get to an audience the size of small cities, the number of problematic members begins to rise sharply. An audience of 20–30 isn't likely to present a major problem. Most people can deal with this quite comfortably. But once the community reaches hundreds of thousands of people – even millions – there is more than likely to be a few troubled members amongst them.

The problems Tim lists in his post are very similar to the problems any gathering of community managers would quickly name. They include stalkers, death threats, harassment, desperate pleas for help, friends with ulterior motives, and increased spam and phishing attempts.

Managing a community makes you a very visible persona amongst a large group of people. It's often not difficult for someone to track down your name (even if your full name isn't displayed). Once someone has your name they can find your social media profiles. Once they have those profiles, they can often track down your hometown, friends, spouse, and possibly even your address.

One community manager I know had her face photoshopped into pornographic images, which were sent to her Facebook friends. Others have had their email, social media, and personal website accounts hacked.

It's sadly common for women managing communities to receive unwanted advances and comments from members of the community. Sometimes these are members 'just reaching out' to community managers through external channels such as LinkedIn and Facebook. Other times comments in the community focus on the community manager's looks or personality.

I strongly recommend all community leaders to consider these risks and take reasonable steps to protect themselves, set appropriate boundaries, and ensure private information remains private. This might include:

1 **Don't use your full name or photo.** In many communities, the community team either use their first name or a pseudonym to prevent personal abuse. This isn't always possible (or acceptable in some professional communities). However, it is a useful barrier to maintain a reasonable level of privacy.

2 **Only engage in the community.** Do not accept requests from members to become friends on Facebook and Twitter unless you have spent time with them in person and know them well. If members attempt to contact you outside of the community, write them a message to let them know it's best to befriend each other on your community platform instead. If you need to

connect with members on WhatsApp or Facebook for work, create a separate work account for these connections and consider using a second phone for work.

3 **Turn the privacy setting up to full on your social media profiles.** This is easier for Facebook, Twitter, and Instagram than it is for LinkedIn. You may wish to reconsider whether you want to list your current place of employment on LinkedIn. Be aware that if you use the same username or images on one account for any other – people can track you down through a Google Reverse Image Search. If you don't want members researching things like your eBay buying history – use a completely different username and photo.

4 **Never reveal location information via social media profiles.** If your social media is not private, it's best never to reveal location information via social media. Once people know the area you live in, it becomes a lot easier to track down your address. It's also wise to avoid broadcasting when you and/or your partner are away from home (especially at company or community events).

5 **Use anonymous domain registrars.** If you have personal websites linked to your name, use an anonymous domain registrar to hide your address. Anyone can 'whois' a website url to reveal the information of people who created the site.

6 **Use two-factor authentication on all email and social media accounts.** Ensure you use two-factor authentication on all your accounts. This makes it far more difficult for people to hack your accounts. For even better security, use an authentication tool (like Google Authenticator) rather than SMS message as your choice of authentication.

This won't deter every possible problem you might encounter. However, it should limit the frequency and severity of the problems you encounter. If you're building a community for an organisation, you should always insist on creating or seeing the internal policy for reporting situations where you don't feel comfortable.

Like most of the risks here, these types of incidents are thankfully rare. Yet they are common enough that you should take measures to prevent and mitigate them.

Execution failure (and benchmarks)

The final kind of risk is probably the one that we fear the most: *failing to attract people to our community*. This is like hosting a house party and no one showing up, only it's a lot more costly. This isn't an irrational fear either. It happens all the time. It's also a reality too few community leaders properly plan for (and subsequently overcome).

If you find yourself struggling to attract enough members, you might get tempted to dream up an exciting batch of ideas to boost engagement. Try to resist that temptation. None of these ideas is likely to work (at least over the long term). Before you can find the right solution you have to know what the problem is.

Your data can really help you here. For example, you might be able to see every action a newcomer takes and identify precisely where you're losing them. However, this raises a new problem. What's good or bad when it comes to metrics? If you can see half of your newcomers are still participating after three months, should you feel bad that you lost half of your audience or should you feel great that you kept half of them active?[14]

We need some benchmarks to help answer these questions. My consultancy, FeverBee, has gathered millions of data points from thousands of communities of all shapes and sizes. After segmenting these into a few key categories, we were able to identify (with a 95% confidence interval) a range of benchmarks below:[15]

Size of community (reg. members)	% of email subscribers who click links in emails	% of visitors who register	% of registrants who make a contribution	% of contributors who remain active after three months
Ex-small (0 to 1k)	2.62%[16]	10%–51%	22%–48%	17%–45%
Small (1k to 10k)	2.62%	4%–12%	14%–24%	16%–21%
Medium (10k to 100k)	2.62%	2%–8%	4%–19%	16%–20%
Large (100k to 1m)	2.62%	0.3%–3%	1%–11%	12%–17%
Ex-large (1m+)	2.62%	0.1%–2%	0.1%–5%	12%–15%

A quick word of caution here. This data doesn't cover every type of community. We have little to no data on platforms like Slack, WhatsApp, and Facebook groups. The rate could easily be a lot higher or lower. We also have little data for private communities like paid-membership communities, employee communities, and those you might hang out in just with your friends (I expect the conversion rates will be higher, but I don't know how much higher).

However, you should be able to use these to begin diagnosing potential problems in your community and find a solution.

WARNING – Conversion rates naturally decline as a community grows!

When a community is launched, it tends to attract the people who know you best and those most interested in the topic. By nature, these are the most engaged types of people. As the community grows, those less interested in the topic tend to drift in. This causes a natural decline in most conversion metrics. You can see the conversion ratios shrink as the community grows.

This could be more important than you imagine. For example, imagine you're given targets to hit by your boss. You don't want to be held accountable for metrics which naturally decline as a community grows. If you are looking for conversion metrics to hit, try to aim for the upper range of the metrics above by the size of your community.

There are a few common problems you're likely to face. Here is how you diagnose and overcome each of them.

1 Failure to gain traction

It's not easy to get enough members to form a habit of visiting and actively participating in the community. The advice in this book should help, but it's not bullet proof. There are plenty of reasons why the community might not spark to life and you need a plan for dealing with them.

Remember, if your community isn't gaining traction, the first step is to diagnose *why*. There are several questions you need to ask yourself here.

1 **Did enough people register to join the community?** The most common problem is not enough people registered for the community in the first place.

In Chapter 5, I mentioned a typical community needs around 100 actively participating members for a community to sustain a critical mass of activity. But if you're not getting enough people registering, you won't be able to achieve a critical mass. The question then is what is the minimum number of people you need to register? This is where our benchmark helps.

You can see above that in an ex-small community (which a new community naturally is), a maximum of 48% (only half) will participate.[17] If we need 100 active participants we therefore need at least 208 people to register for the community.[18]

If your community achieved that number, your problem isn't getting enough people to register, but getting them to participate. You need to focus on what the journey looks like after someone joins. What are you asking them to do? What messages do they receive? What does that newcomer journey look like? You can tweak your user journey and gradually make improvement. You can use our template user journey at www.feverbee.com/buildyourcommunity (or use Smaply.com to create your own).

If your community didn't achieve that number, we have to find out why. This leads us into the next question:

2 **Did we attract enough people to visit the community?** You can't get enough registrants if too few people visited the community in the first place. People typically need to visit before they can join a community. Looking back at our benchmarks again, we can see anywhere between 10% and 51% of visitors might register to join. If we use the best case scenario (i.e. a maximum of 51% of visitors will register),[19] how many visitors do we need to get the 208 registered members we identified above? The answer is about 408 visitors.[20]

If you achieved this number, the problem probably isn't getting enough people to visit but getting them to register. You need to look at what members see on the first visit. Is there an interesting, engaging activity that motivates and that members want to engage in?

Is the registration process easy to get through? Use Crazy Egg[21] or a similar tracking tool to diagnose how members browse your community and reposition the registration option better in the member's journey flow. Look at what most members are doing and make changes accordingly.

If neither of the above works, you have a concept problem. Your community concept isn't resonating with your audience. Reexamine your member research and test different community concepts using webinars, offline events, and content articles until you find an idea that really resonates with the audience.

If you don't achieve this number, then we need to continue our investigation and find out why not enough people are visiting the community.

3 **Did we promote the community to enough people?** For many organisations, the biggest problem is struggling to get enough people to visit the community in the first place. This often happens when you don't have a large email list, social media following, or web presence to begin with.

If we know we need a minimum of 408 visitors (remember this is the most optimistic scenario possible, you might need several multiples of this) and our benchmarks suggest only 2.62% of people click on links in email,[22] we can roughly estimate we need a mailing list of 15,572 people[23] to reach this number.

Don't sweat if your mailing list isn't that big. It definitely helps, but the conversion rate is a little misleading. For example, this isn't a one-shot deal. You can send multiple emails to your mailing list. The click rate will decline over time, but you should be able to get more than 2.62% of your list to visit.

Also a mailing list isn't the only way to promote your community. You can also promote your community through your website, via paid advertising, via promotion and partnerships. Over time, members will also find it via search and referral from their peers.

What matters is that your combined audience(s) (or networks) are somewhere in the 15,000 people. Obviously for private communities this number is a lot lower. But for a public community, it's very hard to get going without an initial audience to invite to join the community.

If you're reaching this number and not many people are visiting, you have a messaging problem. Either members aren't seeing the value of the community or don't trust you to deliver on the value you claim. You need to revise your messaging and try again. By the way, this is why you should be cautious about doing a big launch. You don't get a second chance to make a first impression.

If you're not reaching this enough, you need to grow the size of your initial audience. You need to steadily build up a following (ideally a mailing list) first. This might mean using social ads, forging partnerships with influencers and other organisations in the sector, or creating content and hosting events to get people to follow you.

If it helps, you can use the flow-chart in the following page to diagnose and overcome activity problems:

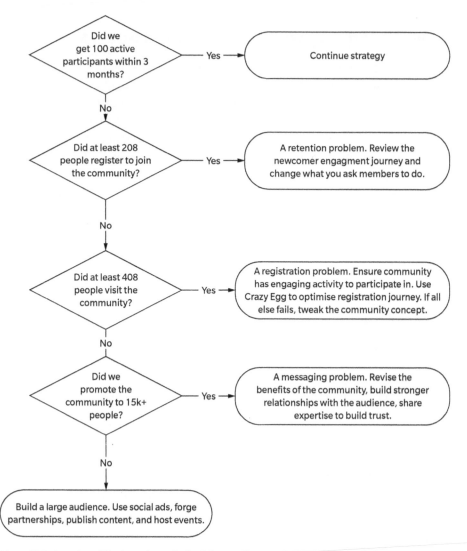

Note: This is a simplified version of a far bigger diagnostic tree. Get the full templates at: www.feverbee.com/buildyourcommunity.

2 Failure to sustain engagement

At some point in your community efforts, you're going to face one of the most worrying problems of all: *declining engagement*. Believe me, no one wants to be at the helm when a previously successful community begins to sink. Don't panic, you're not sunk yet! But you do need to identify the cause of declining engagement and then develop possible solutions.

Declining engagement can be a good sign

In 2016, a client of mine was worried about declining levels of engagement.

We looked at the data and discovered that the number of visitors was higher than it had ever been. But fewer members were registering and fewer newcomers were asking questions. We ran a survey of members and soon uncovered what was happening. Visitors no longer needed as many questions; the majority had already been definitively answered in the community. The community had done exactly what it was meant to do.

Declining engagement doesn't mean you have a problem. Sometimes it can be a great sign of success. Your community might've answered the majority of questions members are likely to have or your organisation might have been fixing the issues which have arisen in the community, resulting in fewer people needing to ask for help.

When you do see a decline in engagement, it's critical to investigate the root cause. If you're working for an organisation, you need the data to back you up if engagement does decline.

If a community engagement begins to decline, it's because one of two things has happened: either something within the community has changed or something outside of the community (i.e. about your members) has changed (or some combination of both).

Changes within the community	Changes outside of the community
• The community design has changed. • The community has answered most questions. • The community has become a less positive experience (slower response time, inaccurate information, noise to signal ratio, more spam/fights).	• Competition from other communities. • Member habits have changed. • Members are different (younger, older, less/more savvy). • Members are less interested in the topic. • Fewer new people are engaging with the topic. • The organisation has fewer customers. • Members have fewer problems/ questions to ask. • Declining search traffic to the community.

This isn't a comprehensive list, but it's a good place to start. You need to figure out which category of problem you're trying to solve. Trust me, this can save you a huge amount of time and resources. It's always tempting when engagement drops to launch new engagement initiatives within the community. But if the cause of the drop doesn't come from within the community, these will have no impact.

In my experience, community leaders zero in on visible problems at the expense of the real problem. One client felt grouchy veterans were driving away newcomers. However, in our survey and interviews, hardly any newcomers mentioned grouchy veterans as a problem. As we dived into the data, we discovered that the real cause of declining engagement was a drop in search traffic caused by a change in Google's search algorithm.

Instead of spending a huge amount of time and energy persuading veterans to play nice, we solved the problem by removing several thousand discussions with very few responses (thin content) and adapting the community to meet the search needs of today. Once we had done this, engagement rose to slightly above what it had been.

The decision tree to fix declining engagement problems is too detailed to fit across a page in this book. If you want a simple process to follow, head over to www.feverbee.com/buildyourcommunity.

3 Losing internal support

I hate to tell you this, but if you're being paid to lead a community, there is a reasonable chance that whoever is paying you will one day decide there are better uses for that money. Many, if not most, community leaders have at least one story of their organisation suddenly deciding to cut the budget for the community team. There are two common causes for this. The first is the arrival of a new senior executive (or CEO). This person has different strategic priorities and sees community as a luxury rather than a necessity. The second is a sudden change in the environment (often an economic downturn or a bad financial year). Many community leaders were made redundant as a result of the COVID-19 pandemic.

This risk can be best negated in two ways. First, develop and continually update the stakeholder analysis we discussed in Chapter 2. You should be reaching out to every stakeholder each month to gather their current views on the community, what they want to see, and how they can be better involved in the process.

Second, send information to each stakeholder in the right format. That's probably not going to be an excel spreadsheet attached to an email at the end of each month. It might be a monthly chat over coffee, a single image, a short video, or stories of members. Every stakeholder has different preferences you need to adapt your knowledge to.

Third, create a community steering committee composed of key community stakeholders who can meet once a month, review progress, address issues, and collaborate together on the way forward. This helps ensure broader understanding and awareness of the community.

Developing your risk analysis

A proper risk plan protects you, your community, and your organisation. It's not just smart to do it, it's a moral imperative to do it. There are three key steps.

Step 1: Identify the risks

Use the table below to identify the risks which are relevant to you. Remember this isn't a comprehensive list. You might want to include other kinds of risk here too. For example, some clients have worried about competitors poaching their customers through their community. Others have been concerned about people from a specific geographical region participating in the community. Drop every feasible risk into a simple table like the one below:

Type of risk	Category	Specific risk
Legal	Superusers	Superusers claiming their roles rose above the threshold of employment.
	Data privacy	Member email addresses, passwords, photos, or direct messages are hacked and leaked into the public sphere.
	Ideation	Members claim credit or royalties for ideas implemented within the community.
	Illegal content	Members sharing copyright material in the community. Members sharing illicit/illegal content within the community.
	Competitions	Competitions are considered gambling. Competition violates laws of member location.
	Minors	Minors join and participate in the community.

Type of risk	Category	Specific risk
Reputation	Bad publicity	Journalists discovering angry customers or hateful posts to write negative stories about the brand.
	Angry customers	Inability to quickly and effectively respond to questions.
		Inability to involve members in decision making.
		Failure to respond to ideas and comments from members.
		Sense of injustice in perceived differences in member treatment.
		Poor behaviour from staff members upsetting members.
	Leak of confidential information	Staff unintentionally revealing confidential information.
		Staff intentionally posting private information (typically recently departed staff).
		Friends of staff posting confidential information.
Risk to members	Conflict	Fights escalating from online to offline environments.
	Harassment	Members releasing private information about another member (phone number, address, hacked information).
		Members making unwanted advances towards each other.
		Members attacking each other via private messages (bullying).
	False information	Members maliciously sharing fake information to trick or trap other members.
		Members writing self-promotional posts.
		Members being unintentionally given bad information by other members, which is not corrected by other members and could cause them grievance or considerable harm.

▶

Type of risk	Category	Specific risk
Risk to staff	Decline in mental health	Environment which compels the community manager to constantly check in during time off.
		Long-term consequences of dealing with vitriolic statements.
		Inability to provide adequate care and support to staff members.
	Victim of personal attacks or harassment from members	Members personally directly abuse the community team inside and outside of the community.
		Members make unwanted sexual advances.
		Community team profiles are hacked.
Risk of failure	Failure to gain traction	Members aren't interested in the community.
		There isn't a big enough audience to reach.
		Members are prevented from joining or participating through bad technology.
	Failure to secure or sustain internal support	Colleagues fail to support the community.
		Change in colleagues.
		New strategic priorities.
	Technology failures	The platform isn't working as specified.
		The specifications were unclear or poor.
		Breakdown in relationship between community team and platform provider.
		Community is flooded with spam.
		Unforeseeable change in circumstance.

It's a good idea here to ask fellow community leaders in your sector what kind of problems they encountered. You might be surprised to learn of potential dangers you hadn't even considered.

Step 2: Estimate the danger

The next step is to estimate the likelihood (low, medium, or high) of each risk and the potential impact of the risk if it does happen (mild, medium, severe).

The likelihood is probably harder to estimate than its level of impact. You can estimate the likelihood by speaking with other community professionals, browsing the web for examples, and asking your colleagues about their opinions.

You can estimate the severity of impact by talking with different stakeholders (notably legal) and using your own judgement. You can see these dropped into the table below.

Step 3: Develop your mitigation plans

Now using the mitigation steps I've outlined so far in this chapter, your organisation's resources, and your own expertise, develop your mitigation plans. You shouldn't be writing this alone. This should be a consultative process. For each risk, outline your steps to either proactively prevent it from happening or resolve the issue quickly if it does occur.

Harm	Likely	Impact	Mitigation	Owner (initials)
Superusers deemed as employees	Low	Medium	Covered in T&Cs. Superusers to be voluntary with minimum required behaviour nor financial compensation.	TM
Lack of quality participation from community members	High	Severe	New member survey and interviews to identify key needs and trends. Determine why members aren't participating. Narrow focus to a few core goals.	RM
Failure to provide quick responses to questions	Medium	Medium	Identify and build relationships with customer support/marketing/internal developers who are happy to jump in to provide questions which are more than 24 hours old.	RM
Release of sensitive information	Medium	Low	Immediate removal of post with a note to the member about the danger of sharing sensitive information.	SB

▶

Harm	Likely	Impact	Mitigation	Owner (initials)
Community is flooded with angry posts/upset customers/ resellers	Medium	Medium	RM to contact direct marketing for an official response on major issues. Deliver with empathy and invite repeat customers to have a call.	RM
Community is flooded with spam/ self-promotion	Medium	Low	If it exceeds 15 posts per day for 2 weeks, GB to set the community to pre-approved accounts for public users.	SB
Serious breach of code of conduct (sexism, racism, etc.)	Medium	Severe	Immediate removal of the member and outreach to the victim. A notification to the community that this behaviour is not acceptable.	SM
Staff posting information they shouldn't	Medium	Medium	Staff training and reminders to new staff members we will encourage to participate in the community.	RM
Losing support from senior executives	Medium	Severe	Stakeholder mapping and engagement process. Schedule meetings with new arrivals and develop executive materials to explain community value.	RM

Step 4: Assign a directly responsible person

As you can see above, we've also assigned a person to be responsible for mitigating each risk.

It doesn't matter how good your mitigation plans are if you don't act upon them. Someone needs to be responsible for each of these. If you're the only person managing the community, you will be this person (in which case review the actions you've taken to mitigate these risks once per month).

If you're working as a team, then set aside time once a month to update on potential risks and see if anything needs to change. During these meetings update the risk and likelihood of each item, check the owner is undertaking the necessary steps, and add any new items which have arisen to the list.

Summary

Launching your community should be an exciting adventure which yields incredible benefits to you and your organisation. Just don't overlook the risks. You can't prevent every possible problem, but you can take reasonable steps to reduce the likelihood and impact of each risk.

Risks tend to fall into five categories. You have legal risks to consult your legal team about. You have reputation risks to discuss with your marketing and PR teams. You have a risk to members which you should discuss with your colleagues. You have personal risks to you and your team. And you have risk of a strategy or execution failure.

Make a list of the potential risks facing your community and then come up with a plan to reduce or mitigate the likelihood or impact of the risk. Assign each step to a specific person and meet once a month to ensure the steps have been taken to prevent that risk from happening.

The purpose of this chapter isn't to scare you, but to prepare you. You should be able to go forward with confidence that you have taken all necessary precautions to ensure your community thrives.

Remember this isn't a one-off process. The bigger your community becomes, the higher the stakes. You have to continually add and adapt your risk analysis and actions. Only then can you build a community with confidence to tackle anything that might come your way.

Checklist

1 Identify the risks you might face when you launch your community.

2 List each risk by the likelihood of it happening and the severity of it happening.

3 Develop mitigation plans to prevent or deal with each risk as it happens.

4 Ensure someone is responsible for each plan.

5 Meet as a team and review or update the plans each month.

Tools of the trade
(available from: www.feverbee.com/ buildyourcommunity)

- Crazy Egg
- Google Analytics
- CMX Hub, FeverBee Experts, and Community Roundtable (consult with other community leaders to identify potential risks)
- FeverBee's Risk Assessment Checklist
- FeverBee's Decision Tree Templates

chapter 10

Building your community strategy

In 2018, I ran a simple poll asking community leaders at large brands if they had a community strategy. The results were stunning. Over half the respondents *didn't have a community strategy!*

If you don't have a strategy, you're flying blind. You don't know where you're going or how to get there. There's a good chance you're showing up each day and responding to what's happening without ever proactively driving what's happening. That's not community leadership.

If you don't have a strategy, you're probably repeating the same activities every day, week, or month without any idea if (a) they are the right activities or (b) that they're having the intended impact. Without a strategy, it's unlikely you have the full support of your colleagues or agreement from the senior leadership team on what you're doing.

If you don't have a strategy, you probably haven't dug deep to discover what your audience needs and desires. You might not have identified what technology you need and what your requirements will be as you grow. You might not even know what skills you need, when you need to recruit more staff, or what the cost of your community will be.

But perhaps the biggest sign of not having a good community strategy is feeling overwhelmed. This feeling of being overwhelmed comes from trying to do too many things at once and not making any progress. A strategy is essentially how you allocate limited resources to achieve the biggest impact. Creating a strategy forces you to prioritise and ensure you're not trying to do too many things. A really good strategy zeros in on the handful of things which really matter to you and your audience and aims to do those things really well. Most importantly, a great strategy takes your community to the next level. If you haven't seen much progress in your community over the past year, or if you're still doing the same tasks as a year ago, it's time to create (or revamp) your community strategy.

This chapter is going to pull together everything we have learned so far to create a clear and coherent community strategy. I'm going to help you develop your community strategy from scratch and ensure it's aligned to every possible best practice.

A great strategy isn't created, it's facilitated

A critical lesson I've learned in the past decade is the only strategies which succeed are those which engage stakeholders throughout the entire process. You can't drop your strategy upon your colleagues 'fait accompli' and expect them to pay much attention to it. That's a sure-fire way to wind up with a strategy which begins collecting dust from the moment it's published.

A great community strategy isn't created, it's facilitated. The goal isn't to produce a 'final document' but instead to produce agreement and alignment amongst everyone to move forward. When I work with a client, I don't sit in a dark room for a few months and create a community strategy in a 'spark of genius' moment. My goal (and your goal when doing this) is to act as a catalyst for change. You need to bring people along with you on the journey.

You bring people together and facilitate discussions to ensure the organisation is making the right trade-offs and is aware of the resources and risks required. Believe me, people want to have input and feel consulted. You can't create a great strategy if you're not going to commit to engaging in dozens, even hundreds, of interviews, workshops, calls, and emails.

Nothing in the final document should be a surprise to your colleagues. The final document is simply the summary of all the discussions you've facilitated along the journey. The real value is building the support and getting the direction to execute the strategy.

What's in a community strategy?

A community strategy is structured into the following sections:

1 Executive summary

2 Defining the problem or opportunity

    a) Community analysis (existing only)

    b) Internal analysis

    c) Audience analysis

    d) Summary SWOT analysis

3 Creating the community concept

    a) Guiding principles

    b) Value statement for the brand

    c) Value statement for members

4 Short-term strategic plan: 0–3 months

5 Near-term strategic plan: 3–9 months

6 Intermediate strategic plan: 9–18 months

7 Long-term strategic plan: 18–36 months

8 Technology requirements

9 Measurement

10 Mitigating risk factors

11 Appendices

Creating a strategy for an existing community is slightly different from creating a strategy for a new community. There are some sections of this chapter which only apply to existing communities. If you haven't started your community yet, you can skip these sections. But try not to skip any other section. Each phase logically leads into the next. If you skip a phase, you're probably taking a 'leap of faith'.

Leaps of faith are great for *Indiana Jones* movies, but they're not so great when it comes to strategy.

1 Executive summary

Every community strategy should begin with a summary for the busy people who won't have time to read the full strategy. While this section appears first, you should write it last (otherwise what are you summarising?)

Your summary should outline:

1 The problem this strategy is trying to solve (or opportunity it will seize).

2 How the strategy will solve it.

3 Key discoveries from research.

4 Key value of the community to you and the audience.

5 Required resources.

6 Key challenges to overcome.

This should be no more than two pages. I often include a simple one-page overview graphic showing the community strategy. If you're working in a large organisation, you probably also want to create a short presentation of five to ten slides here which can be easily shared around and understood.

Your goal in the summary is to make it easy for someone to grasp what you're trying to do and the implications of what you're trying to do, and say 'Yes, go for it!'

2 Defining the problem or opportunity (ref: Chapter 2)

Your community should always solve a problem (or seize an opportunity) for you, your audience, and your organisation. Before you can do that, you need to define this problem or opportunity by undertaking background research we covered in Chapter 2.

This section should *summarise what* you've learned from your research. Try to keep this brief. Selectively use one or two key charts, graphs, and quotes that best support your findings here and drop everything else into the appendices.

This section will usually include the following:

a) Community analysis (ref: Chapters 1 and 9)

If you have an existing community, begin by analysing how it's doing today. Don't simply publish graphs showing metrics going up or down, but explain *why* these are going up or down. We covered this in detail in the last chapter.

You should endeavour to anticipate and answer questions you're likely to get. These questions will usually include:

1 **Is the number of people visiting the community rising or falling?** Look at the overall number of visitors to the community and where your visitors are coming from. This gives you a good indicator of the overall level of interest in your community and where the interest is coming from. Now use the principles from the last chapter to explain why the number is rising or falling. What's changed about the community or its audience?

2 **Are members finding the community engaging?** Look at your total contributions divided by your total number of visitors (or active participants). This shows you if members are finding the community more or less engaging when they do visit. Now find out why. What else has changed during this time period?

3 **Are members performing behaviours that are useful to us?** This is your value and impact metrics. Are members doing the things you need them to do to achieve your goal? If not, then why not?

You can find our measurement spreadsheets at www.feverbee.com/buildyourcommunity to help.

A quick word of warning. In many communities, traffic rises and falls on a seasonal basis. Some communities become noticeably busier or quieter during festive periods and summer holidays. It's usually best to use year on year (YoY) data instead of trends over the past few months. This means it's usually better to compare March 2021 to March 2020 as opposed to, say, March 2021 to January 2021.

Comparing how well you're doing today against three months ago often just reveals seasonal trends. Comparing how well you're doing compared with the same month last year gives you far more useful information. Use this research to write one to three concise problem statements (see box).

Writing a problem statement

A problem statement is a concise summary of an issue and its causes.

For example: 'The monthly level of participation in the community has declined by 15% year on year. While active members still participate at the same level as before, there are fewer active members. This is due to fewer newcomers arriving at the community via search. The decline in search traffic is caused both by a decline of 2.5 places in the community's average search ranking and fewer people searching for those terms.'

A problem statement like this clearly reveals where to focus your efforts to resolve the problem.

b) Internal analysis (ref: Chapter 1)

In the internal analysis you're aiming to assess whether you (or your organisation) have the right goals and the resources (skill, money, and time) to achieve those goals. During this process you want to surface any potential problems or concerns stakeholders might have.

When working with a larger organisation, I try to host a workshop to bring together key stakeholders for a few hours to identify the goals of the community, build relationships, and provide an opportunity for everyone to voice their opinions, objections, and recommendations. Getting two people discussing an issue in the same room is the 'stitch in time that can save nine' later on.

If you can't host a workshop, then interview each stakeholder individually (you can find our interview templates at www.feverbee.com/buildyourcommunity). These interviews should uncover the fears and desires of stakeholders. I typically rank needs and fears by aggregate mentions. You can find an example below:

Priority level	Need/desire/fear
1	Scale support to SMB customers. (want).
2	Avoid conflict between (and with) partners. (fear).
3	Drive high engagement, activity, and adoption rates. (desire).
4	Increase product adoption and usage of all features. (desire).
5	Identify product problems and learn why areas are not intuitive. (desire).
6	Develop an 'award-winning' support experience. (desire).
7	Collect success stories/sales material for community members. (need).
8	Collect and promote great PR stories from the community. (need).
9	Gain coverage in the trade press. (desire).

Your goals for the community should come from this research. Often the goals which pop up most frequently become the goals for the community. Limit your goals to between one to three to get started.

Resources check

During this phase, I also recommend assessing whether your organisation has the skills and resources to execute its plan. For example, many organisations trying to launch a new community from scratch hire community leaders who have managed large communities but never launched one themselves. This is a completely different skillset.

If you want to review the skills of you or your community team, you can use our community accelerator tool: www.feverbee.com/accelerator. You can list any skill or resource gaps in this section too. For example, if you want to launch a superuser programme and no one has done that before – it's a good idea to learn that skill first.

We'll come back to resources later.

c) Audience analysis (ref: Chapter 2)

Now we need to figure out what our audience truly desires.

Remember all the research we did in Chapter 2 to find out who our audience are and what they want? This is where you summarise the results of that research. You should be able to identify the different segments of your audience, who they are, why each segment visits (or doesn't visit) the community, and what they want.

Segment	Summary from research
Newcomers (using our products for 0–1 year)	• Drawn to the community by an immediate product problem and wants a response without being attacked for asking a 'dumb question'. • Looking for examples and guides they can follow. • Worried about being overwhelmed with too much information too soon. • Typically asks for help via customer support and via friends they know who use the product (by email).
Intermediates (using our products for 1–2 years)	• Most interested in Q&A and long-form content if well organised. • Will sometimes browse questions and answer some if they know the answer. • Visit most frequently to get the latest product news and updates.
Veterans (using our products for 2+ years)	• Visits frequently out of habit to see if there is something new they can learn from. • Cares greatly about the signal to noise ratio. Too much beginner-level content in the community. • Likes to quickly scan the community and will open several tabs at once to respond to relevant questions at the beginning of the day. • Wants a more private place to chat with fellow-veteran users and feel a part of the company's mission.

Broader sector changes

You should also use your data to look at broader changes in the sector here. Are more or fewer people interested in your topic? Are you likely to see newcomers drying up or increasing? What specific niches and new trends are emerging? What technologies are rising and falling in popularity? Use a typical PEST analysis (political, economical, social, and technological) if you need a framework to think about trends.[1]

Your community should always be swimming with the tide, not holding out trying to fight current trends. It's best to incorporate new trends as quickly as possible rather than dismiss and fight against them. Be a leader not a laggard!

List any major trends in this section. For example:

Trend	Implication
Rise in video and social media	We need to support our community both inside and outside of a single platform. People ask questions on whatever tools they are most comfortable with.
Rise in privacy concerns	We may want to enable our members to participate anonymously and collect as little data about them as possible.
Distrust in our brand	Members increasingly distrust our brand due to negative experiences and broken promises in recent years. We must not make any promise to members until we are 100% sure we can fulfil it.
Growth in niche	Our audience is increasingly talking about [new thing] and more groups are emerging about it. We should feature this as a key topic of discussion on the homepage of our community.
50% mobile	Our audience use mobile when browsing our website 50% of the time and we should allocate 50% of our developing resources to mobile to match.

d) Summary SWOT analysis

Now you can summarise all the research above into a simple SWOT (strengths, weaknesses, opportunities, and threats) analysis.

SWOT analyses have been a classic feature of business school strategy classes since the mid-1960s. In a SWOT analysis, you list your community's (or organisation's) strengths and weaknesses at the top and the opportunities and threats at the bottom.

The strengths and weaknesses should only cover *internal factors* already present in the community and the organisation. The opportunities and threats are *external factors* that come from outside the community. Some of the typical aspects of these are included below:

Strengths	Weaknesses
List the unique advantages of your organisation or current community. This might include: • size or reach of your organisation • passion or enthusiasm of your customers • momentum you've established • contacts or reputation within your field • internal collaboration and resources • technology platform you're using.	List here the negatives you identified in your analysis so far. This might include the opposites of strengths. • limited size and reach • dispassionate or upset members • declining levels of participation • internal competition/conflict and/or limited resources • poor technology platform.
Opportunities	**Threats**
List here any unique *external* opportunities you have identified. This might include: • new audience segments you can target • other member needs you can satisfy • partnerships with other organisations • new trends or technology to take advantage of • etc.	List here the biggest potential *external* threats to the community. This might include: • potential legal problems (data privacy/security) • competitors • changing member habits or behaviours • sudden change in executive sponsors of the project etc.

You should be able to list all your key findings into a SWOT analysis. It's a good idea to share this document around and solicit feedback in the process. Remember the more input people have had into defining the problem, the more likely they will own the solution.

By this point you should know:

1 The problem(s) you're trying to solve.

2 What your colleagues (or you) want.

3 Who your audience(s) are and what each segment desires.

4 Broader industry and sector trends.

The research is the foundation upon which you build the rest of the community. When a community effort goes wrong, I can usually trace the problem back to a failure to do great research (or worse, ignoring great research).

3 Creating the community concept (ref: Chapter 2)

Now you've done the research, you can start to craft the vision for the community and its value to both your members and your organisation. This is what I call the community concept.

If the concept is right, it becomes the magnet which draws members in and keeps them returning to generate incredible results for both themselves and your organisation.

If the concept is wrong, your community will have flickers of life but never quite catch fire. Typically the solution to a failing community is to relaunch it with a better, more powerful community concept.

Creating a community concept isn't a 'spark of genius' act of creation. It's simply following your research to its natural and logical conclusion. The community concept you are creating (or, for an existing community, refining) should take advantage of your organisation's strengths and opportunities while mitigating its weaknesses and threats.

Consider present multiple options

If you're working for an organisation, it might be handy at this stage of the strategy process to present several community options of what the community could become. This again helps build support throughout the organisation for your community and ensures everyone has had a say in the final outcome.

One way to do this is to separate options by risk. You might have one option which is similar to what you're doing now, one which is a bit of a risk, and one which is a real 'shoot for the stars' approach. Another way is to present different options based upon the different audiences you could serve.

In 2020, I was hired by Sephora to develop the strategy for its successful BeautyTalk community. The community had high levels of engagement but was being buffeted by changing trends and technology challenges.

Instead of presenting a single vision, I used the trends and research to present four possible concepts along with the pros and cons of each. By giving everyone a say in the process, people felt a lot happier with the final solution.

There are three parts to your community vision: (a) your guiding principles, (b) your value statement for the brand, and (c) your value statement for members.

a) Guiding principles (ref: Chapter 2)

Your guiding principles are a set of five to seven constraints which narrow the scope and focus of your community to a few specific areas. Your principles should identify who the community is for (and not for), the value to the organisation, the value to members, what makes the community unique, and possibly a key challenge to overcome.

This is where your SWOT analysis really helps. The purpose of this stage is to *deliberately close off* areas your community could pursue to concentrate all your efforts on a handful of areas you can do extremely well. I would recommend the principles covering the following.

- **Principle 1: Decide the target audience.** Outline who the community is for and who it isn't for. It should be for a specific segment of your audience. If it's for everybody ('all of our customers'), then it's really for nobody. You can always expand later, but start focused on just one or two audience(s) for now.

- **Principle 2: List the unique, powerful value to members.** Explain why this community is satisfying urgent, relevant daily needs members have (which they can't satisfy anywhere else). If the need isn't urgent or relevant to their *daily* lives members won't visit very often. Again, use your member profiles to answer this. You shouldn't have any competition for satisfying this need.

- **Principle 3: List the value to you/your organisation.** What is the indispensable impact your community offers your organisation? You need to be super specific here. What is the urgent problem that only your community can overcome? Is this an urgent, immediate, relevant need for you and your colleagues?

- **Principle 4: List what you need members to do to achieve this value.** As succinctly as possible, identify the key behaviour(s) members must undertake. This is the critical battle of persuasion you must win. What has prevented this from happening so far? What is your unique, new approach to overcoming it?

- **Principle 5: Explain how this will be future proof.** Using your opportunities and threats from above, explain why your community will survive in a world of constant change. What is the sustainable competitive advantage the community will create which will keep people coming back? This might be a unique asset the community creates, a specific focus on the audience, or a philosophy of following the audience whatever platform they may use.

You can add more than five principles if you need them, but try not to go above seven. Your principles restrict your efforts to a few core areas while still allowing plenty of freedom for the strategy to emerge and evolve. These principles serve as the guardrails for the rest of your community strategy.

Examples of strategic principles

If you find yourself stuck, let me share an example from a former client:

- **Principle 1: Our community is for our small and medium business customers**. Other groups (large enterprises and partners) are welcome to join the community but our community's unrelenting mission is to support these two audiences.

- **Principle 2: Our community's unique assets are speed and quality**. Our community will deliver faster and better responses than filing a ticket or using a search engine to get solutions to product questions. Our community will endeavour to rapidly solve every product problem our members encounter and proactively address issues they don't even yet know they have. And we will do so with empathy and respect for the emotional needs of our members.

- **Principle 3: Our community is the best way to scale our support efforts**. Smaller customers can't afford premium support, yet they consume the majority of our support team's time. This community lets us provide rapid, quality responses at scale. We also know our members want to hear answers from people like themselves, and this community provides that support.

- **Principle 4: Our support efforts must become 'community-first' to succeed**. It's critical we drive every possible customer to the community first to seek answers before filing a ticket. At every possible opportunity we will position the community as the priority means of resolving questions.

- **Principle 5: We will treat our superusers like royalty**. Our community lives and dies by the willingness of a handful of members to answer the majority of questions. We will provide top members with a world-class VIP experience at every opportunity to encourage them to answer and solve questions.

- **Principle 6: We will follow our members – wherever they will go**. We recognise members use a growing number of channels to engage with each other and get support. Our community isn't limited by technology, we will meet our members on every medium they use and go wherever they go to provide them the support they need.

As these principles will guide everything else you do in your strategy, make sure you get support for them before proceeding any further. You can do this in a collaboration workshop with colleagues or go through each of them in turn to present why decisions have been taken and address any concerns your colleagues might have.

b) Value statement for the brand (ref: Chapter 1)

Now you can get more specific about how your community helps you or your organisation. You should identify your short-, medium-, and long-term goals for the community along with the key metrics you're tracking. We can look at our roadmap we put together earlier here to create this section.

Short term (0–1 year)	Medium term (1–2 years)	Long term (2–5 years)
Resolve 25% of customer support questions via the community.	Resolve 50% of customer support questions via the community.	Resolve 75% of customer support questions.
Increase customer satisfaction in our support efforts by 15%.	Increase customer satisfaction in our support efforts by 30%	Generate 75 great testimonials.
Gather 5 insights for product development.	Gather 15 insights for product development.	Post 60 approved case studies.
	Validate our engineering priorities using community data and ideas.	Validate our engineering priorities using community data and ideas.
	Generate 25 great testimonials.	Generate 25 great testimonials.
	Post 10 approved case studies.	Post 10 approved case studies.
		Build a knowledge base of customers' best advice.
		Increase retention of newcomers through community mentoring.
		Generate 50+ reviews on key community comparison sites.

This is a process. You're not going to be able to do everything you want from day one. Instead focus on slow, iterative improvement. It's a lot easier to get it right over time than the first time. You're not going to be able to answer every question or recruit a small army of supporters on day one. But you might aim to answer 25% of questions and recruit 5 superusers within three months.

We can now create a simple value statement based upon this roadmap. I always try to make this value statement inspirational. Anyone who reads this should be pumped and excited to help make this happen.

Example of an organisation's value statement

In the **short term** we will:

- Resolve customer problems at a lower cost than any other support channel.
- Improve customer satisfaction by showing deep care for our customers throughout the community experience.
- Hear the beating heart of what our members think and use these insights to improve our products, services, marketing, and more.

In the **long term**, we will do all of the above PLUS:

- Put our customers at the very heart of our decision-making process and use their feedback to guide everything we do.
- Use the community as our primary source for generating authentic reviews, testimonials, case studies, and PR stories.
- Drive all newcomers to the community to be mentored by experienced pros and reduce our churn rates.
- Create a library of constantly updated best practices created by members for using our products and services.

c) Value statement for members (ref: Chapter 2)

Now you need to clearly identify why members will join and participate in your community. What is the value for them? This should come directly from the audience research you've undertaken already.

Example of a value statement for members

This community will enable and encourage our members to:

- Get rapid solutions to every possible product problem and tackle issues before they arise.
- Learn how to get the most from our products and services.
- Feel a special part of our mission and influence our products and strategic decisions.
- Become a leader with a following of people who look up to them for advice and expertise.

It's common at this stage to list every possible benefit members could want. But that's not strategic, that's wishful thinking. You need to ignore the majority of benefits to zero in on the core few that you can deliver on. Don't try to do everything, just do three to five things extremely well.

4 Short-term strategic plan: 0–3 months

Now you know the kind of concept you're trying to create, you can start putting together your plan to achieve it.

a) Strategic plan (ref: Chapters 5–8)

At the beginning of each phase of your strategy, create a simple overview of your strategic plan (see box). Some organisations prefer using 'objectives and key results' framework. This begins with a broad objective (i.e. create a scalable customer support model) and then lists specific activities which must be achieved during that time period (i.e. develop and launch a community, attract 200 active participants, answer 50% of questions organically).[2]

The one-page overview

I've found it useful to create a simple one-page overview of the community strategy at each phase to include alongside the executive summary.

We already have our goals, but now we can be clear about the behaviours we need members to perform, the strategy (motivation principle) we will use to get them to perform the behaviour, and then the tactics to execute this strategy. This should all come from the audience research you've completed.

You can see a completed example below:

Goal	Resolve 25% of customer questions through the community		Increase customer satisfaction in our support efforts by 15%	Gather 5 insights for product development
Objectives	Get 500 newcomers to ask questions in the community instead of via customer support.	Get superusers to answer 50% of questions in the community.	Ensure every question receives a solution within 24 hours.	Get irregulars and superusers to suggest 50 new product ideas.
Strategy	Make newcomers feel the standard behaviour is to ask in the community before calling customer support.	Make superusers feel like VIPs within the community.	Make colleagues feel like this is a smart way of preventing more questions from coming downstream by answering them in a place where other people can see the answers.	Create a sense of scarcity to give specific insights during fixed windows.
Tactics	Position the community as a prominent navigation tab on our homepage. Create an onboarding series of emails to make newcomers feel confident and safe to ask questions within the community. Move the contact us areas to the bottom of the pages and show questions in the community. Turn our community into the primary support page with typical support questions featured later.	Build relationships with top 3–5 members and invite them to join a private group. Link to unanswered questions in the group so members can provide an answer. Share exclusive news first in the private group (requires getting internal approval first). Initiate regular discussions soliciting and responding to advice and opinions from top members on the community. Provide VIP experience at our annual conference.	Design the community to show the average time to respond and the number of responses that receive an answer and try to reduce that time each month. Respond to any unanswered questions within 24 hours and escalate if needed. Host a workshop series encouraging colleagues to engage in the community to prevent more questions later. Embed related questions in the 'contact us' form from the community, which members may wish to try first.	Run a challenge every 3 months to solicit feedback and ideas on a particular topic. Top ideas are added to a shortlist and members can vote on the ones they like best (and add their expertise and refinement to the idea).

b) How to select your tactics (ref: Chapters 5–8)

It's pretty easy to come up with dozens of tactics to achieve any objective (you can find 260+ tactics in a resource on www.feverbee.com/buildyourcommunity). The real challenge is narrowing them to the core few which will have the biggest possible impact.

You can use three-step criteria for thinking about the right tactics:

1 **How many people will the tactic reach?** The best tactics are those which reach the maximum possible percentage of your target audience. By reach, we mean they have not just received a message but opened it and are able to recall it. A mass email, for example, might technically land in the inboxes of everyone but few people will both open and be able to recall it. Changing the homepage might have more reach as members are more engaged with what they're seeing.

2 **To what extent will it change a member's behaviour?** Will the tactic profoundly change a member's behaviour within the community in a positive way? Again, a mass email is far less likely to change behaviour than direct, personal messages from the community manager. Often reach comes at a cost of depth; you may need to find a balance between the two.

3 **How long will the change last for?** Some tactics are novelties which wear off quickly. Others lead to prolonged changes in behaviour. Sometimes you won't know the answer to this question until you've tried it and seen the longevity of the impact.

We can use these criteria to make assumptions about the best tactics for our needs. For example, creating a blog post in the community probably won't be seen by a large number of members, is unlikely to change behaviour much, and whatever change does happen might not last for long.

However, other tactics, such as creating a superuser programme or a detailed newcomer journey, are likely to fare better in all three categories. Use your judgement initially to select the right tactics. As you begin getting data, you can prune the ones which aren't working and test new ideas.

Don't select too many tactics at once

In the reality TV show *Kitchen Nightmares*, one of the first things celebrity chef Gordan Ramsay would almost immediately do is reduce the size of the menu. The reason behind this is obvious. If a restaurant is offering

▶

hundreds of food options, are any of them likely to be any good? Do you even trust restaurants which offer a hundred food options? Instead, it's better to specialise in offering five or six dishes in which a restaurant can excel and delight its customers.

Some of our consultancy projects often feel eerily similar (without the cameras and offensive comments). One of the first things we do is get the community team to list out every tactic they're working on. Typically, we find they're trying to do dozens of things at once. We try to identify the five to seven tactics which really matter and coach the team to execute them extremely well.

Don't fall into the common trap of trying to execute a dozen or more tactics at once. It's impossible to achieve bigger results when you're dividing your time into smaller chunks. Five to seven tactics is usually enough (if they're the right ones). This doesn't mean you should only have five to seven tactics listed at each phase of your strategy. Some tactics might be one-off actions that don't last the entire phase. It does mean that you should only be executing on five to seven at any one time.

c) Identifying resources

For every tactic you aim to undertake you should be able to answer the five key questions below:

Description	Action
Target audience	Who specifically within the community will this tactic target?
Behaviour change	What change in behaviour does this tactic aim to make?
Execution	What are the individual steps required to execute the tactic?
Responsibility	Who is responsible for executing each step required within the tactic?
Resources	What time, money, skills and approvals might be required to execute this tactic well?

Example 1: Create a journey for newcomers

This is an example of a tactic. It includes the target audience, desired change in behaviour, a brief description, the individual steps, and required resources:

Target audience	Newcomers (joined within past 3 months, made fewer than 3 contributions).			
Desired behaviour change	Ask questions in the community instead of calling customer support.			
Description	Create an onboarding series of emails to make newcomers feel confident and safe to ask questions within the community.			
Steps	Meet with the IT team to ensure we have the capability to run an email automation series.	Sign up to the automation system and work with designers to create a standard template.	Create a series of 4 emails each focusing on addressing possible member concerns about sharing in the community and the potential rewards. Use social proof at every turn.	Check open rates and tweak copy at the end of each month.
Time	2 hours	8 hours	12 hours	3 hours
Financial		$2500		

I can't stress enough how important it is not to just come up with a tactic but to break it down into distinct steps and estimate how long each step will take. Often things that seem simple *'let's send out an email to promote the community'* actually take a lot more time if you need to get approval from marketing, hire a designer, and have it proofread beforehand.

In fact, if you want to execute this really well, you might spend time researching which tactics have been most successful in the past, run split-tests, and create a more personalised experience based upon what information members might have already given you.

Example 2: Create a private group for the top three to five members

Let's use a second example based upon some of the material we've covered in earlier chapters. Let's imagine you want to get superusers responding to more questions and your strategy to achieve that is making them feel like VIPs within the community.

You might decide to create a private group for the top three to five members. This seems simple enough. Simply start a group on your site and invite a few people to join. Boom, job done right?

Wrong!

Creating a group is easy, but creating an incredibly successful group is a little more complex. Think about every step along the way. What would this look like at a world-class level? You might first take the time to build a relationship with each person. You can schedule calls, send them messages, ask for their advice, and understand precisely what they need. This might take a few weeks.

Once this has been achieved, you might then send out an invite that is friendly and directly references these previous interactions. You might identify why you are eager to have them join a private group and why you think they will benefit. You can make direct, personal introductions between every member. Once this group is running, you need to drive it like a racing car!

This means initiating and sustaining activity. You might ask members for their opinions on community decisions, offer training on your products, and let them put themselves forward to run or lead areas of the community. You might constantly lobby for them in the community.

Now you can see how executing this tactic at a world-class level takes a lot more time and resources. Fortunately, we've gained the time to do this by reducing the number of tactics down to just a core few.

Target audience	Most active members.
Desired behaviour change	Increase the number of questions answered by the community.

Description	Create a private group for top members to feel like VIPs and become more motivated to participate in the community.				
Steps	Build relationships with top three to five members and invite them to join the community.	Create a private WhatsApp group for staff and our top 3 to 5 community members to provide them with direct access to.	Link to unanswered questions in the group so members can provide an answer.	Share exclusive news first in the private group (requires getting internal approval first).	Initiate regular discussions soliciting and responding to advice and opinions from top members on the community.
Time	3 hours (weekly)	1 hour	1 hour (weekly)	2 hours (weekly)	3 hours (weekly)
Financial	$0	$0	$0	$0	$0

a) Resources and budgeting

It's easy to brainstorm a list of all the things you want to do, but that's not strategy, that's wishful thinking. Strategy is recognising your resources are limited and deploying those resources to achieve the biggest possible impact. For each phase of your strategy, list the time and budget required. Distinguish between those which are 'one off' activities and those which are ongoing. You can see an example below:

Phase 1: 12 weeks		Cost		Time	
Tactic		Weekly	One time	Weekly	One time
Position the community as a prominent navigation tab on our homepage.					5.00
Create an onboarding series of emails to make newcomers feel confident and safe to ask questions within the community.			$2500		25.00
Move the contact us areas to the bottom of the pages and show questions in the community.					2.00

▶

Phase 1: 12 weeks	Cost		Time	
Tactic	Weekly	One time	Weekly	One time
Turn our community into the primary support page with typical support questions featured later.				15.00
Build relationships with top three to five members and invite them to join a private group.			1.00	4.00
Link to unanswered questions in the group so members can provide an answer.			1.00	
Share exclusive news first in the private group (requires getting internal approval first).			2.00	
Initiate regular discussions soliciting and responding to advice and opinions from top members on the community.			3.00	
Provide VIP experience at our annual conference.		$6500		25.00
Design the community to show the average time to respond and the number of responses which receive an answer and try to reduce that time each month.		$3000		8.00
Respond to any unanswered questions within 24 hours and escalate if needed.			10.00	
Host a workshop series encouraging colleagues to engage in the community to prevent more questions later.				8.00
Embed related questions in the 'contact us' form from the community, which members may wish to try first.				3.00
Run a challenge every three months to solicit feedback and ideas on a particular topic.				4.00
Top ideas are added to a shortlist and members can vote on the ones they like best (and add their expertise and refinement to the idea).				4.00
Summary		$12,000	17.00	103.00

This is a good summary, but it excludes the technology and staffing costs. To estimate staffing, we first need to average our one-time hours over the space of 12 weeks and add it to the repetitive weekly activities.

This comes to 25.6 hours per week.[3] If we consider a community manager is likely to be called into other meetings and have the occasional holiday, we can assume this project needs a single community manager at this stage.

Let's estimate a community manager costs $75k per year. We can add this to an estimated platform cost (let's say, $85k per year) to get the full figure.

Summary	($1,000)	$12,000	17.00	103.00
Staffing 1×FT employee (for 12 weeks of 52 weeks)	($1,442)	$17,308		
Platform licence (for 12 of 52 weeks)	($1,636)	$19,615		
Weekly cost	$4078		25.58	
Total cost		$36,935		307 hours

Now you have a fully budgeted community programme. You know roughly how much the community will cost and what skills and resources are needed to achieve it. Perhaps more importantly, once you have a budget, you can make requests for more staff based upon the extra activities that it will allow you to do. Being able to properly budget your community is a tremendous skill to have.

WARNING – Many community costs are front-loaded!

If you're planning to launch a new community on an enterprise platform, be aware that many of the costs are 'front-loaded'. This means you are likely to incur a significant cost at the beginning to get the community up and running. This will make the community seem more costly than it is. It might be best to amortise (or average) these costs over the duration of the entire strategy. You can see we have done this in our example budget.

5 Near-term strategic plan: 3–9 months

Once you know how to complete one phase, completing the remaining phases isn't too difficult. You simply replicate the same process for each phase. Next you can do the short (3–9 months), intermediate (9–18 months), and long-term community roadmap (18–36 months).

As your community grows, the benefits of the community should become increasingly apparent. Therefore, you should anticipate being able to invest more resources in the community. I typically assume an increase in resources in the region of 15%–25% for each phase (or per year). Over time, you can use these resources to satisfy more of the goals identified by stakeholders above.

At this stage you may also begin growing a community team to work with you. Make sure you include what the community team structure might look like, the skills of each team, and what each person will be responsible for. Once you begin to build a community team, you should also include what a team structure looks like and the skills they will need.

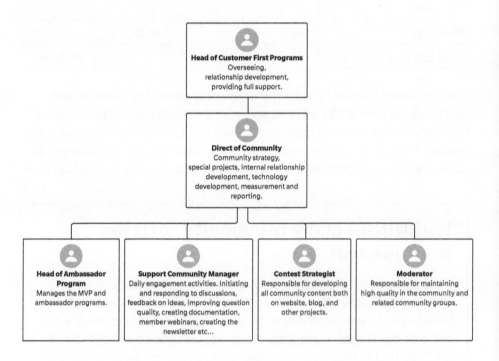

There are plenty of tools you can use to put together your team structure. My preference is to use Lucidchart, which has a handy add-on if you're developing your strategy in Google Docs.

P.S. You can find our community team template structures, skill recommendations for each role, and job descriptions at: www.feverbee.com/buildyourcommunity

Don't reinvent the wheel

Before you introduce new tactics at each phase of the strategy, be aware you will probably get the most mileage from investing more and expand tactics which are already working.

For example, if your superuser programme is going well, invite more people to join it. If newcomers are engaging in the community, then optimise the newcomer journey a little better or create different journeys for each segment of newcomers. Sure, sometimes you need to introduce entirely new tactics to achieve your goals. Most of the time, however, it's best to expand upon what you're already doing.

6 Intermediate strategic plan: 9–18 months

Now you can drop in your longer-term plans in the same format as listed above. At this point you should assume you have 30%–60% more resources than you did at the beginning. If you are looking to move platforms, this might appear in the intermediate term rather than the near term.

Sometimes projects such as a big technology platform migration might take a lot longer than nine months. In these cases a tactic might be mentioned in several phases of the plan. Make sure recruitment is listed as a tactic with a clear list of the relevant skills and resources required. If you're working for a large organisation, you should also spend considerable time in this phase building and sustaining internal support.

Remember, use the same structure as in phase one and update your tactics as necessary.

7 Long-term strategic plan: 18–36 months

Now it's time to think about the big vision for the long term. What will this community look like in three years' time? What is your community at its full potential? After three years you might also assume your resources for the community have increased by 100%–300% and things are beginning to develop quite quickly.

Try and tackle as many of your goals as you have the resources for. Consider what the community team might look like, what kind of skills you need to recruit for, and what kind of systems you will need to put in place to make this vision a reality. Consider the technology implications too. If you have a big technology change in mind, it's best to start seeing the idea and scoping it out over a year in advance.

8 Technology requirements (ref: Chapter 3)

Writing up the technology requirements isn't the most fun part of the strategy, but it's important to do it well. A failure to write good technology specifications can cause innumerable problems later on. Taking the extra time to do this well here will pay off many times over.

If you're launching a new community from scratch, you should go through the same process we went through in Chapter 3. Remember to identify who in your organisation (if you're working for one) needs to be included and bring them along in the journey.

List the category of platform you're using (and why), create your membership projection, and use the objectives you've listed at each phase of your strategy to create your use cases. You should list your technology needs for each phase of the strategy. And remember, each use case should be converted into a specific platform requirement.

Finally, identify the design priorities. Which features and calls to action should be prioritised within the community? These should be the ones which best support your goals. You don't need to develop the entire web specification at this point (that's a separate strand of work), but you do need to have broad agreement about the look and functionality for the community you're creating.

Remember you can find the community experience templates at www.feverbee.com/buildyourcommunity

9 Measurement (ref: Chapter 1)

Great, you've created your strategy! But how are you going to know if it's working?

The next step is to build your measurement framework.

Online communities hoover up a colossal amount of data. You can track almost every click and action in your community. It's easy to become lost in the sea of data flowing through your fingertips. Should you measure how much time members spend on your community? How many visitors register? Or the demographics of participants?

Don't gather copious amounts of data just because you can. Look back at your strategic plan and decide which metrics best reflect if the plan is working. If you've done the strategy well, this shouldn't be too difficult. You should have already set your targets.

Here is an example:

Building your community strategy

Goals	Type	MONTH								
		Phase 1					Phase 2 (etc.)			
		1	2	3	4	5	6	7	8	9
Goal 1 Resolve 25% of customer queries by the community.	**Target**	10%	13%	15%	18%	24%	28%	34%	40%	45%
	Actual									
Goal 2 Increase in customer satisfaction score of community members by 15%.	**Target**	10%	13%	15%	18%	24%	28%	34%	40%	45%
	Actual									
Goal 3 Five customer insights gathered and validated by the product development team.	**Target**	0	0	0	0	0	2	0	2	0
	Actual									
Objective 1 Get 500 newcomers to ask questions in the community.	**Target**	10	20	30	40	50	60	70	80	90
	Actual									
Objective 2 Get superusers to answer 50% of questions in the community.	**Target**	0%	20%	25%	30%	35%	40%	45%	48%	50%
	Actual									
Objective 3 Ensure 80% of questions receive a solution within 24 hours.	**Target**	50%	55%	60%	65%	70%	73%	77%	80%	85%
	Actual									
Objective 4 Get superusers to submit 50+ product ideas.	**Target**	0	0	0	10	15	0	0	10	15
	Actual									

Notice now we're only measuring the things that reflect whether our strategy is succeeding or not. We're being clear what the targets are before we begin and we'll notice very early on if we're falling above or below this line.

How you gather the data and calculate each metric will vary by the platform, but the precise metric you're using should be consistent regardless of the platform you're using.

But what about engagement metrics?

In my previous book, *The Indispensable Community,* I noted that most people measure the level of engagement not because it's the best metric, but simply because it's the easiest thing to measure. The best use of engagement metrics (outside of those within your strategy) are when something isn't going wrong.

For example, if you're not hitting your target engagement metrics can help you find out why. You will usually find the tactics you're executing aren't reaching enough people, aren't having the desired impact, or the impact doesn't last for long enough. This can help you refine or replace the tactics you're using.

10 Mitigating risk factors (ref: Chapter 9)

In this section you should identify and mitigate the risks involved in launching a community. You can use our table from the previous chapter here to drop these in and your efforts to mitigate each risk factor. Remember to assign a person responsible.

Harm	Likely	Impact	Mitigation	Owner (initials)
Superusers deemed as employees.	Low	Medium	Covered in T&Cs. Superusers to be voluntary with minimum required behaviour nor financial compensation.	TM
Lack of quality participation from community members.	High	Severe	New member survey and interviews to identify key needs and trends. Determine why members aren't participating. Narrow focus to a few core goals.	RM

Harm	Likely	Impact	Mitigation	Owner (initials)
Failure to provide quick responses to questions.	Medium	Medium	Identify and build better relationships with customer support / marketing / internal developers who are happy to jump in to provide questions that are more than 24 hours old.	RM
Release of sensitive information.	Medium	Low	Immediate removal of post with a note to the member about the danger of sharing sensitive information. If happens too often, send a pop-up warning to all members.	SB
Community is flooded with angry posts/upset customers.	Medium	Medium	RM to contact direct marketing for an official response on major issues. Deliver with empathy and invite customers to join a call to address their concerns.	RM
Community is flooded with spam/self-promotion.	Medium	Low	If exceeds 15 posts per day for 2 weeks, GB to set the community to pre-approved accounts for public users.	SB
Serious breach of code of conduct (sexism, racism, etc.).	Medium	Severe	Immediate removal of the member and outreach to the victim. A notification to the community that this behaviour is not acceptable.	SM
Staff posting information they shouldn't.	Medium	Medium	Work with HR to include community participation guidelines on staff training materials. Create a separate deck and host a workshop for staff to attend before they are allowed to post.	RM
Losing support from senior executives.	Medium	Severe	Stakeholder mapping and engagement process. Schedule meetings with new arrivals and develop executive materials to explain community value. Regular value of community meetings.	RM

This section of the strategy is a great place to address the concerns stakeholders have raised and assure them you're taking it seriously. You're far more likely to get the support of your colleagues if you first take the time to truly understand their concerns and ensure you have a plan to resolve them.

11 Appendices

Finally you can add in your appendices which contain the research, background information, any important models or philosophy and further reading. This shouldn't be a data-dump to prove how hard you've been working. It should be a carefully curated set of supporting information to answer most of the likely questions that might be raised.

Summary

A strategy is the difference between an amateur and a professional. An amateur enjoys visiting the community, responding to activity, and seeing how things go. A professional works hard every day to proactively develop the community. Professionals have a strategy – a strategy which pre-emptively answers most of the questions they're likely to encounter.

A community strategy provides you with the technical recommendations you need. It highlights the skills you're going to need when recruiting staff. It helps you prioritise what you should work on now and how to do it well. Perhaps, most importantly, it ensures you're allocating your limited time and financial resources to have the biggest possible impact.

Remember that strategy is a collaborative process. You shouldn't be writing this alone in a dark room. Nothing in the final strategy you present should be a surprise to your colleagues – it's simply the outcome of countless discussions you've had with them along the journey.

If you do this right you will have a strategy that aligns everything you do towards achieving clear goals, with your colleagues on board. The strategy will pinpoint what your audience needs and desires and ensure you're supporting and satisfying those needs and desires. A great strategy is how you and your organisation give the best experience to members and harness the most benefits from the community.

Checklist

----

1 Undertake a detailed community analysis to determine how your community is doing today and what changes are needed. Get to the bottom of every problem and write clear problem statements.

2 Interview stakeholders to determine their hopes, fears, and goals. Create a priority list of these to help you determine your goals.

3 Research your audience to identify unique segments and the needs of each segment.

4 Create a SWOT analysis summarising all your research.

5 Create your community concept (guiding principles, value to the organisation, and value to you). Build a community roadmap.

6 Develop a clear overview for each phase of the strategy and list out every tactic you will deploy.

7 Detail your technology requirements at each phase.

8 Create your measurement framework and share it with your team.

9 Create your risks analysis and proactively mitigate risks.

10 Drop any supporting material into your appendices.

Tools of the trade
(all available at www.feverbee.com/ buildyourcommunity)

- Community Strategy Template
- Community Roadmap Template
- SWOT Analysis Template
- Risk Analysis Template
- Measurement Framework and Dashboard
- Strategy Guide (www.feverbee.com/strategy)
- Richard Millington–The Indispensable Community: Why Some Brand Communities Thrive When Others Perish (available from Amazon)
- Strategic Community Management Training Course (http://ondemand. feverbee.com)

What's next?

By the time you read this book, many things might have changed.

New tools might have emerged which present exciting (and, at times, confusing) opportunities for engaging your members. Many of the communities featured in this book will have risen and fallen in popularity. New events will have probably rocked the economic and political climate you work within.

Even as I write these words (April 2020), the COVID-19 pandemic is causing turmoil across the planet. Some communities are struggling to cope with a surge of activity. Others are experiencing a rapid decline in participation. No one knows what the future looks like in a few months, let alone a few years, from now.

As the cliché goes, change is the only constant. Every year or two, a new 'game changing' wave of technology and social trends threatens to crash down upon us. And sure, each wave will undoubtedly leave its mark upon our communities in ways that are impossible to predict. But this doesn't mean you should spend your time trying to surf at the crest of each new wave. While some aspects of communities will be affected, the core principles will remain the same.

This book is about those principles. It's about the things that unite members into communities. It's about creating a community that's indispensable for you and your members. If you stay focused on these, you can survive any change.

Creating a community is one of the most challenging and rewarding things you can do. When you connect strangers together under your roof, you unlock energy which can supercharge your organisation. You create the kind of value that for your audience is impossible to replicate anywhere else.

A huge part of this value is expertise. The only true expert is the one who realises how little they know. No one has all the answers. But the collective wisdom of a community is unparalleled. Whether you're trying to fix your iPhone or you're worried about an upcoming health treatment, the experiences and wisdom of a community surpass any single book or white paper. After all, what is Wikipedia if not simply the documented knowledge of a community on a global scale?

But the other part of this value is emotional. If your iPhone is broken, you're frustrated and angry. You don't just want the answer, you want to know someone sees your anger and they care. You want to know that you were listened to and not dismissed. If you have an upcoming cancer treatment, you want to feel like you're not alone. You can't put a value on having a network of people, who have been through your exact situation, guide you through every step of the journey.

Even this doesn't cover the true impact of a community. Communities help us collaborate better together and coordinate our activities. Communities help us feel respected, appreciated, and wanted. The connections you make when you launch a community can help you support more of your audience better than ever before. You can harness your members' best ideas to deliver a better experience for them. You can spread the best expertise from your top members to newcomers. Almost every area of your work, whether it's recruitment, marketing, sales, engineering or more, can benefit from your community.

But a word of warning here. Be realistic. Not every topic is one which lends itself to creating a strong sense of belonging. Look around you right now. You probably don't want to spend your time hanging out in the community hosted by companies that manufactured the chair you're sitting on right now, the refrigerator you bought, or for the producers for most of the items in your fridge. But that doesn't mean these and millions of other companies shouldn't have communities. It just means the value of those communities is different.

If your internet connection breaks, you probably don't want someone to try and be your friend, you simply want someone who can give you a good, empathetic, answer. Better yet, you want to find the answer without having to ask the question yourself.

Don't underestimate just how important it is to nurture a handful of top leaders, superusers even, in your community. They are the ones who will ultimately determine if the community thrives or dies. In fact, it might only be a handful of top members who are 'true' community members. They might be the ones who feel a true sense of belonging with you and with each other – and that's perfectly fine!

When you do build a community, you need to deeply understand and emphasise with your members. Commit the time to get to know them well. Learn their needs and desires. If they just want to ask questions and get answers in a community, that's great. You can build a community to satisfy that desire. If they want more – perhaps to get expertise and tips, discover how people like them are tackling similar issues, and attend upcoming events, then you can build a community for that too. Every extra minute you invest in getting to deeply understand your members pays off many times over later down the road.

When you get started, try to start small, test your ideas, use a platform that's relatively inexpensive. Once you're sure your concept works, then you can begin expanding and investing in areas that deliver more value to members. You might build a powerful reputation system to reward and support the members who want to lead your community. You might start creating content and hosting events for your members to better share information and connect with one another.

Be deliberate in the culture you want. Every decision has trade-offs. Focusing strictly upon high-quality contributions will make the community difficult for newcomers and limit participation. But if you head too far in the other direction your community might become filled with spam and be of no value to anyone. All major decisions about rules of a community are made somewhere along this kind of continuum. You need to find a balance while ensuring that your community isn't 'just another community', but has a unique position in the minds of your members.

Don't be naive about the risks involved in connecting people. Just because people are interacting in your community doesn't mean those interactions are good. If members share harmful information with one another, attack one another, or look to cause mischief, you need to anticipate and have a plan to deal with that. You can't prevent every possible problem, but you can identify the majority of them and mitigate the impact of many of them.

Finally, if you want to be a professional, you need to have a strategy. You shouldn't be waking up each morning and simply reacting to what happens in your community. You should be proactively driving the community to where it needs to go. You should know what you're trying to achieve and what the plan is to achieve it. This strategy should be fully resourced and costed. A strategy is what takes your community to the next level and ensures both you and your community achieve your full potential.

Find your community

Community leadership can feel like a lonely job. Many of us doing this work are the only people in the organisation responsible for it. So don't do it alone. You can go deep into the meta of our work and join communities of people that lead communities. There are plenty of them out there.

I recommend you join the CMX Hub group on Facebook and consider a membership to the Community Roundtable. I recommend you join our community at www.feverbee.com and attend the events hosted by CMX, Khoros, Higher Logic, and many others. You can also follow the #CMGR (community manager) on Twitter and keep abreast of the latest conversations taking place in this field.

Of course, once you have found your community of like-minded community leaders, be sure to share your experience and expertise too. Even if you're a newcomer to the field, you know what it's like to be a newcomer to the field and the kinds of questions you have. The people who come after you will find that truly valuable. Even the smallest contributions to our community compound over time to help the masses.

Take your skills and knowledge to the highest level

I also strongly recommend you take your community skills to the highest possible level. Remember that ultimately the success of your community depends not on the technology you use but in your own abilities. Far too many people leading communities have received no training and are forced to learn on the job.

In 2011, we created the first professional community management course and over the years have trained 1300 community leaders today. If you want to advance your skills, then you can head over to www.feverbee.com and take our training courses.

You can also read some of the top books in this field. I recommend those below:

- Jono Bacon – *People Powered: How Communities Can Supercharge Your Business, Brand, and Teams* and *The Art of Community: Seven Principles for Belonging*
- Charles Vogl and Carrie Melissa Jones – *Building Brand Communities: How Organizations Succeed by Creating Belonging*
- Priya Parker – *The Art of Gathering: How We Meet and Why It Matters*
- Bruce Patton, Douglas Stone and Sheila Heen – *Difficult Conversations: How to Discuss What Matters Most*
- IDEO.org – *The Field Guide to Human-Centered Design*

- Peter Block – *Community: The Structure of Belonging*
- Douglas Atkin – *The Culting Of Brands: When Customers Become True Believers*
- Rob Kraut and Paul Resnick – *Building Successful Online Communities: Evidence-Based Social Design*[1]

You can also read my two previous books:

- *Buzzing Communities*
- *The Indispensable Community*

Need more help? Drop me a line

If you want an organisation who can design, create, and/or manage your community for you, you can drop me an email at richard@feverbee.com.

FeverBee has helped 300+ organisations develop their communities including organisations like Apple, Facebook, SAP, Novartis, and many more. We're eager to develop your community strategy, create a fantastic community website experience, and train your team. Whether you just want a check up on what you're doing or someone to guide you through the process, we've got the experience to help you.

And even if you just have a question about something you've read in this book, drop me a line. I'm only too happy to help.

Good luck!

I wish you tremendous luck on your community journey. You're doing work that matters and I can't wait to follow your success.

Notes

Chapter 1 Why create a community?

1. These taxonomies aren't mutually exclusive.
2. https://www.amazon.com/Group-Dynamics-Forsyth/dp/9386650932.
3. https://www.amazon.com/Logic-Collective-Action-Mancur-Olson/dp/B001AZMNCC.
4. Kopelman, S. (2009) 'The effect of culture and power on cooperation in commons dilemmas: Implications for global resource management'. *Organizational Behavior and Human Decision Processes*. 108: 153–63.
5. ROI stands for return on investment.
6. https://www.amazon.com/Indispensable-Community-Communities-Thrive-Others/dp/1947635107.
7. It's important that your goal isn't to drive as much engagement as possible here.

Chapter 2 Who is your community for?

1. https://www.fentybeauty.com/you-did-that.
2. https://greatbrook.com/survey-statistical-confidence-how-many-is-enough/.

Chapter 3 Creating your community experience

1. Discourse and Vanilla have both open source platforms and enterprise options.
2. Fitbit actually does all three – but it's an outlier.
3. https://www.feverbee.com/communityparticipation/.
4. https://basecamp.temenos.com/s/.

Chapter 4 Setting the rules

1. https://mitpress.mit.edu/books/high-noon-electronic-frontier.
2. https://www.amazon.com/Art-Gathering-How-Meet-Matters/dp/1594634939.
3. Site hosted by Reddit.
4. Qi, M. Edgar-Nevill, D. and Mousoli, R. (2009) 'Spam and Social Effects', Symposia and Workshops on Ubiquitous, Autonomic and Trusted Computing. Brisbane: QLD, pp. 498–501, doi: 10.1109/UIC-ATC.2009.89.
5. Bevans, B., DeBruhl, B. and Khosmood, F. (2017) Understanding Botnet-driven Blog Spam: Motivations and Methods. In DH.
6. Markines, B., Cattuto, C. and Menezer, F. (2009) 'Social spam detection' in Proceedings of the 5th International Workshop on Adversarial Information Retrieval on the Web (AIRWeb '09). New York, NY, USA: Association for Computing Machinery, 41–48. DOI: https://doi.org/10.1145/1531914.1531924.
7. Buckels, E.E., Trapnell, P.D. and Paulhus, D.L. (2014) *Personality and Individual Differences*. Vol. 67, pp. 97–102. Available at: https://doi.org/10.1016/j.paid.2014.01.016.
8. Torgersen, S., Kringlen, E. and Cramer, V. (2001) 'The prevalence of personality disorders in a community sample', *Arch General Psychiatry*. 58(6): 590-6. DOI: 10.1001/archpsyc.58.6.590.
9. https://www.syfy.com/syfywire/how-star-trek-darkness-just-ignited-wikipedia-grammar-war.
10. https://www.slideshare.net/FeverBee/justin-isaf-how-to-reduce-your-moderation-costs.

11. Matias, J. N. (2019) 'Preventing Online Harassment and Increasing Group Participation Through Social Norms in 2,190 Science Discussions'. *Proceedings of the National Academy of Science*. Available at: https://doi.org/10.1073/pnas.1813486116.

12. https://www.wired.com/2015/01/inside-the-largest-virtual-psychology-lab-in-the-world/.

Chapter 5 Attracting your first members

1. https://www.feverbee.com/datacommunities/.

2. http://community.geotab.com.

3. https://www.jmir.org/2019/11/e14421.

4. Ridings, C. M. and Gefen, D. (2004) 'Virtual community attraction: Why people hang out online'. *Journal of Computer-mediated communication,* 10(1), JCMC10110.

5. Velasquez, A., Wash, R., Lampe, C. and Bjornrud, T. (2014) 'Latent users in an online user-generated content community'. *Computer Supported Cooperative Work (CSCW)*, 23(1), 21–50.

6. Rodgers, S. and Chen, Q. (2005) 'Internet community group participation: Psychosocial benefits for women with breast cancer'. *Journal of Computer-Mediated Communication*, 10(4), JCMC1047.

7. Nimrod, G. (2012) 'The membership life cycle in online support groups'. *International Journal of Communication*, 6, 23.

8. Lee, J. and Suh, A. (2015) 'How do virtual community members develop psychological ownership and what are the effects of psychological ownership in virtual communities?' *Computers in Human Behavior*, 45, 382–91.

Chapter 6 Nurturing superusers in your community

1. Airgetlam is a pseudonym.

2. An active contributor is a member who created a post or discussion within the previous month.

3. It's difficult to analyse internal communities and those on platforms like Facebook, Slack, and other channels.

4. https://en.community.sonos.com/members/airgetlam-7880809.

5. https://www.amazon.com/People-Powered-Communities-Supercharge-Business-ebook/dp/B07R4YN5JR.

Chapter 7 Keeping members engaged

1. https://sparktoro.com/blog/resources/10x-content-by-rand-fishkin/.

2. https://stackoverflow.blog/newsletter/.

Chapter 8 Rewarding your members

1. https://www.amazon.com/Community-Building-Web-Strategies-Communities-ebook/dp/B004SHDFH6/ref=sr_1_1?dchild=1&keywords=community+building+on+the+web&qid=1586769072&sr=8-1.

2. Kuo, M. S. and Chuang, T. Y. (2016) 'How gamification motivates visits and engagement for online academic dissemination–An empirical study'. *Computers in Human Behavior*, *55*, 16–27.

3. Kuo, M. S. and Chuang, T. Y. (2016) 'How gamification motivates visits and engagement for online academic dissemination: An empirical study'. *Computers in Human Behavior*, 55, 16–27.

4. Mekler, E. D., Brühlmann, F., Tuch, A. N. and Opwis, K. (2017) 'Towards understanding the effects of individual gamification elements on intrinsic motivation and performance'. *Computers in Human Behavior*, 71, 525–34.

5. https://lithosphere.lithium.com/t5/Science-of-Social-Blog/Applying-the-Gamification-Spectrum-Part-1-Solving-Business/ba-p/184812.

6. Farzan, R., DiMicco, J. M., Millen, D. R., Dugan, C., Geyer, W. and Brownholtz, E. A. (2008) 'Results from deploying a participation incentive mechanism within the enterprise'. In Proceedings of the SIGCHI conference on human factors in computing systems, April, pp. 563–72. ACM.

7. Hamari, J. and Koivisto, J. (2013) 'Social Motivations to Use Gamification: An Empirical Study of Gamifying Exercise'. In *ECIS*, June, Vol. 105.

8. Hamari, J., Koivisto, J. and Sarsa, H. (2014) 'Does Gamification Work? A Literature Review of Empirical Studies on Gamification'. In *HICSS*, January, Vol. 14, No. 2014, pp. 3025–3034.

9. Hanus, M. D. and Fox, J. (2015) 'Assessing the effects of gamification in the classroom: A longitudinal study on intrinsic motivation, social comparison, satisfaction, effort, and academic performance'. *Computers & education*, 80, 152–61.

10. Sailer, M., Hense, J., Mandl, J. and Klevers, M. (2014) 'Psychological perspectives on motivation through gamification'. *Interaction Design and Architecture Journal*, (19), 28–37.

11. Farzan, R., DiMicco, J. M., Millen, D. R., Dugan, C., Geyer, W. and Brownholtz, E. A. (2008) 'Results from deploying a participation incentive mechanism within the enterprise'. In Proceedings of the SIGCHI conference on Human factors in computing systems, April, pp. 563–72. ACM.

12. Mekler, E. D., Brühlmann, F., Tuch, A. N. and Opwis, K. (2017) 'Towards understanding the effects of individual gamification elements on intrinsic motivation and performance'. *Computers in Human Behavior*, 71, 525–34.

13. Hamari, J. and Koivisto, J. (2013) 'Social Motivations To Use Gamification: An Empirical Study Of Gamifying Exercise'. In *ECIS*, Vol. 105.

14. Tsay, CH-H, Kofinas, A. K., Trivedi, S. K. and Yang, Y. (2020) 'Overcoming the novelty effect in online gamified learning systems: An empirical evaluation of student engagement and performance'. *J Comput Assist Learn*. 36: 128–46.

15. Hamari, J. (2013) 'Transforming Homo Economicus into Homo Ludens: A Field Experiment on Gamification in a Utilitarian Peer-To-Peer Trading Service'. *Electronic Commerce Research and Applications*. 12. 236–45. 10.1016/j.elerap.2013.01.004.

16. Anderson, A., Huttenlocher, D., Kleinberg, J. and Leskovec, J. (2012) 'Discovering value from community activity on focused question answering sites: a case study of stack overflow'. In Proceedings of the 18th ACM SIGKDD international conference on Knowledge discovery and data mining (KDD '12). New York, NY: Association for Computing Machinery, 850–8.

17. https://support.apple.com/en-us/HT209033.

18. https://help.salesforce.com/articleView?id=networks_reputation_points_setup.htm&type=5.

19. You could theoretically relaunch the gamification program and award people all the people they've already earned as 'bonus points' but it's tricky to do and requires some technical development.

20. Li, Z., Huang, K. W. and Cavusoglu, H. (2012) 'Quantifying the impact of badges on user engagement in online Q&A communities'.

21. Mutter, T. and Kundisch, D. (2014) 'Behavioral mechanisms prompted by badges: The goal-gradient hypothesis'.

22. Bornfeld, B. and Rafaeli, S. (2017) 'Gamifying with badges: A big data natural experiment on Stack Exchange'. *First Monday*, 22(6).

23. Cavusoglu, H., Li, Z. and Huang, K. W. (2015) 'Can gamification motivate voluntary contributions?: the case of stack overflow Q&A community'. In Proceedings of the 18th ACM conference companion on computer supported cooperative work & social computing, pp. 171–4. *ACM*.

Chapter 9 Overcoming problems

1. https://www.sun-sentinel.com/sports/fl-xpm-2012-11-09-sfl-mike-tyson-explains-one-of-his-most-famous-quotes-20121109-story.html.

2. Rev. Williams, H.K. (1919) 'The Group Plan' (excerpt) in 'Young People's Service', January. *The Biblical World*, Vol. 53, No. 1, Religious Education, pp. 80–1, Col. 2. Chicago, Illinois: The University of Chicago Press.

3. At the time of writing, the potential repeal of section 230 of the Communications Decency Act in the USA may make hosts of online communities in the USA liable for the content posted by community members.

4. https://archives.cjr.org/the_news_frontier/aol_settled_with_unpaid_volunt.php.

5. https://www.polygon.com/2018/5/29/17406254/microsoft-layoffs-twitter-support-xbox-ambassadors.

6. https://www.extremetech.com/gaming/270234-microsoft-replaces-xbox-support-reps-with-unpaid-volunteers#comment-3925594642.

7. https://hrdailyadvisor.blr.com/2018/01/04/can-accept-volunteer-labor/.

8. https://ofm.wa.gov/state-human-resources/compensation-job-classes/compensation-administration/fair-labor-standards-act-flsa.

9. https://www.theguardian.com/business/2019/oct/15/wework-sack-staff-workers-adam-neumann.

10. https://cmxhub.com/cmx-summit-code-of-conduct/.

11. https://www.theverge.com/2017/12/29/16830626/call-of-duty-swatting-prank-kansas-man-dead-police-shooting.

12. Self-care was the theme of the 2020 Community Management Appreciation Day.

13. https://tim.blog/2020/02/02/reasons-to-not-become-famous/.

14. It's actually an outstanding achievement, kudos to you!.

15. 95% confidence intervals.

16. Click-through data is not scrapable and is instead gathered from Mailchimp's industry reports, available at: https://mailchimp.com/resources/email-marketing-benchmarks/.

17. This applies to small communities; it would not include customer support communities.

18. We calculate this by using the highest range of registered members who participate (48%). Thus 100/48 × 100 (needed members) = 208.

19. This feels ridiculously high to me.

20. We calculate this per above using the highest possible range who might register (51%). Thus 100/51 (the conversion rate) multiplied by the number of people we need (208) = 408.

21. A heatmap mapping tool.

22. https://mailchimp.com/resources/email-marketing-benchmarks/.

23. 100/2.62 × 408.

Chapter 10 Building your community strategy

1. https://www.mindtools.com/pages/article/newTMC_09.htm.

2. https://en.wikipedia.org/wiki/OKR.

3. 103 hours / 12 weeks + 17 one-time hours.

What's next?

1. You can find a full list of community books here: https://medium.com/@growingcommunity/resource-books-on-online-community-127c981732ef.

Index